TALKING TO THE DEAD

LeRhonda S. Manigault-Bryant

talking to the dead

RELIGION, MUSIC, AND
LIVED MEMORY AMONG
GULLAH/GEECHEE WOMEN

Duke University Press   Durham and London   2014

© 2014 Duke University Press
All rights reserved
Printed in the United States of America on acid-free paper ∞
Designed by Heather Hensley
Typeset in Quadraat by Graphic Composition, Inc., Bogart, Georgia

Library of Congress Cataloging-in-Publication Data
Manigault, LeRhonda S.
    Talking to the dead : religion, music, and lived memory among Gullah-Geechee women /
LeRhonda S. Manigault-Bryant.
        pages cm
    Includes bibliographical references and index.
    ISBN 978–0–8223–5663–9 (cloth : alk. paper)
    ISBN 978–0–8223–5674–5 (pbk. : alk. paper)
    1. Gullah women—Religious life—South Carolina. 2. Gullahs—South Carolina—Religion.
3. Spiritualism. 4. South Carolina—Religious life and customs. I. Title.
E185.93.S7M36 2013
200.89′960730757—dc23
                                                                            2013048707

TO JAMES

Who inspires me daily

Who supports me absolutely

And who loves me unconditionally

CONTENTS

ACKNOWLEDGMENTS

To articulate in writing a practice that is utterly metaphysical is an exercise of faith. Thankfully, I have not walked this faith journey alone. To the seven women who took part in this project—Ruth, Yenenga, Roberta, Lucille, Beatrice, Lucinda, and Faye—your sacred memories, stories, and selves are the heart of this work. I cannot thank you enough for allowing me into your homes and hearts, and I hope that you find my humble attempts to capture the depth and complexity of your stories to be an accurate glimpse into your fascinating lives.

A substantial part of this project unfolded during my years of graduate study at Emory University. My graduate mentors Don Seeman, Gary Laderman, and Dianne Diakité supported me and continue to encourage me with their wisdom, advice, and willingness to engage. Don, thank you for helping me construct my own methodological language. Gary, you always reminded me not to get too hung up on death—I am so glad that you were "the death guy" for a time. Dianne, you have been an incomparable advocate. Thank you for all of your support, and especially the intangibles that coincide with mentoring graduate students. Many others who were at Emory during my tenure there—Luther Smith, Theresa Fry-Brown, Alton B. Pollard III, Sonja Jackson, and the incomparable Pescha Penso—made being a graduate student a humanizing experience for me. My comrades Kent Brintnall, BaSean Jackson, Wylin Dassie Wilson, Anjulet "Nina" Tucker, Claudette Anderson, and my best sister friend Stephanie Sears helped me remain sane with lots of laughter, great food and drink, sustaining conversation, and, of course, karaoke.

While the bulk of this work evolved during my graduate years, the idea for this project took root while I was an undergraduate at Duke University. Encouragement from Rod Clare to pursue the PhD (feel the pain indeed!) and becoming a Mellon Undergraduate Fellow (Deborah Wahl, you are amazing) altered my life course for the best. Since that time, ongoing support from the Andrew W. Mellon Foundation and the Social Science Research Council have reminded me in the best ways that "once a Mellon, always a Mellon." Generous funding from The Ford Foundation, The Louisville Institute, and the Fund for Theological Education (where would I be without you, Sharon Watson-Fluker?) ensured that I had the resources necessary to get the work done. These opportunities, alongside a generous research leave during my term at Wake Forest University, gave me sufficient time to revise, revisit, and revamp as necessary.

I would be remiss if I did not thank Miriam Angress and the team at Duke University Press (Susan Albury and Heather Hensley especially) for their diligent work, their attention to detail, and the willingness to take my work seriously at every stage. Rare is it these days can an academician in the humanities can find a press that cares so much about the author and her work. Miriam, you have been such a great conversation partner, and you set the standard of what it means to usher a writer's work through the publication process. I am so very appreciative and grateful that our paths have crossed.

Collegiality has been pivotal to my success in this profession, and there are so many people who have given me encouragement through the years. Although everyone cannot be named, my colleagues at Wake Forest, in Africana Studies (hotep!) and Religion at Williams College, and in the profession at large (especially Corey D. B. Walker, Elise Edwards, Bernard "Chris" Dorsey, Derek Hicks, "Mama" Nyasha Junior, Lisa Allen-McLaurin, Roger Sneed, Tim Lake, Quinton Dixie, Stéphane Robolin, and Evie Shockley) have been instrumental to this work in tangible and intangible ways.

To my very good friends old and new—Roneka Ravenell-Price, Lisa Hughey, Melva Sampson, Darrick Young, Jasmine Mena, Khalil Saucier, Candis Watts Smith, Tim Lebestky (aka "White Chocolate"), and Aaron and Charlotte Kelton—you have been the ever-important sounding boards, drinking buddies, sports watchers, and vacation and holiday partners. To my "bff" Caron Cox-Branch, thanks to you, Chris, and the boys for truly being my family (not just relatives) and for always sharing laughter, crude advice, and honesty with me. To my dearest homie Erica R. Edwards, I am so glad that thousands of miles have not managed to separate us in any significant way. You are an "ideal coconspirator" indeed, and the laughs, video chats, and conversations about life, Beyoncé, and "Blackberry Molasses" have sustained me in ways that you cannot know. Much love to you and Deb.

It is often said that "you can't go home again," but in all truth, this project would not exist if it were not for home. I simply would not be the person I am without my rural, Southern upbringing, and I am eternally grateful for that. To all my people in Moncks Corner, I thank you for allowing me to have a space to which I could always return, even as my visits are not as often as one might wish. To my mother, Gwendolyn, and my brother, Maurice, I may not say it enough, but I love you both very much. The memory of my grandmother, Annie Mae, carried me through this work during the most difficult moments. As I write, I am thinking of all fifteen of my nieces and nephews, my sisters Sonya Bryan and Nicole Martinez, and through them, all of my extended family. I hope seeing this work in print gives you some sense of what "Auntie Rhonda" has been doing all of these years.

Rest in peace to Quest, the best dog ever. If you ever had the chance to meet him, you understand well why canine companionship warrants acknowledgment in a book.

To my husband, James, in whom my imaginings of love have been made real, gratitude in the form of words can never be enough. From the very beginning you modeled how fulfilling mutual engagement can be, and I am with you as I am with no other—completely free to be myself. We have had such a rich journey over the years, and your editorial sensibilities, valuing of equity, strivings for balance, advocacy for me to remain true to my passions, and the space you have given, have pushed me to be the best person I can. The journey continues for us, and I am so very excited to embark on this next phase with you and our beautiful son, Cy. I dedicate this work to you, as life with you exemplifies the mutuality and sustenance that only the best lover, partner, and friend can provide.

Lastly, to those who believe in communicating with the dead, keep talking.

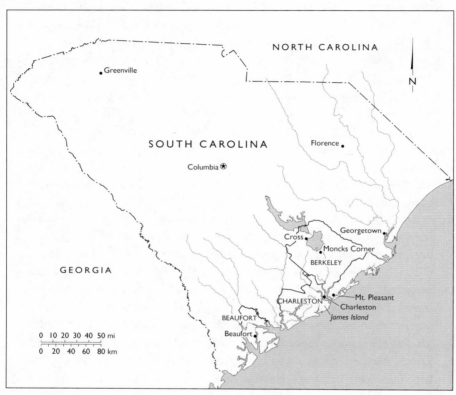

South Carolina.

Talking to the Dead

"Gyal, Ah tulk to de dead all de time!" one of my informants impatiently exclaimed when I recounted my experience of nearly fainting in Charleston's City Market during a middle-school field trip. In preparation for the trip, we received information about the numerous historic homes and museums that make up a part of Charleston's rich heritage. Upon arrival, we went to the Battery on Charleston Harbor, the place where Charleston residents witnessed the first shots of the Civil War at nearby Fort Sumter. It was not my first time visiting downtown Charleston, but I was fascinated by the cobblestone streets and captivated by the feeling that I had stepped back in time. That sense of being a part of history remained with me for the duration of the excursion.

The experience of recognizing my own place in historical time became an especially distinct reality, however, when we visited the City Market. Built between 1804 and the 1830s, the City Market had always been utilized as a space for the public selling and trading of goods. Comprising three buildings located between four cross-streets, the City Market continues to be a tourist hotspot in the downtown area today, and is open 365 days a year. Each corner within the City Market contains more than one hundred open-air sheds filled with clothing, jewelry, antiques, toys, souvenirs, food items, paintings, and crafts of all kinds for sale. For those without a vendor's permit for space inside the City Market proper, stands also take up considerable space between the A, B, and C Buildings. In addition to being close to historic hotels like the Andrew Pinckney Inn and the Planters Inn, as well as such contemporary lodging as the Charleston Place Hotel and the Doubletree Suites, the City Market is in near proximity (within two blocks) of at least twelve restaurants and eateries. It is also currently and conveniently located across the street from The Shops and Charleston Place, a high-end shopping venue that features such stores as Gucci, Louis Vuitton, and St. John. When visiting the City Market today, one is likely to cross paths with tourists and visitors from all over the world, as well as local residents. The City Market, as you can imagine, is a very busy place. Any visitor will immediately encounter a wide variety of goods crammed into a fairly restricted space yet will be simultaneously struck by the ease with which the space is navigated by hundreds of people at a time.

Designed much like a flea market, the City Market was thriving in its original purpose during the late 1980s when my class took our field trip. I saw vendors selling T-shirts, jewelry, and other handcrafted items including sweetgrass baskets. I was excited by the hustle and bustle surrounding the space and looked forward to a full tour of the area. Upon entering the City Market from East Bay Street, however, the cool dampness of the space overtook me and left me with the distinct sense that I was no longer in the place that was before me. I became overwhelmed by the most intense sense of agony, anguish, and pain that I had ever felt or imagined. People—black people—were reaching for me and silently crying out to me, some so horrified that their mouths were agape, and no sound emitted.[1] Though I was not afraid of the women and men, the experience startled me. It felt so real that I stumbled to the ground and had to be helped up and out of the space. My teacher simply thought I had become overheated and needed some air. I did not reenter the City Market, but waited outside for the class to return from the tour.

This was the experience I shared with my informant who exclaimed, "Gyal, Ah tulk to de dead all de time!" during a 2004 visit to her home on James Island. The impatient manner in which she uttered those words suggested that she saw nothing new or strange about what had happened to me. After recovering from my initial shock at her comment, I asked her to explain what she meant, and she described the rich connection she shared with her ancestors who "been long gone but is still yeh with me"—that they were not simply a part of the past but have remained with her in the present. Something about what she described resonated within me. It reminded me of my connection with those who had gone before me, whose presence I had rationalized as exceptional. I had not previously thought of any connection with the dead or spirits as something distinctive about lowcountry

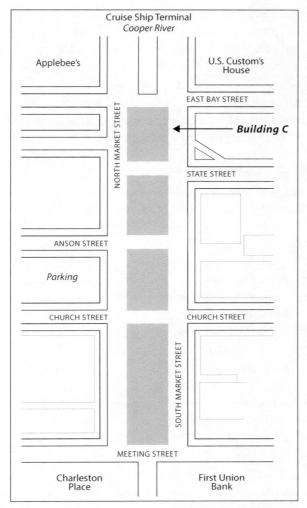

Fig.Prologue.1. Charleston City Market. Art by Pearl Delaine.

culture, so I began to ask other women. And from their responses, I discovered that it resonated with them too, although in different ways and for different reasons.

After the incident in the City Market, I continued to feel surrounded by the presence of forces that were not physically "real" but would visit me and were often visually apparent to me. At the age of twelve, I awoke in the middle of the night and went to tell my grandmother that a woman from our church had come to me in a dream. Moments after I relayed my dream to her, the phone rang—it was another member of the church calling to tell my grandmother that the woman in my dream had passed away. Growing up, there were numerous occasions when I would tell my mother and grandmother about people I had seen and spoken to, all of whom were long-since dead. This happened too many times to recall. Initially diagnosed as nightmares, these occurrences became conflated by my family as symptoms of "the hag," a communal interpretation of a bewitching spirit-woman who would possess, torment, and literally "ride" her victims, paralyzing them so they could not move, speak, or scream. By the time I was fifteen, my family simply attributed these visions and dreams to the "third eye," which to many blacks throughout the rural south and the Caribbean means that one possesses the ability to see things that average humans cannot see—or will not allow themselves to see.

These experiences have continued into adulthood, although they occur with less frequency. My "third eye," which I now consider to be a gift, has given me the uncanny ability to "know things" about complete strangers that I should not know and to have an advanced awareness of events, such as the death of a family member and the pregnancy of a friend. Despite reconciling these experiences, I still have difficulty entering the City Market. I even struggle to walk past the Old Slave Mart on Chalmers Street, the official location where the slaves who entered the port of Charleston were kept until they were sold.[2] The images, smells, and sounds that come to me are still too much to bear.

While conducting interviews for this project, I asked my informants to talk about their connections with their history, which always evolved into a discussion of music and ancestral presences—mothers, grandmothers, siblings, church elders—who continued to be present even though they had passed on. Each of the women in this study related experiences of having an ongoing connection with the dead. When I described my experience in the City Market to Yenenga, Lucille, and Beatrice, they each nodded in agreement. Yenenga and Lucille intentionally avoid the City Market because of their own (or their family's) experiences of a kind of "haunting" in the space. Beatrice, who has a sweetgrass stand located a few blocks away from the City Market, has described that she chose not to have her booth in the market on purpose because of the fees, but also because "the spirits talk too much there." I have no doubt that my own ability to talk to the dead was instrumental in alerting me to the continued significance of the practice—a custom that has been well documented in the generations of scholarship on Gullah/Geechee culture.

Inevitably, I too had to come to terms with the ways that my own ties to the lowcountry and my past connected me with forces that were not completely of this world. While I do not self-identify as Gullah, I cannot deny the Gullah cultural influences that exist in my hometown (Moncks Corner) and in my life. I do not know of anyone in Moncks Corner or the nearby areas of Cross, St. Stephens, and Bonneau who creates sweetgrass baskets, which is one of the many distinctive markers of the Gullah people. Until I began the ethnographic phase of my research, I had never heard of anyone in these areas talk about "seekin'" in order to join a church, nor had I heard anyone refer to him or herself as Gullah or Geechee. Once I learned about the familiarity the women of this study had with talking to the dead as a common practice, however, I reconsidered the ongoing connections. There are many similarities in the speech patterns of the longtime residents of Moncks Corner, the Sea Islands, and the surrounding areas—enough similarities to suggest a common heritage. I have little difficulty understanding the Gullah dialect, but I speak it only minimally. Occasionally, though, I unintentionally draw from the little dialect I know in such a way that only friends and family from the lowcountry can understand my meaning.

My ability to comprehend and speak to the women in their own language, my familiarity with aspects of lowcountry life, and my former existence as a Christian smoothed my entry into the communities of the women included in this book. I did not feel uncomfortable attending worship services, had no difficulty understanding the expressions of faith that emerged in our individual conversations, and was able to adapt to their habits and practices with ease. Although I do not have any shared commitments with the women in a Christocentric, theological sense, I share their experiences of talking to the dead (which is arguably not limited to Christian expression), I recognize the importance of their traditions, and I value lowcountry culture and the ways black women navigate those spaces. The women never questioned my religious identity (and thankfully did not try to proselytize), even when they discovered that in my "normal" life I did not regularly attend church nor have a "church home." They presumed—rightly so—that for me to have interest in the kinds of questions I raised about their faith meant that I too accepted belief in a "higher power," and at the very least valued their perspectives.

As a native of Moncks Corner with the surname Manigault (which is quite common in the lowcountry), I gained an advantage while conducting this research: Everyone I spoke with immediately recognized my name and would ask me who "my people" were. All of the women interviewed treated me as a long-lost relative or family member. As a result, I had little difficulty getting the women to open up and to share their experiences with me, even though initially many were suspicious because they could not understand why I thought documenting their experiences was so important.

My familiarity with the culture, while beneficial in some respects, proved also to be challenging on occasion. Although I made it clear to the women I spoke with that I had only spent my formative years in the lowcountry and had not lived there since 1995, I found that they often made assumptions about what I knew. Moreover, I had to temper my presumptions about the practices and meaning of things, which I did by asking them about everything, even the things I thought I knew. There were times when all of my questioning about things the women thought I should have known, compounded by differences in our ages and disparities in our education, made some of our interactions demanding. With one exception, none of the women had attended college. Because of their unfamiliarity with graduate school requirements, let alone institutional review boards, they had some difficulty understanding the exact purpose of my study. In the beginning stages of my research, the women repeatedly asked me to explain what I was doing and why I was interested in writing about them. On multiple occasions, I had to provide lengthy explanations about why informed consent was so important. Although it was an unintentional result of my inquiries, all of the women in the study were old enough to be my mother, and most treated me as a daughter. While that was usually endearing, there were occasions when their concern for me as a young, and, at that time, unmarried woman proved taxing—especially including the efforts they made to set me up with their family members and their oft-expressed concern about me "travelin' da roads alone." All of these features had a direct impact on the types of questions I raised and also on the ways that the women responded to me. Hence, throughout this research I delicately negotiated my roles as both insider and outsider of this culture.

Moncks Corner is not an island, at least not literally, but being there has a special quality. This is certainly because it is a small southern rural town and because spending time in rural towns almost always gives one the sense of stepping back in time. Moncks Corner is now the proud home of a Super Walmart and an Applebees, and recently a CVS and a Brooks Pharmacy. The main grocery store is Piggly Wiggly, most people continue to get their prescriptions filled at the locally owned Delta Pharmacy, and the only "upscale" place to shop is Baron's Department Store. Being in the lowcountry also feels different because there is something unique about hearing "Ma Beck" (an elderly woman from my community) say, "Gyal you been gone a minute any?" when I visit after being away for extended periods of time. I have had friends visit my home only to tell me that they felt like they were in the Caribbean because of the thick dialect of the people. Even one of my Jamaican-born friends has described visiting Moncks Corner as giving her a sense of going home.

What makes me most willing to embrace the connections between Moncks Corner, other inland areas, and the Sea Islands is the structure and performative style of the music produced in their churches. Over the years, I have attended numerous services throughout the lowcountry and have been amazed at the overlap in the singing style and rhythmic patterns across denominations. I have also been fascinated by the presence of what I call the "lowcountry clap," a uniquely synchronistic meter accompanied by an uncannily blended harmonious style of call and response. The lowcountry clap, as demonstrated in the accompanying audio, can alter the tempo, sound, and feeling of a hymn, spiritual, or contemporary gospel song. I do not think it is by accident that these musical styles continue to reverberate from the windows and walls of lowcountry churches. These practices are alive and well in Moncks Corner, which is a mere fifteen minutes east of Cross, thirty minutes north of James Island and Mt. Pleasant, and ninety minutes north of Beaufort—the areas in which the women included in this study reside.

My research for this project has led me to conclude that these factors demonstrate the many ways that cultural influences operate like the tides: The ability or inability of the water to reach certain parts of the shore depends on the location of the sun, moon, and earth, as well as the time of day and the pull of gravity. The rich religious culture of the lowcountry functions in much the same way. Rather than occurring in a vacuum, it is a continuous ebb and flow, a dynamic process of give and take that is influenced by—and influences—the people involved, the practices transmitted, the stories shared, the prayers prayed, and the songs sung. All of these ingredients bring this work together.

Gullah/Geechee Women

In the film *Daughters of the Dust*,[1] Julie Dash captures the struggles of the Peazant family, three generations of lowcountry women who, at the turn of the twentieth century, consider whether they should relocate from the Sea Islands of South Carolina to the "mainland." While elder members of the family are not in favor of relocating, younger members support the move inland. Flashbacks in the film reveal the longstanding importance of ancestral communication, folk traditions, faith, and music within the family. This may sound like a fairly typical rendering of generational differences. However, there is much at stake because the senior family members associate the move with a loss of sacred traditions. The younger members view the elder members' reliance upon tradition as dated, and consider the change necessary.

Daughters of the Dust, according to Yvonne Chireau, is an important source for interpreting religious signifiers in African American culture. In *Black Magic: Religion and the African American Conjuring Tradition* (2003), Chireau emphasizes the film's concluding scene, where Nana Peazant transfers heirlooms to younger family members. Nana's gift, coupled with the young women's departure from the island, signals the merging of religion and magic. Nana's charm allows the family to collectively remember their past as participants in conjuring and faith traditions while celebrating an unknown future. Chireau suggests that *Daughters of the Dust* "might be read as an allegory of the religious sojourn of blacks in America, with Nana's charm as a metaphor for the legacy that some have chosen to preserve, and others to reject."[2] The film's storyline of preservation and rejection invokes the question that is central to this project: How do Gullah/Geechee women negotiate traditional practices associated with their cultural identity in the midst of significant historical and generational change?

An immediate response to this inquiry is that the seven women of this study talk to the dead. Talking to the dead is a perceived ongoing exchange between living and deceased members of these communities. The practice occurs during traditionally "religious" customs, such as prayer and the singing of Christian sacred songs, but is also facilitated by sociocultural activities, such as storytelling and sweetgrass basketry. Talking to the dead strengthens a sense of unity among members of these communities and gives individuals a way to communicate with deceased relatives. I argue that whether facilitated by customs traditionally interpreted as religious, through the performance of cultural and folk activities, or through the act of remembering, talking to the dead is a longstanding yet underexplored spiritual practice. For Yenenga Wheeler, Faye Terry, Beatrice Dixon, Lucinda Pinckney, Ruth Kelly, Roberta Legare, and Lucille Gaillard, talking to the dead facilitates their relationships to the past, and is relevant to the ways they navigate and live out their faith.[3] This project offers a narrative of a broader community's negotiation of change by weaving together its memories, folk traditions and mythical practices, sacred worldviews, music, and history. Embracing what Sheila Smith McKoy calls "limbo time"—the fused, contested space that black diasporic cultures negotiate between linear and cyclical time[4]—this book takes the reader through a "figurative journey"[5] that crosses the boundaries of time.

Scholars, journalists, and laypeople alike have taken interest in the Gullah/Geechee and noted their cultural distinctiveness. The Gullah/Geechee are the unique African American inhabitants of the Sea Islands, a 250-mile area of barrier islands off the coast of Georgia and South Carolina. They are also residents of the lowcountry[6]—the coastal lowlands of South Carolina—who, while not inhabitants of a barrier island, bear the imprints of coastal culture.[7] I characterize the Gullah as those who inhabit the Sea Islands, and the Geechee as those who inhabit the lowlands and interior, nonisland dwellings within five to forty minutes from a barrier island.[8] Although "Gullah" is now generally accepted as a combination of the abbreviated form of Angola and the Gola tribe of the Windward Coast,[9] in the nineteenth and early twentieth centuries sources labeled all blacks who spoke the unique patois[10] of the lowcountry as "Gullah," and applied this label to African Americans as far inland as Goose Creek, St. Stephens,

Walterboro, and Georgetown. Today, while there is a clearer demarcation between Gullah and Geechee as those who are from the Sea Islands and those who are not, these terms are employed with an understanding that the distinctions between Gullah and Geechee are not historically concise.

The inhabitants of the coastal lowcountry are considered by scholars and local residents to be among the most interesting microcosms of African American culture in the United States. Until the brink of the Civil War, interstate and intrastate trading systems resulted in ongoing transportation of enslaved blacks throughout the lowcountry. Historically, lowcountry culture developed, at least until the mid-twentieth century, in relative geographic isolation, as many residents had only marginal contact with people from outside the Sea Islands and accordingly fostered dynamic intercommunal relationships.[11] These factors contribute to the rich cultural viscosity that has always been part of lowcountry life.

This cultural fluidity has become threatened within the past half century by the influx of modernity. Television advertises the wider world and encourages local residents to expand their horizons beyond their roots. Bridges now connect the majority of the islands with the mainland, and the isolation that once helped to maintain cultural distinctiveness has given way to a much more commercialized exchange of culture. Despite efforts by lowcountry residents to preserve their culture, it is becoming increasingly difficult to distinguish the unique character of the Sea Islands from that of any other place. The rapid increase in resort development, diminished access to maritime resources, and the migration (forced and unforced) of African American landowning families away from the lowcountry—and most significantly, away from the waterfronts—have dramatically altered the physical, social, and cultural landscapes.

Attitudes have also changed with respect to the religious practice of talking to the dead. Although the custom is alive and well in the lowcountry, contemporary shifts are affecting the practices of such traditions. Some community members believe talking to the dead is an irrelevant, archaic tradition.[12] Others are reluctant to speak of it out of concern that it will be perceived as anti-Christian. Yet an appreciation of the practice has persisted, and increasingly, prototypically "Christian" rituals are utilized as a means of talking to the dead. Many community members—including the women of this study—still draw from the rich repertoire of Gullah/Geechee culture to remember their pasts while celebrating their faith in God. The women who practice talking to the dead in no way view it as antithetical to their Christian identities. Like many communities that have responded to increased tourism and the "sale" of Gullah/Geechee culture by celebrating their cultural heritage, lowcountry religious practitioners have embraced their historical antecedents.

Reared thirty minutes from the Sea Islands, I am well aware of the distinctive aspects of Gullah culture, from the soul-stirring harmonies and polyphonic rhythms of its music to the artistry of its sweetgrass baskets. My interests in the culture of the lowcountry thus stem from my roots as a Geechee girl who grew up connected to and intrigued by the extraordinary qualities of life on and around the Sea Islands. They also emerge from a personal commitment to documenting the histories of these communities— which are swiftly changing. The implications of such efforts are potentially far reaching, for they will contribute to larger discourses about religion in American culture, and respond to lapses in an academic canon that has largely omitted the voices of women like those included in this work.[13] What follows is the perspective of a subset of what has been characterized as a unique diaspora culture, where the prominence of folk ancestral practices present in Gullah/Geechee music, faith, and memory speak to the importance of talking to the dead for Gullah/Geechee women.

Women's Work and African Cultural Retentions

Gullah/Geechee women are key contributors to African American religion and culture because they have been constant participants (i.e., members and supporters) and leaders of lowcountry faith systems. This includes traditions that can be identified as formally "Christian" and those that are interpreted as "folk." In the South Carolina lowcountry, women have historically been conjurers, praise-house leaders, worship leaders, and spiritual parents, which were all equally valued in terms of perceived spiritual power. Those writing about lowcountry culture have not always recognized these roles; written representations of Gullah/Geechee religion have omitted or misrepresented the contributions these women have historically made and continue to make. This is in large part due to the fact that women have not held the more prominent, visible role of pastor—the position that has received the most attention in the literature on Gullah/Geechee culture and American religion broadly.

Scholars have focused more on the communal quality of religion than on the individual function of religion to practitioners and believers. This, in my view, continues to be one of the largest omissions within research on Gullah/Geechee culture. Despite efforts to incorporate a more comparative analysis that historicizes religious practices within Gullah/Geechee culture, as in recent works by Michael Wolfe and Jason Young, what is glaringly absent from the historiography of Gullah/Geechee religion are the ways that Gullah/Geechee women have navigated, negotiated, and continued to practice their religiosity within these spaces. Because interest in Gullah/Geechee culture has centered upon their numerous "peculiarities," the omission of women's narratives of religion within these communities is striking. *Talking to the Dead* fills a gap in this literature.

Religious experience and spirituality facilitate change and help women in America broadly and black women in particular negotiate class, age, race, sexuality, and power.[14] As recent scholarship by Rosetta Ross, Marla Frederick, Anthea Butler, and Judith Weisenfeld and Richard Newman supports, religion is an especially important lens through which to analyze black women's experiences because of the role faith plays in women's activism and survival.[15] The study of religion also bears great significance in the South Carolina lowcountry because of the role religion has played in the historical quest for African cultural retentions. Anthropologist Melville Herskovits famously defined Africanisms as elements of culture in the New World that are traceable to an African origin.[16] Herskovits believed that the *religious* practices of blacks in the diaspora were the most viable means of identifying cultural retentions. According to Herskovits, if one cannot find African influences in religion, there are no Africanisms to be found.[17] Following Herskovits's lead, nearly all written materials about Gullah/Geechee culture reference the "African" nature of lowcountry religion.

The question of cultural retentions is therefore significant to any study of lowcountry culture, as one cannot talk about the Gullah/Geechee and ignore the discourse of Africanisms.[18] Many who have heard the unique patois and observed the various artistic and cultural practices of the Gullah argue that they are African in origin, and thus establish connections between the Gullah and various west and central African groups.[19] Efforts to pinpoint African cultural continuities have dominated discussions of lowcountry culture since the 1930s. Lorenzo Dow Turner's *Africanisms in the Gullah Dialect*[20] was the first text[21] to explicitly engage the influence of African culture upon lowcountry inhabitants, and it continues to be the among the most highly cited texts about the Gullah.[22]

Efforts to identify Africanisms in lowcountry culture have proven valuable. They have illuminated the meanings of various cultural practices and shaped theories of traditions particular to the lowcountry, which include use of the Gullah dialect, sweetgrass basketry, and music traditions such as the "lowcountry clap." The quest for Africanisms has also substantiated claims of the ingenuity of lowcountry blacks, who combined their African and American heritages to form a distinctive culture. Moreover, Margaret Creel, Samuel Lawton, Patricia Guthrie, and others have successfully identified African continuities within religion and expanded the historiography on Gullah/Geechee culture to provide new analytic lenses to engage lowcountry culture.[23]

When I began studying Gullah/Geechee culture, the question of identifying Africanisms was central to my research. I explored literature on the transatlantic slave trade to determine where in Africa lowcountry inhabitants could trace their heritages. I studied religious practices, rituals, myths, and symbols to determine if they could be linked to specific areas or ethnic groups throughout Africa. As my research progressed, however, I discovered that the complex dynamics of the slave trade and the challenges of conveying abstractions, such as experience and memory, made it difficult—if not impossible—to identify an item of culture as exclusively or predominantly "African." I also realized from my earliest interactions with lowcountry residents that scientific observations of Africanisms collected by Herskovits, Turner, and others obscured the lived experiences of the Gullah—especially Gullah women. I swiftly came to recognize the shortcomings of seeking "isms" to sum up a culture, and that more work needed to be done to address gaping omissions in the literature.

Subsequently, I focused my efforts on three limitations within the scholarship on Gullah/Geechee religion. First, that the earliest generation (1863–1950) inadequately accounted for the dynamism that resulted from the merging of Christian and African-derived religious practices, and simply characterized Gullah/Geechee religion as an example of "primitive heathenism."[24] Although the treatment of religion improved within later generations of Gullah/Geechee scholarship (1974–1999 and 2000–2010), religion was nonetheless treated as a secondary factor that influenced lowcountry culture; the limited exploration of religion within these discourses was a critical deficiency. Second, most of the literature provides a historical reckoning of Gullah/Geechee culture and does not sufficiently account for the changing meanings of religious practices over time. The third limitation, which is most important to this study, is the striking absence of Gullah/Geechee women, who are largely excluded from examinations of the significance of religion in lowcountry life. Lowcountry women have not been viewed as leaders within Gullah/Geechee communities and are only peripherally included in descriptions of communities as performers of songs, shouts, and dances. Furthermore, detailed descriptions of the activities and names of women were often only provided insofar as they validated negative ideas about black religion. Scholars of the Gullah/Geechee have allowed the focus on Africanisms to overshadow, oversimplify, and at times misrepresent the meaning of religion to lowcountry women.[25] The quest to identify cultural retentions compounded the silencing of Gullah/Geechee women, whose experiences have on the whole been excluded and whose communal roles have been grossly overlooked.[26]

Thus, the focus on African cultural continuities, while inherently valuable, has not emerged without cost. While it is important to acknowledge the continuities of lowcountry tradition with those of specific African communities, it is just as significant—if not more so—to understand *what these practices have historically meant and continue to mean* within lowcountry communities.[27] A search for Africanisms that excludes analysis of the meaning of cultural practices among lowcountry inhabitants, in order to prove the value and significance of black culture and disprove white claims of black inferiority, is no longer sufficient. "Pinpointing Africanisms" creates a rigidity that does not best fit the nature of religion or culture, which is always a fluid, ongoing exchange that does not occur in a vacuum. The goal of contemporary work on Gullah/Geechee communities should not be to identify African retentions or to verify any type of "authentic blackness." Instead, the objective should be to understand the meaning and impact of religious practices and religio-cultural associations with Africa to lowcountry inhabitants today. This is at the forefront of *Talking to the Dead*.

Black Atlantic Studies

In *Rituals of Resistance: African Atlantic Religion in Kongo and the Lowcountry South in the Era of Slavery*, Jason Young calls for analyzing cultural dialogues without getting entrenched in dialectical debates. This challenge is important to consider in a study that explores the religious lives of lowcountry black women. In *Talking to the Dead*, religion is crucial for delving into how black women have navigated the traditions, spaces, and places that have been instrumental in Gullah/Geechee religious culture. This includes explorations of their conversion experiences, their roles in the church and praise house, as well as their positions as "sanctioned" religious leaders and as root-workers and conjurers. This work centers the ways that Yenenga, Ruth, Roberta, Lucille, Lucinda, Beatrice, and Faye live out their faith. Quite noticeably, their present lives and their faith are heavily informed by the histories that they see themselves as being a part of. This includes how they "seeked" their religion (how they became members of their respective churches); why they sing certain songs; how they were positively influenced by older women (formal and informal spiritual leaders) in their communities; and how they share communal understandings about talking to the dead. The experiences of the women—whether their music practices, their relationship to Africa, or their communications with the dead—are part of a longstanding history, which influences their present realities and helps these women determine what their faith in God means and how to live out that faith.

My efforts to translate the ways that conceptions of God and faith and the role of ancestors are present in contemporary Gullah/Geechee communities necessitates some exploration of how these worldviews are triangulated between African, Caribbean, and black American diasporas. I also explicitly engage the ways that seven women from different towns, cities, and areas of the lowcountry recognize their symbols, histories, religion, and heritage as African (or not). Because of these features, this investigation continues to be part of a historical discussion about African cultural retentions, while it engages contemporary discourses about transnationalism located in black Atlantic studies. Although I make little effort to pinpoint the "Africanness" of the Gullah/Geechee or to explicitly connect Gullah/Geechee practices to comparable diasporic communities, this work becomes part of conversations emerging in black Atlantic studies, exemplified by Paul Gilroy's *The Black Atlantic*, Bayo Hosley's *Routes of Remembrance*, Saidiya Hartman's *Lose Your Mother*, J. Lorand Matory's *Black Atlantic Religion*, and Young's *Rituals of Resistance*. Unlike these important works, my project does not emphasize transnational dialogues through a comparative analysis of cultures. Rather, it extends these discussions by addressing how self-identification among Gullah/Geechee women reflects an ongoing engagement with modern interpretations of the "image" and memory of Africa in lowcountry religion, the fluidity between past and present that influences how contemporary women enact their faith, and the ancestral practices of talking to the dead.[28] This is a way of including women's narratives in the histories of the lowcountry, and in the broader discourse on black Atlantic thought, while placing these women's stories at the forefront of investigations into lowcountry religious life.

My attempt to understand the contemporary meanings of religious practices among these women is one faithful way to bridge gaps between the narratives of scholars and those of lowcountry residents. Another effort is related to conversations about transnationalism, of which translocalism is a part.[29] Again, because this text grapples with the meaning of customs that are not exclusively African or American, this project is in conversation with these discourses. What makes these discussions important to the present study is the ways they expand our understanding of seemingly "local" customs and utilize comparative data to account for similarities between distinct cultures. Transnational discourses are also contestations of the cultural retention "debate." Rather than essentializing Gullah/Geechee culture as having any singular "origin," these conversations free cultural practices from being identified as any single thing, or being reduced to any singular locale. Similarly, these discourses enlarge our perspectives about the bounds of local and national communities. This project focuses on "local" perspectives (as the genre of anthropological ethnography has traditionally done), but by taking the fluidity of the formation of Gullah/Geechee religious culture seriously, it avoids the methodological baggage of translocal exclusion that has historically accompanied anthropological ethnography. The focus on the local certainly provides a means of accessing the translocal, national, transnational, and even transatlantic, for there truly is no way to understand Gullah/Geechee religion and culture without some recognition and awareness of their ongoing and varied cultural, social, and historical influences.

An Ethnohistorical Approach

To better situate Gullah women's experiences while attending to diverse religious practices in the lowcountry, I employ an interdisciplinary methodology that joins religious studies, gender studies, ethnomusicology, history, and anthropology in a way that is ethnohistorical. The ethnographic portion of this project involved spending time with, interviewing (audio recorded when permitted), observing, and documenting the experiences of seven women of James Island and Mount Pleasant (Charleston County), Cross and Moncks Corner (Berkeley County), and Beaufort (Beaufort County), South Carolina.[30] These women represent different perspectives from multiple communities throughout the lowcountry. All profess to be Christians.[31] As women of deep faith, they vary in their denominational affiliations (Baptist, Methodist, Pentecostal, Presbyterian, and Disciples of Christ) and in their understandings of what being Christian means.

Between March 2003 and March 2007, I spent a substantial amount of time with these women.[32] I stayed at their homes and attended church and Bible study with them. I also went with them to the grocery store, helped them wash vegetables from gardens and market stands, ate and cooked with them, and spent months driving between their churches, residences, and jobs. I sat with them while they worked, rested, and praised God, spent time with their families, and examined their daily lives. While observing, I asked questions about their identities as Gullah/Geechee women, as black women in the South, and about their understandings of their roles in their communities' histories and religious practices. I strove to create spaces where the women felt comfortable and open, and always invited them to candidly describe their personal beliefs and religious experiences. Since my fieldwork was completed, Faye Terry has passed away, but too-infrequent visits and phone calls keep me in touch with the remaining six.[33]

From my time with these women, I acquired some knowledge of their lives. I recognize that my knowledge was merely a glimpse into their daily existence. Hence, what I did not understand or could not interpret, I asked them to clarify, and what I thought I knew or understood, I asked them to confirm. By spending time with these women and observing them in various settings, I utilized the technique Clifford Geertz called "thick description," which entails gathering data by selecting, observing, and interviewing informants, but also by describing to the best of one's ability the variety, depth, breadth, and texture of their life-worlds with special attention to what is significant to them.[34] I believe that there is great cultural value in having these women's experiences documented, in part because of the general exclusion of the narratives of Gullah/Geechee women in textual representations of lowcountry religion.[35] When applicable, I utilize the women's original wording and dialect or offer translations that are closest to its original meaning and structure, despite the controversy over Lorenzo Turner's reading of the origins of Gullah/Geechee patois. This is a part of my ethnohistorical approach; I consider those representations to be as important as published materials and thus reproduce these black women's experiences using their own words and expressions. Most significantly, I contend that documenting their experiences is valuable because of what it reveals about individual appropriations of religious practice, theological interpretation, and the spirituality of black women, which potentially show larger patterns for understanding black American religious experience specifically and American religious experience broadly.

My ethnographic approach is distinct in two ways: First, it employs a comparative analysis of published and unpublished historical sources and treats those sources as active, informing "voices" rather than the typically utilized contextual "voice." Second, my ethnographic method utilizes black feminist and womanist theory as an analytical framework for approaching and interpreting the information collected through ethnographic means. Ethnography allows us to understand what we can learn when black women's voices are viewed as authoritative. This study therefore privileges the ideas, experiences, and narratives of African American women and builds upon the womanist tradition espoused by Alice Walker, who defined a womanist as, among other things, "a black feminist or feminist of color."[36] It relies upon approaches set forth by black feminist anthropologists[37] and womanist theologians.[38] While womanist scholars have intentionally taken up the significance of religion for black women, black feminist anthropologists have not consistently explored religion as a dominant or viable lens through which to interpret black women's experiences.[39] At the same time, womanist scholarship has been limited by its commitment to theology, ethics, and biblical hermeneutics, features that are only addressed in this project insofar as they naturally evolve from the written, oral, and experiential narratives provided from the sources utilized in this work.[40] This study is therefore centrally located at the intersections of womanist and black feminist thought because it critically engages the implications of black women's unique location at the junction of race, sex, and class—a fundamental characteristic of black feminism—and the impact of religion alongside these intersectional effects upon black women, a prominent feature of womanism.

The historical aspect of this approach involved analysis of source materials that reference the Gullah/Geechee and, in particular, Gullah religion. This included the systematic analysis of nonfiction, published materials on the Gullah from 1863 to 2010; exploration of published documentation and unpublished, archival materials from the South Carolina Historical Society; and the incorporation, when possible, of materials housed in local churches and the homes of lowcountry residents. Gullah/Geechee historiography has been significantly expanded by the work of social historians, linguists, and anthropologists, who have produced more than a century of scholarship on Gullah/Geechee culture. What is of central importance to this project, however, is the treatment of Gullah/Geechee religion within this genealogy.

Descriptions of Gullah/Geechee religion within the first generation, 1863–1950, fall into three categories, the first including unpublished, nonfiction, first-person accounts that were not devoted exclusively or predominantly to documenting religion, but which reveal significant features of religion. The extensive archival documentation of John Bennett[41] and Jane Heyward exemplify this category.[42] A second subset of materials includes published articles between 1863 and 1910 that were thematic in scope and focus, such as essays published by Charlotte Forten and Charles Raymond.[43] The third genre includes published and unpublished monographs that detailed Gullah/Geechee life and practice. Significant contributions within this category include Guion Johnson's *A Social History of the Sea Islands, with Special Reference to St. Helena Island, South Carolina* (1930),[44] Mason Crum's *Gullah: Negro Life in the Carolina Sea Islands* (1940),[45] and the diaries of Laura Towne and Charlotte Forten, which were published nearly one hundred years after they were penned. Samuel Miller Lawton's unpublished dissertation, "The Religious Life of South Carolina Coastal and Sea Island Negroes" (1939) is significant because it was the first work devoted exclusively to the study of lowcountry religion.[46] An important additional contribution to this first generation is Turner's *Africanisms in the Gullah Dialect*. Although Turner did not focus predominantly on religion and his analysis has since been contested, his research transformed how subsequent scholars focused on Africa as a means of understanding the life, dialect, and culture of lowcountry blacks.

Many of the articles and unpublished materials from this first generation offer a sympathetic perspective on Gullah/Geechee life. For example, lowcountry native Jane Heyward, a white, middle-class woman whose father owned slaves, toured the Southeast offering recitals of Gullah folk stories. Heyward, a self-professed "Gullah dialect recitalist" prefaced a presentation to her dialect recitals with, "Close contact of the races, brought a love with reverence blent [sic]."[47] Like many early sources on Gullah/Geechee culture, Heyward noted the uniqueness of Gullah communities—their dialect, their ways of thinking, and their practices—and in her own way attempted to document the "peculiarities" she observed within Gullah culture. What also links several of these writers are the ways that accepted racist notions of intellectual superiority influenced their conclusions and observations about Gullah culture. During an introduction to one of her Gullah dialect recital programs, Heyward stated: "What I want to give my audience by these true stories, I will tell, is an understanding of the love which existed in the old Plantation days between the White folks in 'The Big House' and the Black folks in the Quarters. And something of the loyalty which survived for long years after the [N]egro had been told he was 'Free.' We of the South feel such a responsibility to help the simple ignorant ones, that really sometimes it becomes quite a burden."[48] I have approached documents like these with caution, care, and criticism. That these authors meant well and tried to give the most accurate descriptions in their representations of blacks of the lowcountry is not in question; however, genuine attempts to depict the life, religion, and culture of South Carolina's African Americans should not obscure and does not excuse the racism and paternalism prevalent throughout many of these works.

Engaging antebellum-era and reconstruction-era sources that document "romantic racialist conceptions" of black life has proven particularly challenging over the course of this project.[49] This is especially so because I begin this project by writing about marginalized African Americans in a period when they did not document their own experiences because they could not write, were not allowed to write, or only minimally recorded their experiences through writing. Before blacks became increasingly literate beginning in the 1900s, it was almost exclusively white writers who provided descriptions of African American culture. This is the case with South Carolina's Gullah/Geechee communities, who—with little exception—had their experiences, customs, and practices recorded by white Americans. This feature has proven particularly challenging in uncovering the experiences of the Gullah—a struggle reconciled by directly confronting how the uncritical use of these historical sources is indicative of a larger negation of black thought. In other words, to continually rely upon these sources as accurate representations without interrogating their paternalist and racist ideologies is to perpetuate the limited perspectives they articulated.[50] Therefore, I use in-depth historical analysis to demonstrate how these sources have led to continuous negative characterizations of Gullah/Geechee religious practices.

The second generation of materials on Gullah/Geechee culture (1974–1999)[51] took Lorenzo Turner's lead and made explicit efforts to identify African cultural continuities in lowcountry culture, including religion.[52] Key texts within this generation include *Down By the Riverside: A South Carolina Slave Community* (1984), by Charles Joyner; the 1977 dissertation "'Catch Sense': The Meaning of Plantation Membership on St. Helena Island S.C.," by Patricia Guthrie, which later became *Catching Sense: African American Communities on a South Carolina Sea Island* (1996); *When Roots Die: Endangered Traditions on the Sea Islands* (1987), by the late Patricia Jones-Jackson; the seminal work on lowcountry religion, *A Peculiar People: Slave Religion and Community-Culture among the Gullahs* (1988), by Margaret Creel; and *The Gullah People and Their African Heritage* (1999), by William Pollitzer.[53] Also included within this generation are the anthologies *Sea Island Roots: African Presence in the Carolinas and Georgia* (1991), by Mary Twining and Keith Baird; *The Crucible of Carolina: Essays in the Development of Gullah Language and Culture* (1994), by Michael Montgomery; and *The Legacy of Igbo Landing: Gullah Roots of African American Culture* (1998), by Marquetta Goodwine. These works represent a resurgence of academic inquiry about the Gullah, and are characterized by serious consideration of religion as a central aspect of lowcountry culture. This shift in part resulted from two critical interventions: (1) movements within social history where scholars treated the exploration of African American culture as a viable area of critical inquiry—due in part to responses to Melville Herskovits; and (2) queries by academics of religion who argued that it was a fundamental means for understanding African American history and culture.

The most significant transition in this discourse was the discussion of the *positive* impact of African cultures on lowcountry religious practices. As a result, scholars no longer treated religion and the widespread practice of African and folk traditions as a reflection of the "heathenism" of lowcountry blacks. Instead, scholars viewed Gullah/Geechee culture and religious practices as an example of religious and cultural "syncretism." Hence, perspectives that actively explored the pervasiveness of living African gods and vibrant African culture as a means of understanding Gullah/Geechee religion emerged. This shift did not fully come to the fore in the literature on lowcountry religion until the late 1970s. Pivotal to this shift was Albert Raboteau's landmark study, *Slave Religion: The "Invisible Institution" in the Antebellum South* (1978), which treated African American religion in the South as an ongoing process of formation between Christian, Muslim, and practices from African and African-derived traditions. Raboteau's assessment of the fluid and integrated quality of black religion in the South transformed the way that black religion was understood.

> It is important to realize, however, that in the Americas the religions of Africa have not been merely preserved as static "Africanisms" or as archaic "retentions." The fact is that they have continued to develop as living traditions putting down new roots in new soil, bearing new fruit as unique hybrids of American origin. African styles of worship, forms of ritual systems of belief, and fundamental perspectives have remained vital on this side of the Atlantic, not because they were preserved in "pure" orthodoxy but because they were transformed. Adaptability, based on respect for spiritual power wherever it originated, accounted for the openness of African religions to syncretism with other religious traditions and for the continuity of a distinctively African religious consciousness.[54]

Raboteau's work was the direct result of the movement to uncover examples of African cultural retentions. It had a profound impact on how African

American religion has been understood broadly and on how investigators of Gullah/Geechee religion have analyzed lowcountry religious practices.

Scholarship since the year 2000 makes up the third generation of research on Gullah/Geechee religion and culture. Trends in this generation—eight doctoral dissertations and three monographs—include (1) the continuation of efforts to identify specifically "African" identities of the Gullah, with an emphasis on scientific testing; (2) an expansion of scholarship that emphasizes the cultural impacts of commodification upon Gullah/Geechee culture, of which conversations of cultural survivals are a part; (3) the broadening of linguistic studies of Gullah/Geechee, with a focus on literary contributions; and (4) the central placement of religion as a vital means of exploring Gullah/Geechee culture.[55] The monographs salient to this project include *The Abundant Life Prevails: Religious Traditions of St. Helena Island* (2000) by Michael C. Wolfe and Jason Young's *Rituals of Resistance* (2007). It is noteworthy that two of the three recently published monographs on lowcountry culture have focused on religion as the primary lens through which to examine the Gullah/Geechee. This trend within the latest generation indicates the recognition of religion as an understudied area within Gullah/Geechee studies and signals the value placed on the critical exploration of religion as a means of understanding numerous aspects of culture.

This ethnohistorical study is simultaneously *constructivist* and *collaborative*[56] and utilizes five approaches to data collection: archival research, review and analysis of published source materials, participant observation, structured and unstructured interviews, and audio recording. This method integrates the materials by placing what lowcountry women say about themselves in dialogue with what writers have theorized about them, and noting similarities and differences between the interpretations. The project thus engages Gullah/Geechee women's ideas and experiences of race, gender, religion, and identity with writers who in their descriptions of lowcountry life addressed the same topics. This allows us to learn what contemporary women view as most important in their everyday lives, preventing written texts from being interpreted as the main voices of authority in descriptions of human experience. This approach promotes written works as *supplemental* rather than *primary* sources. I do not uphold written over "live" sources (or vice versa), nor do I categorize sources as "primary" or "secondary." As Patricia Hill Collins eloquently states, "The ability to rank scholarship into categories of primary, secondary and tertiary importance reflects the power of those who classify."[57] Instead, in an effort to challenge Western hegemonic classification processes, I combine ethnographic and historical approaches as a means of placing the living and the dead in conversation.[58] This metaphor of navigating between the past and the present influences the lived experiences of Gullah/Geechee women and my attempts to capture their meaning. It is especially apt given that talking to the dead is a practice with which these seven Gullah/Geechee women identify.

Talking to the Dead—A Critical Approach

I use the phrase talking to the dead to connote three different features of the practice: first, actual lived experiences that lowcountry residents have with the dead that they interpret as real, even as the presence of an apparition likely does not exist (which is exemplified in my own experience in Charleston's City Market); and second, engagement in what I call religio-cultural activities (singing, storytelling, sweetgrass basketry, prayer, and dreaming) that calls one's forebearers to mind—often through a performance or (re)enactment—and can sometimes lead to the experience of connecting with the dead. These two manifestations of the practice are the main ways in which I employ the phrase. A third category of talking to the dead refers to the communal belief in the act of "living memory" or remembering. Talking to the dead is one of several ways that the women see themselves as remembering their pasts and living out their memories. This third category is the most difficult to describe because it also includes practices that can invoke talking to the dead (storytelling, prayer, the performance of music that has been passed on generationally, etc.), as well as ancestral communication. As a result, the first two features become subsumed under the third, which makes talking to the dead a general reference to the act of remembering.[59]

I could certainly categorize these three configurations in other terms. For example, I might call the act of speaking to a deceased ancestor "direct encounter," and connecting with the dead through certain acts "practice-mediated, indirect encounter," and give an entirely new name to the act of lived memory. However, as much as it might prove easier to a reader outside of these communities to categorize these "forms" of talking to the dead, the challenge of making these distinctions is that they do not represent how these women experience, identify, and understand what talking to the dead means. There is no categorical distinction for Roberta when she has a conversation with her dead sister in a dream, for how Lucinda talks to her dead mother when she sings "Sendin' Up My Timbah," or for how Beatrice talks to her dead grandmother while she is making sweetgrass baskets. Although the means by which they "encounter" the dead may be different, their interpretation of the meaning of the experience—that their deceased relatives are communicating with them—is exactly the same. My use of talking to the dead emphasizes the importance of lived memory among the women individually and in their communities, and places this project within subsequent conversations in memory studies that question how the use of memory can enhance and complicate ethnographic research.[60]

In *Black Magic*, Yvonne Chireau raises the question, "Is there an intermediate category in which to place ideas of the ways that humans have engaged in a reality beyond their own, a reality delineated by the presence of divine beings, forces and other invisible entities?"[61] I believe that talking to the dead as experienced and expressed among these seven women gestures to that category, which harkens to McKoy's interpretation of "limbo time":

> Tradition bonds African culture across space and time to the extent that the living are responsible for answering to their ancestors for their behavior. In essence, tradition binds Diaspora cultures to their African roots across space and time in that the ancestor—the mythical and spiritual embodiment of another time—maintains a constant relationship with the living. In effect, there exists a living transcendental pact that is grounded in another temporal space. Not only does tradition provide kinship ties, but tradition determines progress in the sense that both scenes of culture and the events derived from them can be replicated and depended upon through time. Perfection resides, not in the surpassing of groundwork laid by the ancestors, but in the value placed on the perfect replication of such cultural moments.[62]

The mediation between space, time, and invisible entities that McKoy and Chireau gesture toward are ever-important considerations in black diasporic culture, and especially in the case of the Gullah/Geechee. For Lucinda, Roberta, Faye, Ruth, Yenenga, Lucille, and Beatrice, talking to the dead is the manifestation of the liminal space between the living and the dead *and* the past and the present.

It is not coincidence that all seven of the women who talk to the dead have held formal leadership positions within their churches and have been spiritual leaders within their communities. Talking to the dead thus provides a unique means of framing just how important Gullah/Geechee women are to the continuation of lowcountry religious and spiritual practices, a feature missing in the literature, while introducing readers to a distinctive custom within the region. Although the act of talking to the dead may be different in its orientation for each of these women, what they share is that the outcomes of talking to the dead have direct bearing on their understanding of their faith, their participation in their churches, the way they live their daily lives, and their relationships to their pasts. Talking to the dead is viewed as a sustaining practice among the women because it has significant consequences in the decisions and life choices that many of them have made and will make. Talking to the dead greatly informs how they negotiate changes in their own lives and within their communities as it helps determine their actions and reactions while simultaneously gesturing to the histories and past experiences that inform their present. The relationships these women each share with the dead are very special and reflect a deep spiritual connection that surpasses denominational or formal church affiliation and seamlessly coincides with their Christian identities.

Relating Religion, Methodology, and Structure

When Robert Orsi, Danièl Hervieu-Léger, and David Hall began talking about "lived religion" as an area of analysis within religious studies in the late 1990s, they were responding to what they saw as a significant disparity between how academics (especially theologians) theorized religion and how people of faith lived out their religious identities. They wanted to give religious practitioners a chance to speak on their own terms and without the confines of "armchair theologians," who interpreted systems of belief with limited experiential knowledge. This turn toward focusing on the function of religion for its believers (what is in many camps now called "practical theology") became a counter to theoretical treatments of religion that lacked substantive engagement with the people about whom arguments were being made.

This disparity between what is theorized and what is lived is echoed in studies of the Gullah/Geechee, which have largely grouped these communities in terms of geographic and cultural distinctions without really attending to the nuances of their religious faith from the perspective of individual practitioners. Gullah/Geechee women have been excluded from examinations of the history of lowcountry religion and are not treated as significant contributors to the continuation of Christian faith today. To further efforts to allow individuals to speak about the importance and practice of their faith for themselves, it is important to rely on Gullah/Geechee women's voices to see how they are creative agents in their theological development, how they personally understand their religious practices, and how their experiences make unique theoretical contributions of their own. We must simultaneously consider the history of American religion as a collection of particular practices with theological meaning that are connected to specific social contexts.

Central to my analysis is the understanding that religion and religious expression are deeply embedded in our social contexts. One cannot examine religion or religious experience without understanding the powerful social forces that the women of this study find themselves dealing with. My use of these terms emerges both from the perspective of the project's informants as well as from an amalgamation of pivotal texts within religious studies. *Religion* is one aspect of culture and emerges from the complex processes by which humans make sense of their world, their place in the world, and their relation to others. This is often (though not exclusively) expressed in the form of belief, order, judgment, and ritualized practice. *Religious experience* therefore refers to the events and moments that inform how humans make sense of and act in the world. Experience can be characterized as ongoing behaviors and thoughts as well as special, memorable moments that stand out amidst everyday events. Not all experiences are deemed "religious." Yet what sets a religious experience apart is not belief in a divine presence or an increased level of spirituality but the fact that it is specifically interpreted, labeled, and/or acknowledged by the person(s) as a religious experience.[63] This caveat is especially significant to this work because there are several experiential practices that would not typically be identified as spiritual or religious (storytelling, for example). To the women, however, these practices are prototypically experienced as powerful religious events that connect them to their deceased ancestors.

I contend that there is something particular about Gullah/Geechee religious experience, which I describe primarily through the lens of talking to the dead. In other faith systems within African diasporic communities, such as Santería in Cuba and Vodun in Haiti, the meeting of African-derived practices with Christianity (in those cases Catholicism) resulted in a distinctive merging of African rituals with traditions and epistemologies of Catholicism to form a new faith system with its own rites. Similarly, when we look at the formation of spiritual churches in a North American locale such as New Orleans (which is highly studied because of the folk practice voodoo), the influences of Spiritualism, Catholicism, Pentecostalism, and Voodoo resulted in a syncretic but distinct faith system with its own rituals and customs. By contrast, in the South Carolina lowcountry, African-derived folk customs such as talking to the dead and conjure do not become conjoined with Christianity, but are maintained as separate yet accepted spiritual practices that do not conflict with Christianity, which functions as the primary faith system. As a result, the symbiotic, fluid relationship between their staunch Protestant faith and their ongoing belief in and support of African-derived practices and African American folk traditions (of which talking to the dead and conjure are a part) makes Gullah/Geechee religious experiences distinctive. More specifically, the women's appropriation of Christianity, music, sweetgrass basketry, storytelling, and belief in conjure, coupled with their ability to use these practices to talk to the dead, without causing any disruption to their theological and epistemological frameworks, exemplifies this fluidity.

The structure of this project coincides with this fluid understanding of religion and religious experience. Chapter 1, "Culture Keepers," introduces Lucille, Roberta, Lucinda, Ruth, Yenenga, Faye, and Beatrice through descriptions of their lives as well as their social, political, and cultural contexts. I use their narratives to contest the ways that lowcountry women were historically treated as peripheral or even negative actors in the perpetuation of black religion and religious expression. I also compare the representation of women in written narratives of lowcountry religion to their lived experiences, using interviews with the women to document the centrality yet fluid appropriation of Christian faith. As Julie Dash's cinematic focus on intergenerational relationships between three Gullah women suggests, there is something very special about women of the lowcountry. This chapter examines the significant role women play in the maintenance and sustenance of a dynamic religious culture within the lowcountry. I characterize Gullah/Geechee women as "culture keepers," persons who have great responsibility in shaping the structures of religious history, as well as their current (Christian) faith and practice.

The unique contributions of Gullah/Geechee women stand out when we examine their influence in folk practices. In chapter 2, "Folk Religion," I discuss the historical pervasiveness of folk traditions such as conjure within Gullah/Geechee communities, as well as the contemporary prevalence of folk traditions among the women. Lucinda's role, in particular, as a local herbalist and perceived conjure woman reflects an ongoing acceptance of folk traditions as symbolized by the merging of folk and Christian practices among the Gullah/Geechee. This chapter documents the numerous elements that make up the diverse features of black religious expression in the lowcountry, and sets the stage for the subsequent discussions of contemporary religious identity and practice, including the continued significance of talking to the dead.

I turn to a fuller exploration of talking to the dead in chapter 3. There, I unpack the religious and religio-cultural manifestations of talking to the dead among the women and integrate additional details about how their religious practices facilitate talking to the dead. Though not an exclusively female custom, it is unclear why women largely maintain it. What is transparent, however, is that women are the keepers of the practice. For the women included in this work, "talking to de dead" represents an ongoing exchange; the process occurs in their daily practices of leading prayer trees and communicating with friends, visiting the sick, telling stories, and weaving sweetgrass baskets. Talking to the dead influences their interpretation of the meaning of religion and the relationship between church membership and individual practice. All of these women communicated with the living dead through their experiences of "seekin'," the process by which each woman joined her local church. During this experience many of the women encountered deceased ancestors during intense periods of fasting and prayer or while dreaming in the midst of the process. Seeking was thus essential to their recognition of the fluid connections between the living and the dead. Communicating with the dead was seen as one of the most prominent folk traditions in the lowcountry. Chapter 3 therefore emphasizes how significant talking to the dead is among these lowcountry women. While some of the activities above may not be considered "religious" in a traditional sense, they are nonetheless central to these women's lives and are tightly interwoven with religious imagery and concepts. By documenting the significance of women in lowcountry religious practice, I demonstrate how women continue to maintain substantial roles within lowcountry communities as the main preservers of Gullah/Geechee religious culture.

Any meaningful understanding of African American religion must look at the musical traditions associated with it, and in chapter 4, "Sendin' Up My Timbah," I examine the ways in which sacred music traditions have played and continue to play a particularly significant role in the religious lives of lowcountry women and how sacred music becomes a means of expressing their faith as well as facilitating their communication with the deceased. I contend that music in the lowcountry functions as performative memory; that is, musical practices and traditions among Gullah/Geechee women are one way that memories of the past are transmitted and sustained into the present. These traditions become identifiable via bodily performative practices and rituals in addition to written texts. In this way, music functions as its own mode of language and acts as a medium between the living and the dead. The attitudes these women share about the meaning, value, and function of music demonstrate how music operates as a lived representation of "tulking to de dead." Unlike earlier generations of literature on lowcountry music practices, I center women's participation in music, which helps us understand the spiritual significance of music in Gullah/Geechee culture in general. It is through the shouting, dancing, and singing traditions that these lowcountry women connect to their past and act in their present. Music is the single most important element of Gullah/Geechee culture that ensures its continuation as a distinctive African American community. To these women, music is second in importance only to belief in God. Moreover, music, like the seeking process and active participation in the church, unites the women in this study. I capture the deep meaning and performative ritual aspects of music in the companion website,[64] which documents the women in the study singing, shouting, and demonstrating the significance of sacred music in their lives.

For all seven of these women, remembering is a sacred, spiritual practice that ensures ongoing connections between the living and the dead. In chapter 5, "Lived Memory," I explore how talking to the dead through remembering continues to be important among the women, especially through celebration of the memory of Africa as a shared heritage and sacred home. I examine contemporary meanings of Africa to these women to understand how remembering Africa has been an important part of talking to the dead. My exploration of how these women see and remember Africa reveals important differences among them. Remembering Africa as a way of talking to the dead is changing due to cultural commodification, as culture becomes tied to market forces. Disparities in how the women of this study remember Africa reflect significant fragmentation in Gullah/Geechee culture. I discuss these changes and engage how contemporary efforts to remember Africa by way of "Gullah Festivals," "Gullah Tours," and even the *Gullah/Geechee Cultural Heritage Corridor Act* (2006) have complicated the ongoing significance of talking to the dead.

I envision this project—in its methodology, content, and scope—as a critical response to an absence in scholarship. In the broader landscape of work on American religion, little about the Gullah/Geechee in the American South exists, and even less addresses the role of women in lowcountry religious practices. Despite contemporary sources that explicitly engage black women's religiosity, the fact remains, as Weisenfeld and Newman noted in the late 1990s, "the religious lives of African-American women loom as a substantial yet largely undiscovered terrain in the study of religion in America."[65] I therefore view my technique of investigating black women's lived experiences alongside representations and absences in written texts to be a critical intervention. As such, I have made intensive efforts to return to the lowcountry to follow up with the women with whom I spent so much time and to ensure the fairness and accuracy of my descriptions. This is an essential aspect of contemporary ethnography, which I view as a collaborative effort that includes getting feedback from my informants about my representations of their narratives and experiences. My investigation into their lives adds to a limited but growing body of literature about these communities and expands the existing scholarship by engaging how women in the lowcountry interpret their own histories. It is my hope that this project will contribute to an ever-broadening landscape of studies of African American women, of black religion in the South, and of the use of ethnography as a viable approach to religious studies.

In their introduction to *Not Only the Master's Tools*, Lewis R. Gordon and Jane Anna Gordon contend that dismantling the master's house, as Audre Lorde described, is a "misguided project." Instead, scholars of black studies must utilize the imaginative creativities of the enslaved and formerly enslaved to transcend the limitations of Eurocentric, Western-based thought and build houses of their/our own.[66] This project emerges in that spirit. Its goal is not to invalidate historical representations and writings about Gullah/Geechee religion, but to demonstrate how women of the South Carolina lowcountry have utilized, reconfigured, and transcended those representations. I contend that Gullah/Geechee frameworks, specifically from a religio-cultural perspective, offer great insight into the past and present imagination of a population.

When one considers representations of black religion in the lowcountry that have been documented over the past century and a half, it should be apparent that Gullah/Geechee religious expression was both diverse and dynamic. Whether through the presence of black deacons and preachers who were appointed by whites and affirmed by blacks; the significant role of the praise house/church as a meeting space for black community members; or the belief in and presence of conjurers, root-workers, and hoodoo practitioners, it is certain that while they have become predominately Christian over time, religious traditions in the lowcountry have existed alongside, and at times competed with, folk religious customs such as conjure. Embracing this rich religious culture should certainly influence our understanding of religious practice among the Gullah/Geechee in a historical sense, but also should guide our interpretations of the practices of today.

CHAPTER 1

Culture Keepers

A Modern Context

Driving into the South Carolina lowcountry is certain to arouse a deep sense of nostalgia. Whether entering from Columbia via a southeastern route on I-26, through Savannah on I-95 north, or by way of a southern trek past Georgetown and Myrtle Beach on Highway 17, the meandering country roads, scenic patches of undeveloped forest, and small, sleepy, seemingly deserted towns give the distinct feeling of a slower pace. If you dare risk opening a car window—especially between the months of June and September!—prepare to be engulfed by a jarring humidity that makes clothes and hair cling. That hot, heavy, sticky dampness, combined with the potpourri of honeysuckle, ocean, fish, and salt marshes, evokes heartfelt appreciation for the luxury of air-conditioning. The ninety-two-mile drive between Beaufort, Charleston, and Moncks Corner includes at least an hour on two-lane highways, many of which are flanked by clusters of oak trees and palmettos. In the lowcountry, the rich, lush green of grasses and tree leaves suggests exceedingly fertile soils. Stepping out onto a porch or the beach for a closer glimpse of the ocean reveals skies laden with hues akin to the azure-blue of the Caribbean. Make no mistake, once you enter the lowcountry, you cannot help but relax—if only a bit—and to appreciate the meandering pace of time.

At first glance, this same sense of ease prevails in the towns of Cross and Moncks Corner, and the cities of Mt. Pleasant, James Island, and Beaufort. Yet a closer look reveals notable demographic differences. Cross and Moncks Corner are geographically the smallest and least populated of these areas. Although Cross's status as an unincorporated town limits the quantity and quality of available statistical data, the seemingly inverted ratio of white to black residents between Cross and Moncks Corner is noticeable. As part of Berkeley County, the largest in the state, these two towns have median annual incomes that are a representative average of broader county statistics, but below South Carolina's statewide income average of $45,000.[1]

Lucille Gaillard, a fifty-nine-year-old resident of Moncks Corner, travels twice a week to attend Sunday worship service and Wednesday Bible Study at Poplar Hill Christian Church (Disciples of Christ) in Cross. The drive "is a straight shot up Highway 6" and takes about twenty minutes. However, Lucille spends a quarter of the year at her family home in Beaufort, a city ninety miles away whose greater metropolitan area boasts a total population of nearly fifty thousand residents. The contrast in geographic size and population has directly influenced Lucille's decision to keep her family in Moncks Corner and attend church in Cross. To her, "Beaufort jus' too big, too busy, and too white!"[2] Lucille's social reading of Beaufort coincides with its demographics, as its nearly 70-percent white population contrasts strikingly with the racial makeup of Moncks Corner. Santee Cooper, a state utility company that was established during the New Deal, is Berkeley County's largest employer, and Lucille's husband Donald worked there until 2007, when he retired at the age of sixty-three. Increasingly, however, as more people recognize Moncks Corner's proximity to Charleston, local employment is shifting toward the primary industries of the city of Charleston: tourism and the rapid development of resorts and gated communities.

Lucille lives in the area of Moncks Corner known as Kittfield, a predominantly black community historically divided into "up top," where the smaller white population live, and "the bottom," where African Americans reside. Kittfield is the area where I grew up, but I did not know Lucille well as a youth because she lived "up top." I did know of her, however, and began cultivating a professional relationship with her during one of my visits to South Carolina in 2004. Lucille was posting flyers near the neighborhood baseball field advertising a "Gospel Sing" at her church in Cross. Given that most residents of the community attend local churches near town, I was surprised to learn that Lucille traveled "so far" to attend church, and that she did so multiple times per week. I soon discovered that Lucille spends a great deal of her life traveling throughout various areas of the lowcountry. ". . . I [used to] go to Beaufort all the time, I'd go back and forth to see my family and to go to Mt. Sinai Baptist Church and New Hope Christian Church, which were my parents' churches. Then I found Poplar Hill and so

I stayed in Cross and started going to church there." A curvaceous, dark-brown-skinned woman who "doesn't enjoy cooking as much, but loves to eat good food," Lucille sees Poplar Hill as instrumental to her survival during difficult times in her life. Lucille continued attending Poplar Hill, even after her first marriage failed and she moved to Moncks Corner. "Man, that was a hard time in my life and that church really supported me you know, it really did. So I just kept going."

Kittfield is also home to Lucinda Pinckney, who lives down the road from Lucille but admits they are not well acquainted. Their unfamiliarity is in part due to their age difference. At eighty-nine, Lucinda is a spry, lean woman who could easily pass for sixty. Standing over six feet tall, she has maintained relatively good health and has outlived her husband, seven younger siblings, and one of her four children. The daughter of a local itinerant Baptist preacher and a well-known seamstress, Lucinda has long been retired from her job as caretaker, and spends the bulk of her time "in the service of the Lord" and "checking in on [her] kids." Lucinda—or Ms. Cinda, as she is known within the community—has a commanding presence that makes many community members uncomfortable. She is not belligerent or mean, but also does not exude the traditional conviviality associated with southern women. Her very dark skin, prominent cheekbones, jutting chin, onyx-colored eyes, silver eyebrows, and jet-black hair contribute to her striking appearance. When combined with her imposing height, Ms. Cinda's arresting facial features—which are often couched in a stern expression—give her a no-nonsense persona. Lucinda is well aware of the community's perception of her, and she shrugs it off, "I don't pay these folks no mind, me and God got our own thing."

Moncks Corner is also where close friends Faye Terry and Roberta Kelly reside.[3] Roberta lives in a small, brown, tin-roofed, three-bedroom house with yellow vinyl siding. As a resident of the historically African American section of town called the West End, Roberta is within walking distance from Wesley United Methodist Church (hereafter Wesley UMC), the church that she, Faye, and Lucinda regularly attend. Roberta and Faye, who met shortly after each moved to Moncks Corner when they were newly married, have a great deal in common. Faye owned a home and lived a few streets over from Roberta in the West End before moving to the mostly white area of Pinopolis, closer to her husband's job. After his death, Faye relocated in 2005 to an apartment in the predominantly black neighborhood of Haynesville. In addition to being members of Wesley UMC, being born at the brink of the Great Depression, and having children and grandchildren close in age, both women contributed to their families' income by working as maids, cooks, and caregivers for white families, and both women's husbands worked for the Berkeley County public school system.

I first met Yenenga Wheeler in 2003 at her residence on James Island, which is forty-five miles from Moncks Corner. After driving fifty minutes, crossing the James Island connector that links the island with the city of Charleston, traveling down Folly Road and onto several unpaved side roads, I reached the driveway of her blue, single-story, ranch-style house with a white awning and a matching porch. Her house was the only one on what appeared to be at least an acre of land, and a blue and white sign that read "Storytelling in the Gullah Language" welcomed me onto the porch. A slender, fair-skinned woman with shoulder-length dreadlocks, Yenenga came to the screen door and greeted me warmly with a hug and memorable words of welcome, "God's good." Casually dressed in green slacks, a tan blouse with lace sleeves, white socks, and brown, open-toed sandals, she sat down with me for our initial conversation only after I accepted a glass of water and declined (multiple times) her offer of food. Yenenga's home is large and spacious, comfortable and roomy, but not flashy or extravagant in any way. The room I became most familiar with, the sitting room, has cherry hardwood floors that accentuate walls decorated in muted pinks. The interior has an island feel to it, with soft pinks complemented with varied shades of green, including numerous live plants. The large, soft chairs were not merely showpieces, but received many guests.

Yenenga did not introduce to me to Ruth Kelly, but she had a direct hand in our meeting as she sent me to the church they both attend. It was there, at St. James Presbyterian, where I first met Ruth, a young, spirited woman in her late forties. I was sent to Ruth by their pastor, who believed she would be a good person for me to talk to in order to gain an understanding of the church and the role it played in the community. St. James was our ongoing meeting location, which is significant because of what it reveals about how much time Ruth actually spends there, doing what she calls "church work." When I first met her, Ruth embodied the style, dress, and persona of the consummate church professional, yet she has an infectious laugh that belies her professionalism. She wore her relaxed hair in an upswept bun with bangs and was dressed in dark slacks and a blouse. She was hospitable and punctual, and provided in-depth explanations about her personal experiences while placing them within the spectrum of church activities. It was clear from our meetings that Ruth was an effective communicator who had an air of maturity that seemingly surpassed her literal age—a trait she attributed to the fact that she "always used to hang out with the old folks."

Yenenga and Ruth are both members of St. James Presbyterian and life-long residents of James Island, a Sea Island community that, like the city of Mt. Pleasant, has a complicated relationship with the city of Charleston because of its proximity. One half of James Island lies within Charleston's city limits, while the remainder is either part of the Town of James Island or is unincorporated. All that separates James Island from Charleston is the James Island connector. Similarly, the Cooper River and the historic Arthur Ravenel Bridge distinguish Mt. Pleasant from Charleston. Their respective locations place both towns within the Charleston–North Charleston Metropolitan Statistical Area, and people often buy residences on one of these two islands to avoid the higher costs associated with living in downtown Charleston. James Island and Mt. Pleasant also share hospitality, tourism, and urban development as their primary industries.

This is where the obvious similarities end, however, for Mt. Pleasant has almost double the population and median income of James Island; in addition, the contrast in the racial makeup of the cities is striking, especially when one compares the percentage of residents in each town living below the poverty line. Beatrice "Ms. Bea" Dixon, a nearly seventy-year-old woman who has lived all of her life in Mt. Pleasant, is well aware of the implications of racial and economic disparities in her town: "There ain't nothing but gated communities 'round yeh [here]. It used to be so that we could get together and maybe even get a little piece of land if you didn't inherit any. Now I can barely afford to pay the tax on my property since these white folks done come in an take over so."[4] Ms. Bea feels the stress that the economic disparities of the tourist industry can induce, as her primary income derives from making baskets out of the natural warm-season sweetgrass found in coastal dune areas.[5] Lulls in the tourist season, the natural ebb and flow of the market economy, and periods of poor weather mean that there are times when the money from making baskets does not meet her family's needs. In addition to providing food for her husband, four adult sons, and adult daughter, Ms. Bea also prepares enough food for her six grandchildren and fourteen great-grandchildren, who come to her house after school several days a week, as well as every Sunday. As a result, twice a week she travels forty minutes south to Beaufort where she cleans the home of and runs errands for a more elderly white woman.

It is noteworthy that Faye, Roberta, Lucinda, Lucille, and Beatrice have worked or continue to work as in-home domestics for white families, and all have a high-school-level education.[6] It is therefore not merely coincidence that the five of them did not achieve a class status beyond the positions of poor and working-class domestics; as Angela Davis has noted, there are historically explicit connections between black women's level of education and their level of class attainment.[7] According to Patricia Hill Collins, "Black women domestic workers remained poor because they were economically exploited workers in a capitalist political economy. . . . [H]istorically, many White families in both the middle and working class were able to maintain their class position because they used Black women domestic workers as a source of cheap labor.[8] Ruth is exceptional in that she has worked as an office manager, and she attended a four-year college after graduating from high school. After college, she returned home and went into church ministry. She counts herself as "lucky to be able to work for the church full time now," and she has been a paid employee of the church since shortly after completing college.

That Faye, Roberta, Lucille, Beatrice, and Lucinda have worked as domestics coincides with the historical treatment of black women as mammies, cooks, and other domestic figures within white households and communities. It is even more striking that well into retirement age Beatrice and Lucille both continue to be employed by white families as domestics. If these women hold a seeming sense of disdain for white people—or "buckra,"[9] as the Gullah/Geechee often call them—it is because they are well acquainted with what Roberta calls "the wills and ways of 'dem white folks." All five of the women are well aware of the stigma associated with their positions as servants.[10] Faye noted that white people frequently referred to her as "Mammy" or "Mauma" for as long as she could remember, even after she retired as an in-home caretaker for a white family. That these women continue to be relegated to these positions speaks to the lasting implications of their particular positions as black women with limited education in the South, and supports contemporary examinations that note modern reinscriptions of these historical forms.[11] These women's class status is especially important to consider because of the ways it also affects their religious lives, where women continue to dominate positions within the religious sphere such as church mothers, hospitality committee members, and nursery providers— positions that are frequently deemed as "caretaker" in nature.[12]

At best, Lucinda, Faye, and Roberta can be viewed as examples of the poorest levels of working-class women. Although the subject of their specific incomes was never broached, their frequent references to their economic struggles and to their stated trust in God to help them "get through," the material items within their homes, and the homes themselves—while well kept, inviting, and comfortable—reflect a borderline impoverished lifestyle. Lucille and Beatrice, on the other hand, could be characterized as working class because they are property owners, have larger (though not bountiful) homes and land, have cars (both, coincidentally, own Ford vehicles), and have appeared to retire with some level of economic comfort. Yet they both "come out of retirement" to "clean house" or run errands for white people to supplement their income as necessary, which occurs in Lucille's case from time to time even though she has a debilitating heart condition; she is a skilled seamstress. Their current positions reflect the perpetuation of the black servant-class culture common to southern cities and communities.

Of all the women, Yenenga appears to be the most financially stable. Her situation is distinctive, as she has multiple cars (including a luxury vehicle) and owns several acres of land within her local neighborhood as well as "prime" real estate in downtown Charleston. Before retiring, her husband was locally employed as a construction site manager and was what Yenenga calls the "primary breadwinner." Yet Yenenga contributed to the household finances as a musician, business owner, and entrepreneur. She is a talented pianist and was an organist at St. James Presbyterian Church from the time shortly after she "seeked" her religion at the age of twelve until she retired from her work as the primary church organist in 1995. She also owns a store across the street from her house, which she inherited from her parents. She sells candy, potato chips, and beverages, as well as "down-home dinnas" featuring traditional southern cuisine, including macaroni and cheese, collard greens, and fried chicken. She has a liquor license, and used to sell fresh cuts of meat before the local supermarket became more popular. While the store does not do as well financially in the winter months of November through February, business overflows during the summer months when local baseball and softball leagues are active at the community baseball field next door. She opens the store "mostly in the afternoons" during the week when children are getting out of school, as they are her biggest candy customers. Yenenga speaks openly about her economic independence, noting, "I don't devote all my time to the store, but gyal I be out there tellin' stories and [doing] church work." She now makes most of her money from storytelling, for which she reportedly charges between $25 and $300 per hour, depending on the event. She is happy that she "punches her own time" and is able to run the store, do the work she feels called to do for the church, and tell her Gullah stories—all "how she wanna run it."

She is well aware of just how fortunate she is economically compared to her family, friends, and other members of the community. "I can only say that it's God who brought me thus far."

This notion of being brought "thus far" by faith, as the popular African American hymn celebrates, resonates with each of the women. Even though the majority of them struggle financially, and they have each faced various forms of racial and gender discrimination in their respective communities, they see themselves as fulfilling the purposes that God has destined for their lives. This does not mean that they live their faith blindly, and that they are not at times troubled by the difficulties they face. Rather, they envision themselves as rising above their circumstances and being empowered by their faith in God, which is in part lived out through their participation in local African American churches.

The Contemporary Black Church

As in many locales throughout the South, churches are more readily accessible and numerous than grocery stores. This is the case in the small towns of Cross and Moncks Corner, as well as in the larger cities of James Island, Mt. Pleasant, and Beaufort. Wesley UMC, Poplar Hill Christian Church, St. James Presbyterian, and Greater Goodwill African American Episcopal Church (hereafter Greater Goodwill AME) are among more than one hundred churches in Moncks Corner, Cross, James Island, and Mt. Pleasant.[13] For example, although the town of Moncks Corner has fewer than ten thousand residents, it has fifteen churches. This is indicative of a broader trend within the southern United States and signals the perceived significance of religion within these communities. Comparing the structure, style, and membership of the four churches the women of this study attend can reveal a great deal about similarities and differences within contemporary Gullah/Geechee religion specifically, and about the broader influences of the black church.

Historically, the phrase "The Black Church" has been signified by black participation in seven mainline Protestant Christian traditions that developed from the mid-eighteenth through the nineteenth centuries; these include the African Methodist Episcopal Church, Christian Methodist Episcopal Church, National Baptist Convention, National Baptist Convention America, Progressive National Baptist, and the Church of God in Christ. As sociologists of religion C. Eric Lincoln and Lawrence Mamiya describe in their landmark text, *The Black Church in the African-American Experience*, these churches were important because they provided a space for blacks in America to forge their own spiritual, religious, and worship identities. These denominational churches emphasized black liberation from the economic and social limitations established by a white plantocracy, as well as from temporal, physical, and corporeal oppression. According to Lincoln and Mamiya, these denominations led to the black church's capacity to function simultaneously as a cultural broker of American values and a preserver of black cultural heritage. Contemporary debate exists about the usefulness of this phrase given the vast religious diversity among black Americans, its exclusive focus on Christian traditions, and a diminished sense of significance among black Americans.[14] The four churches the women in this book attend are mainstream, Protestant Christian denominations that are predominantly black in their orientation and membership. I therefore use the phrase "black church" or "the black church" to broadly refer to black Christian churches, which also gestures to the historical use of the term, but is distinguished by my use of lowercase letters.

In the South Carolina lowcountry, black churches continue to be dominated by mainstream Protestant denominations (Presbyterian, Methodist, Baptist, Episcopal, Lutheran, Congregationalist, and Reformed), but current shifts have resulted in the presence of more nondenominational churches. This increase is reflected in larger society, where dissatisfaction with mainline denominational church polity and liturgy have led to the development of more churches that profess their own organizational systems. At the same time, however, mainline denominations have relied on their longstanding histories, and as exemplified by the mainline church membership of all seven women in this study, remain relevant because of their established pasts. Poplar Hill Christian Church, like Wesley UMC, is a smaller church, with a membership roster of approximately one thousand and average Sunday church attendance of two hundred.[15] Greater Goodwill AME and St. James Presbyterian are significantly larger churches. The average Sunday attendance at Greater Goodwill is five hundred, and St. James averages closer to eight hundred active participants per Sunday. Community demographics have a direct impact on each church's respective population. If we presume the kinds of cars that people drive to be relatively indicative of their economic (or at the very least social) status, St. James and Greater Goodwill are frequented by individuals who drive typically higher-end vehicles in terms of style, make, and model: these churches also have larger numbers of luxury sedans and SUVs—especially Mercedes, BMW, and Lexus—in their parking lots. Wesley UMC and Poplar Hill parking lots are more often peppered with American-made Ford, Buick, and Chevrolet four-door sedans and pickup trucks.

St. James Presbyterian Church is notable for what distinguishes it from and what it shares in common with the three other churches. St. James is near the geographic center of the island. Founded in 1866, St. James began just like Wesley UMC—as a place of worship where blacks and whites gathered collectively, but sat separately.[16] As was also common in the lowcountry, at its founding the church had more black members (235) than white (35). According to St. James's history, the majority of blacks moved to Methodist and Baptist churches postemancipation, but St. James was able to retain many of its black members because of the efforts of Reverend Ishmael Moultrie, who encouraged black members to remain at St. James "while they waited for a minister out of training."[17] Currently, Reverend Doctor Charles Heyward holds the pastorate of St. James, which now has more than four thousand communicants (members) on its roster and is the largest black Presbyterian congregation on the Charleston-Atlantic Presbytery. Of the churches the seven women in this study attend, St. James is the largest in terms of its size, roster, and regular Sunday attendance. The church's brick exterior belies its size, for it can easily hold more than a thousand people. Its interior is ornate—solid oak pews, deep-red carpet, and stained-glass windows—without being flashy or gaudy.

St. James differs from Poplar Hill Christian Church, Wesley UMC, and Greater Goodwill AME in denominational affiliation, physical size, and the class diversity of its members, yet it is remarkably similar in its physical organization, liturgical content, and worship structure and style. Although it is physically larger, St. James's most important interior space—the sanctuary—is organized exactly the same as the sanctuaries in the three other churches. The sanctuary is divided into two rows of pews, which contain copies of the hymnal and the New International Version of the Bible, flanked on either side by smaller aisles. The space is divided in the center by a wider, single aisle, where the pastor and choir process to the front of the church at the beginning of the worship service. The front of the sanctuary is the center of the space. When one sits in the pew, spaces to the far left and far right are designated for the choir(s) and, when applicable, for esteemed visitors and guests. Immediately in front of the choir stands are two podiums, and the pastor generally preaches from the one to the audience's left, while announcements and readings by other speakers or guests are delivered from the podium to the audience's right. The space is highlighted by two focal points: the altar, which is in front of and centered with respect to the podiums, and a large, three-dimensional crucifix, which is centered upon the front wall of the sanctuary.

St. James publicly professes a Christ-centered ideology, which it announces in its mission statement: "A Body of Believers: inviting people to **Joyfully Worship** God through **Active Fellowship** in the church family, preparing them as **Matured Disciples** of Jesus Christ; and sending them for **Evangelism** in the community and **Service** to the world." As this statement embraces the principles of the Presbyterian Church broadly (evangelism, service, and mature disciples), it also celebrates its own take on worship and fellowship (joyful and active). Similar mission statements and mottos guide the other churches. At Poplar Hill, their vision is "To Make Disciples of Christ"; Wesley UMC's motto is "The Church Where Christ is the Head of Our Lives." Each church creatively incorporates aspects of popular culture into its worship, service, and life. While attending a service at Greater Goodwill AME, I heard the pastor repeat, "Can you hear me now? Can you hear me now? Can you hear me now?" in reference to the popular Verizon Wireless commercial, in order to get the congregation's attention. Wesley UMC has used Rick Warren's *The Purpose Driven Life* as a Bible-study aid. In 2009, Poplar Hill held a "woman thou art loosed" seminar to help female church members identify their respective callings within and beyond the church. Certainly, as these church leaders find ways to reach their members, aspects of prosperity-gospel ministries popularized by prominent black and white ministers, such as Joel Olsteen, T.D. Jakes, and Rick Warren, have entered the churches. None of the lowcountry churches described here, however, can be clearly identified as a prosperity-gospel-directed church.[18] For example, St. James uses quotes from Rick Warren on its website, but does not emphasize the notion of giving to get blessed that typifies prosperity-gospel ministries.

These churches also share numerous similarities in terms of worship structure and liturgical content. All four have Wednesday night Bible study at either six or seven in the evening, which is usually modestly attended. St. James, however, holds two Bible studies on Wednesday, one at noon and the other at seven o'clock. Whether church begins at 10:00 A.M. (Poplar Hill, and on first Sundays at Greater Goodwill), 11:00 A.M. (Greater Goodwill on second–fourth Sundays and every Sunday at Wesley UMC), or is marked by two services (8:00 and 11:00 at St. James), Sunday worship is the highlight of the week. Getting ready "to go to church" is certainly a form of ritual performance for Lucinda, Roberta, Lucille, Faye, Yenenga, Ruth, and Beatrice. Whether they "dress down" and wear a simple skirt, blouse, and sandals, or "dress up" in a full-skirted suit with a church hat and panty hose, they put great thought into what they wear and how they look on any given Sunday.

In all four of these churches, Sunday worship is treated as a performance event in terms of the efforts made to get ready and be "presentable for God," as Beatrice explained. Sunday worship is also heralded as a special, uniquely sacred event where one can be healed and restored. Although the women do not always immediately experience the deeply liberative aspect of sacred worship, Lucinda's statement, "I don't always get as much as I'd like outta the services, but I always get something, and it's always what I need," captures their belief in the power of transformation inherent in the worship experience.

The Sunday morning worship includes liturgical components, such as the call to worship, the hymn of praise, *Gloria Patri*, select scripture readings, congregational readings, the offering, and the sermon. Other elements include varied selections from the choir, the reading of announcements and the welcoming of visitors. Although called different things by the different denominations ("prayer of confession" at St. James Presbyterian is the same as the "prayer for illumination" at Greater Goodwill AME), the elements are largely the same. The programmatic content echoes general trends within Protestant denominations across the country. Another characteristic these churches share is their comparable worship styles, a feature I call Protestant-Traditionalist-Pentecostal worship. The Christ-centered focus of the service itself denotes its Protestant orientations. Worship within these churches is highly spirited in terms of outward, audible expression, and in this way embraces more traditional forms of black religious expression, including call and response and syncopated clapping on the two and four beats. The services are also notably spirit-filled in that they specifically invite and expect the presence of the Holy Ghost. The frequent occurrence of shouting and glossolalia, or speaking in tongues, during worship service denotes shared Pentecostal influences.

The Hammond [organ] was turned up and everyone remained on their feet. Many began to lift one or both of their hands, many had their eyes closed. The tune was repeated at least twice. While the congregation was singing, Pastor Heyward encouraged people to worship "voluntarily, not out of compulsion." He also called out words like "Power!" and "Hallelujah" as the song was repeated. "Feel it! Feel it!" he said. "Let's give God a praise offering!" Many people were clapping their hands (against the rhythm of the song) and shouted exclamations that matched the pastor. "Hallelujah!" "Thank ya Jesus!" Then the minister of music led the congregation in the tune "Thank You Lord." The church continued to clap, sing, and lift their hands in celebratory praise. One woman nearby began to sob. The woman sitting next to her attended to her by putting her arm around her and giving her tissue. We continued to sing and repeated the song once more.[19]

On another Sunday the youth choir sang the popular gospel selection "Perfect Praise." As soon as they began to sing, a small number of people began to stand, and as the song progressed, more folks followed. A woman four rows to my right rocked back and forth across the pew. Another woman on the same row jumped up and down screaming, "Yeah, yeah, yeah!" By the time the song was over, at least forty people were standing, and many were crying. Notably, women and men began crying out and applauding, and offered the exclamations "Hallelujah!" and "Praise Him!" when compelled. A woman toward the front, right side of the sanctuary began to speak in tongues, softly at first, then loudly. No one seemed surprised. At the end of the song, many remained standing. The pastor exclaimed, "Come on church! Praise Him, praise Him, praise Him, praise Him!!!" The woman speaking in tongues continued, but louder. Eventually, she was the only one standing and speaking. The pastor stood up after a few moments and although the woman was still speaking (and at that point crying too), he began to move on with the service.

As an observer, what I found most striking in these moments was the worshippers' heartfelt expression. Hands were raised not out of rote or obligatory expectations, but as people genuinely felt connected with the music, the message, and the moment. The song "Thank You Lord," was ushered in as a call to its hearers—to say thank you was to reflect genuine gratitude for being blessed by God generally, and in the most immediate sense being able to stand and offer praise to God for whatever one was grateful for. Although I had long since left the Christian faith, and I was not compelled to lift my own hands, I was reminded in a deeply familiar way of what it meant to participate in a community of shared faith. This type of audible, spiritual expression is commonplace and expected within the four churches, and derives from a longstanding lowcountry tradition of worship.

A Space to Pray and Praise

In the lowcountry, the antecedent of the contemporary black church has directly influenced modern religious practice. Historically, the socioreligious needs of African American communities in the lowcountry were met mostly in a physical meeting space—the local church or "praise house." Planters created these meetinghouses after 1840 to give the enslaved opportunities to worship on their own and in direct support of the efforts to spread the Gospel to rural communities in the late nineteenth century. In a description of religious life among Sea Island blacks, George C. Rowe, pastor of Battery Colony Congregation Church in Charleston, stated: "The churches are the meeting places of the people, where they worship, and where occasionally the more enlightened preachers of the various denominations give instruction, but where for the most part the local preachers hold up the dimly-lighted spiritual torch to those who are walking in darkness."[20] Similarly, in 1903 Niels Christensen Jr. confirmed, "The Negro hereabout is a great churchgoer. One of the colored ministers estimates that seventy-five percent attends church."[21]

The church/praise house was the central locale for religious expression and for transmitting explicitly Christian, folk, and social customs during worship services. Also called the "pray's house," many among the Gullah/Geechee employed the term to refer to all religious meeting buildings. In the early 1930s, social historians Guion Johnson and Mason Crum each examined the impact of the plantation system and structure on the Gullah/Geechee communities on St. Helena Island and wrote of Gullah/Geechee religious practices and their weekly "praise house" meetings, where attendees sang "sperichils," prayed, and shouted.[22] During the same era, Samuel Lawton described worship on St. Helena Island in the following way: "The Pray's house activities of today include an evening devotion three times a week of Bible reading, prayer, and singing; a speech of exhortation and instruction; a period of free religious expression; and occasionally the shout, affording social pleasure with a degree of religious sanction; once each quarter a covenant meeting characterized by heart-searchings and rededications; an examination of candidates for church membership; and an examination of prodigals who wish to return to church membership. The Pray's house is a check to the recalcitrant and a place of instruction and solace to the faithful." Lawton posited that the praise house functioned as a spiritual and moral intermediary within the local community and the church by "aiding the church in maintaining acceptable Christian living on the part of the church members." In addition to reminding members "of their weakness, their mutual need of prayer, and their common dependence upon the Deity for power to live right," the praise house leaders also deterred members from breaking church restriction with "cautions, warning, and threats."[23]

The praise house functioned as a meeting space for religious and social gatherings, including weddings, baptisms, and other local events. In 1862, at least nine African American couples were married in the church on St. Helena Island (which also functioned as the community's school during the week) after the conclusion of the worship service.[24] That same year, two officers of the Union army visited the church to recruit soldiers. In March of 1863, armed African American soldiers hid in the rear of the church during school while trying to capture someone. On Sunday, September 13, 1863, members raised $107 during worship to build a monument for Colonel Robert Shaw, a beloved commander of the Fifty-Fourth Massachusetts Regiment, a black troop, who had been killed in the line of duty. They also agreed to donate potatoes for the soldiers on Morris Island.[25] The diversity of these accounts illustrates just how functional these "religious" spaces were.

The church/praise house was the place where the black community participated in the rite of baptism, which occurred throughout the year and on "baptizing Sundays." Often, as Laura Towne described, candidates for baptism were examined immediately following the worship service:

> This morning there was no white preacher. After church Father Tom and his bench of elders examined candidates for baptism and asked Ellen to record their names. We stayed. Each candidate, clothed in the oldest possible clothes and with a handkerchief made into a band and tied around the forehead, stood humbly before the bench. Father Tom, looking like Jupiter himself, grave, powerful and awfully dignified, put the most posing questions, to which the candidates replied meekly and promptly. He asked the satisfactory candidate at last, "How do you pray?" Then the soft musical voices made the coaxing, entreating kind of prayer they use so much. A nod dismissed the applicant and another was called up. There were sixty or seventy to examine.[26]

It is unclear whether the candidates were baptized then, merely questioned, or if this was one aspect of the baptismal ritual. Yet this description is significant because it demonstrates the role of a particular group of black religious leaders in the community—elders. Elders played a large part in the religious lives of community members and during the process known as "seeking," which African Americans underwent to join local churches. These examples reflect how the ebb and flow of socioreligious life of lowcountry black communities was built around the function and utility of the church or praise house, which was often the largest and most accessible place to meet.

Above all, the church/praise house was where the members of the community came together for worship. Worship in the lowcountry was simultaneously structured around Christian traditions, African traditions, folk traditions, and the deeply embedded labor structure of the plantation system—all of which were maintained long after emancipation. While there were some Saturday evening services where white preachers visited and preached exclusively to the African American members (though whites were often also present), Sundays were the days that African Americans most frequently gathered. The structure and style of worship varied throughout the lowcountry. In the larger Methodist, Presbyterian, Episcopal, and Baptist churches in downtown Charleston, for example, white parishioners ran the Sunday morning services. Local white ministers preached to the white members seated in the lower levels of the church, while the African American constituents listened from the gallery. On the Sea Islands and in more rural areas of the lowcountry, whites were statistically fewer in number and church buildings were smaller. White parish ministers, when available, delivered the sermons, but African American members of the communities—preachers, deacons, and elders alike—played major roles in the worship service. In these smaller churches the few whites present worshipped alongside and sat next to black members. In the formidable text *Slave Religion*, Albert Raboteau has suggested that enslaved blacks "felt inhibited by the presence of whites, so they preferred to worship at a separate service by themselves."[27] In the South Carolina lowcountry, however, having a space to pray and praise was as much about desire as it was about the feasibility and accessibility of such spaces.

Whether on Saturday evenings or Sunday mornings, the worship services devoted to and led by the African American members of the community bore a distinctive style and format. Services began with a devotional period, when men and women would offer several songs and recite prayers and scriptures. The aim was to invoke God's spirit, to uplift communal songs, and to prepare the audience to hear the word of God delivered in the sermon. Devotion was followed by a sermon, which was usually delivered by a white missionary or minister or a black preacher. After the sermon, a prayer was offered, usually by one of the black deacons or elders, and the white preacher would provide a benediction. When there was no white minister present, community elders or other religious leaders (including deacons) would continue on with the services.[28] Charlotte Forten described the historical significance of the praise house and worship services in the lowcountry in great detail:

On this [Seaside Plantation on St. Helena Island], as on several other large plantations, there is a "Praise-House," which is the special property of the people. Even in the old days of Slavery, they were allowed to hold meetings here; and they still keep up the custom. They assemble on several nights of the week, and on Sunday afternoons. First, they hold what is called the "Praise-Meeting," which consists of singing, praying, and preaching. We have heard some of the old negro preachers make prayers that were really beautiful and touching. In these meetings they sing only the church-hymns which the Northern ministers have taught them, and which are far less suited to their voices than their own. At the close of the Praise-Meeting they all shake hands with each other in the most solemn manner. Afterward, as a kind of appendix, they have a grand "shout," during which they sing *their own* hymns.[29]

Religious rituals, meetings, and ceremonies were not limited, however, to the church/praise house. Throughout the lowcountry, blacks were frequently baptized in a local creek or river rather than in a church. In 1863, 150 men, women, and children on St. Helena were baptized in the creek near the church. Led by the parish minister, the candidates filed to the relevant body of water, "many of them in white aprons, and bright dresses and handkerchiefs."[30] On another occasion, an elderly woman who adamantly desired to be baptized could not make the walk, and was carried to the creek: "An old woman was baptized to-day who is a hundred and twenty years old, they say. That of course they can't prove, but it is a fact that her daughter's granddaughter has a granddaughter, so that makes six generations living together. She has 'tried to pray' all her life, but was always 'turned back,' and to-day she was triumphantly baptized, with all her family about her. She sat up, but could not walk at all, and it took two elders to take her to the water."[31] The performance of baptism beyond the parameters of the church may have been pragmatic, as large numbers of women, men, and children could not fit inside the church building. In addition, the meaning of baptism as a communal and individual religious practice was significant. Being led to the water by the symbol of the Christian religious community—the parish minister (and presumably on occasion by black preachers)—communicated the importance of religious leaders, conveyed the personal faith of the individual, and confirmed individual belief within the larger community of believers.

Funerals and shouts were two other occasions where lowcountry blacks gathered in religious celebration beyond the walls of the church. These meetings were held outdoors under large trees, or in other communally designated meeting spaces, such as at the home of a member of the community. Funerals were directly affected by the plantation work schedule, and they were usually held on Sundays, the sole day of rest that the enslaved were offered.[32] On occasion, funerals were commemorated long after the death of an individual if a special privilege was granted to the family of the deceased and a black funeral preacher was called. As these preachers were governed by the wills of the planters and the plantation work structure, it may have taken some time for the itinerant preacher to arrive. Charles Raymond described this type of occurrence when he was invited to hear a local minister named "Uncle Phil" preach the funeral of a local woman named Sally Green. Sally had reportedly been dead two years, but the slaves "waited for Phil." According to Raymond, the ceremony was "performed as a duty which the survivors among the relatives and associates owed to the memory of their deceased friend."[33] Whether held shortly after the passing of the deceased or commemorated long after their death, funerals resonated communally as opportunities for residents to honor the dead and to gather with prayer and devotional hymns.

Praise meetings were an integral component of religious celebration in the lowcountry. Also known to locals as "shouts," these meetings, which were most often held on Sundays *after* church, allowed blacks to gather and worship in a service not governed by whites. While the frequency of the shout varied, documentation by John Bennett, Charlotte Forten, and Laura Towne suggests that shouts occurred at a minimum on a weekly basis.[34] Laura Towne confirmed the frequency of shouts on St. Helena Island. On Sunday, May 4, 1862, she wrote, "Last night we heard the negroes singing till daylight. Rina said they thought as they had Sunday to rest they would keep up their meeting all night. It was a religious meeting."[35] These occurrences inside and outside the walls of the church/praise house demonstrate how African American inhabitants of the lowcountry utilized every opportunity they could to gather and cultivate their spirituality beyond the parameters of the traditional Sunday morning church meeting.

One praise house on St. Helena Island was described as "small, private, hidden-away buildings . . . the interiors are plain and bare with wooden benches or chairs. Each contains a podium and a naked light bulb hanging from the ceiling."[36] In the lowcountry, the praise house or black church meeting space served a purpose far greater than its often-diminutive physical size and modest furnishings would indicate. The existence of these meeting spaces created an important social, cultural, and religious space for lowcountry blacks to gather around and within, and became a physical means for them to form community bonds within the sanctioned parameters of religious expressions. Although many folk practices, religious rituals, and ceremonies were not limited to the walls of the praise house, it was the central locale for religious expression. As the primary meeting space for weddings, baptisms, and funerals, it was essential for transmitting the rituals and customs of local faith systems. The praise house literally emerged as a place for lowcountry blacks to learn, pray, praise, and shout with members of their faith communities, and to cultivate *their own* religious and spiritual identities—often under the leadership of women.

Women Within and Beyond the Praise House

The praise house was important in the lowcountry because of its role as a sacred space, and also for how it allowed religious leaders to facilitate spiritual development among the Gullah/Geechee. Although every community, enslaved or free, has its own sets of leaders, deacons and preachers have historically had the most visible ecclesial positions in the lowcountry. This visibility is directly related to the Christian missions movement that began in South Carolina during the 1830s.[37] According to Luther Jackson, the rise of black deacons and preachers was the result of how ". . . the field of religious instruction for a community was entirely too big for any one pastor to cover," and as such, white ministers appointed "a leader or watchman among Negroes on every plantation with two or three helpers to assist such a leader."[38] Deacons, as Samuel Lawton suggested, were "second only to the minister in ecclesiastical power."[39] They were faithful and often quite zealous, and were responsible for visiting, praying with, and exhorting the sick; conducting prayer meetings; watching over the youth; and acting as moral guides. They were highly respected religious and moral exemplars who wielded great power in the community. In particular, deacons had "great moral influence over the people," which the people "always regard[ed] as legitimate authority." Members of the slave community believed that the deacons' "spiritual power ha[d] been conferred by the imposition of official dignity."[40] The office of deacon was thus not merely an ecclesial position, but extended beyond the religious community as a socially significant part of the plantation community.

Also of pivotal importance were black preachers. In his 1940 text *Gullah* Mason Crum described the black preacher on St. Helena and Edisto Islands as "the most respected person in the community, and to his support they contribute liberally according to their means."[41] Samuel Lawton suggested that black preachers received the utmost respect because they were "called by God."[42] As divinely appointed authorities, they were afforded exceptional treatment even if their position was openly questioned outside the walls of the church and the preaching moment. Raymond's writings detailed the primacy of the black preacher, and identified him as a key member of the socio-religious rural plantation community in South Carolina. According to Raymond, all that the slaves learned and knew about their lives, their futures, and the world as presented in the Gospel came from the preaching they witnessed. More than the white preacher, the presence of a black preacher held particular significance within black communities. Generally, black people were disinterested in and unaffected by white preachers. If a white minister delivered the sermon, "no matter how great his shoutings," attendees would sleep or intermittently interject, "Amen! Bress de Lord!" to express their interest. "But let the congregation be surprised by the unexpected visit of some colored preacher, or let the exercises consist, wholly of prayer, exhortation, and singing, and the fervor, vivacity, and life of the meeting would continue for the hour without diminishing."[43]

Although not the predominant focus of this study, deacons and preachers are important to acknowledge because they were often the most visible in terms of religious leadership, and were key players affording lowcountry blacks some semblance of autonomy within and beyond the plantation structure. It is through some of the historical detail provided by Raymond, Crum, and Lawton that we learn how religion and spirituality were a substantial part of everyday life in the lowcountry, and especially how this quotidian quality of religion was best exemplified in the roles of deacons and preachers. Deacons and preachers were exclusively men, and their positions were held by men who were viewed as maintaining the most upright moral standing within the eyes of a white pastor or planter. This fact has led scholars to determine erroneously that Gullah/Geechee women (like women throughout American religious communities) were omitted from spiritual leadership. However, these men were also endorsed or supported by the black community at large, which certainly included women. For example, during services where deacons were selected, black members of the church would elect him by a majority vote. At these election meetings, "often no white person except the pastor would be present." The pastor would consult with the existing deacons regarding "the Christian character and standing, and whether the church [would] be pleased with the election." The meeting continued with a devotional service, or the offering of songs and prayer, followed by the presentation of the candidate and a description of the diaconal duties. The meeting would then conclude with the vote of approval by black members, who typically offered their unanimous response "by uplifted hands."[44] By lifting their hands and being counted, lowcountry women had a great deal of say, even if they were not included in the earliest narratives of "sanctioned" religious leaders within their communities. As scholars of African and African diasporic religious traditions have acknowledged that women were historically active participants, many of these authors have nonetheless interpreted the histories of black religious leadership as being synonymous with male leadership. This also equates visibility with importance.[45] The perspective that men were the most important religious leaders while the women worked "behind the scenes" was sustained during and after the period of slavery and has continued well into the present. Yet we would be remiss if we did not consider how in their affirmation and endorsement of more visible community members, Gullah/Geechee women also contributed significantly to the spiritual and religious life of lowcountry communities.

It is unfortunate that women's roles with the Gullah/Geechee communities did not receive greater attention. Source materials between 1863 and 1929 did not generally cite women as formally appointed or elected leaders within lowcountry churches and praise houses. However, in his 1939 study of religious practice in various lowcountry communities, Samuel Lawton concluded that "Customarily, the leader [of the praise house] is a man; however, women do serve in this capacity." He further described: "In three out of five Pray's house services attended, there were Negro women who voluntarily led in prayer during the informal part of the service. The brethren seemed to approve of these prayers as shown by the fact that while the women were praying, they joined in with other women in making such exclamations as, 'Amen, sister, dat's de trut,' 'Yes, Lawd,' 'Hab mercy.' Such remarks on the part of both men and women accompanied the prayers, whether the one praying were a man or woman. There seemed to be no appreciable difference."[46] Lawton's observations suggest that even though women were not frequently cited as leaders within the first generation of scholarship, they nonetheless fulfilled important positions within lowcountry religious communities.

In the second generation of Gullah/Geechee scholarship (1974–1999), women were more frequently noted as facilitators and leaders of religious practices and, as such, began to be described in ways that acknowledged their positive contributions to lowcountry religion. In particular, lowcountry women were portrayed as active participants in the praise house or church. In *Catching Sense* (1996) Patricia Guthrie countered Lawton's argument about the presence of women as praise house leaders and noted that women did not traditionally serve in that capacity. Rather, the praise house leader maintained a role that was different from that of minister or deacon in the praise house system. While deacons and preachers traveled throughout the community exhorting, praying with and for the sick, and visiting community members, praise house leaders were primarily responsible for the functions of the praise house itself: collecting money (offerings), leading praise house meetings, ensuring that the order of service went as scheduled, and, on occasion, speaking (as opposed to preaching) at funerals. Although women were not often praise house leaders, they did, however, frequently attain the offices of "committee person" and "deaconess." While men could not simultaneously hold the office of deacon, praise house leader, and minister, the standards were different for women: "Women serving as committee persons can hold the church office of deaconess while also functioning as committee persons. Island Baptist church deaconesses sit together in the front of the church during Sunday service. They set the tone and example for girls and women of the church. Unlike leaders, however, committee people are chosen by the local praise house leader and confirmed by the praise house members. The office of committee person seems to be an end unto itself; it is not a stepping-stone for obtaining other praise house or church offices."[47]

Similarly, in *A Peculiar People* (1988), Margaret Creel documented the prominence of women in lowcountry religious culture. Directly influenced by Guthrie's emphasis on the communal quality of religion rather than the function of religion itself, Creel treated religion as the key factor that united South Carolina's Gullah communities, and argued that religion and religious instruction "provides powerful, persuasive belief systems, symbols and images of cosmic order which act as realistic explications of human experience and/or the human condition." According to Creel, Gullah women were critical to the ways lowcountry religion shaped communal and social life, especially during enslavement. Creel relied upon source materials that included references to numerous named and unnamed women, and in so doing, relayed examples of women who, during slavery, utilized their ingenuity and skill to actively resist servitude, to undermine plantation discipline, and to refuse their master's conceptions of moral behavior. Women and men actively chose mates without the permission of or formal recognition by white planters or ministers and created their own moral codes for conjugal relations that were often antithetical to those of whites. Creel also utilized examples of women from previously untapped source materials—archival, unpublished, and published—to demonstrate how women served as moral exemplars within the enslaved community. To Creel, Gullah religion was not only a contract between God and the individual, "[i]t was a mutual agreement among themselves which implied that they could not love God without loving each other."[48] Women were at the heart of expressing this religious love. In addition to working laboriously to produce crops for their plantation owners, they also toiled to provide for their families and for other members of the community to ensure that no one went without food or care.

In the more recent text *The Abundant Life Prevails* (2000), historian Michael Wolfe acknowledged the importance of women on St. Helena Island as leaders and active transmitters of lowcountry social and religious culture. He described women on St. Helena who cooked and taught other women how to cook, as well as how to preserve and pickle fruits and vegetables. He recounted how an unnamed female cooking teacher at Penn School organized "Homemakers Clubs" where, after opening with prayer and devotion, "the women launched into discussions about improving home life with leaders listening carefully to the women's needs." The Homemakers Clubs were monumental because they "initiated a nutrition revolution" by teaching Sea Islanders about the value of fruits and vegetables, thereby "establishing a higher standard of diet." Wolfe also described how women served as religious and communal leaders; he documented the narrative of one Sea Island man whose primary guide during the seeking process was a "spiritual mother." Wolfe's text suggests that much of life on St. Helena would not be what it is today if women had not taken a primary role in the perpetuation of local practices. He therefore concluded that lowcountry women "played an especially significant role in maintaining the values of the ancient faith while propagating the teachings of the modern. Often, more than the ordained clergy, island women functioned as the primary storytellers and held responsibility for transmitting, maintaining, and perpetuating inherited Gullah culture."[49] Though brief in its references to women, Wolfe's text is important because of the attention it pays to lowcountry women's unique contributions.[50] *The Abundant Life Prevails* lifted up the influence of lowcountry women without relegating their actions to larger themes of community, family, or religion.

Lawton, Creel, Guthrie, and Wolfe made laudable efforts to shed light on the contributions of lowcountry women to Gullah/Geechee religious practices. Yet, even as their works discussed women in greater detail than the earliest writings on Gullah/Geechee religion, they failed to tell the stories of the importance of religion to the women who actually practice religion, and to capture the significance of an active and enacted sense of faith. Narratives expressed by Gullah/Geechee women who are continuing to live out their religious identities are especially important because they tell a somewhat different story from historical depictions about women's roles. Rather than merely capturing the specific positions Gullah/Geechee women functioned in, or denoting that they prayed, shouted, danced, and praised God,[51] the perspectives of women who are living out their faith day-to-day reveals that faith in God is never exclusively or predominately about what they "do." Rather, faith is about who they are, how they see themselves, and how they live their lives based on their belief. In sum, religion has always meant and continues to mean more to those who are living their lives out in specific faith traditions. These differences in meaning and interpretation can only be fully grasped by engaging historical narratives with the perspectives of contemporary women.

Faith in Action

Like most mainline denominational churches in America, the four churches that Yenenga, Ruth, Roberta, Lucille, Lucinda, Beatrice, and Faye call home are dominated by the presence of women. The most prominent formal leadership role—the position of pastor—continues in the tradition as outlined above and is held by a man above the age of fifty. Exceptions to this include Poplar Hill Christian Church, where the head minister, Reverend Brown, is a woman, and St. James Presbyterian, where Reverend Carolyn Heyward is the church's associate pastor. Reverend Brown has been the pastor at Poplar Hill for over seven years, and her ministry has been so successful that she now also faces the demands of shepherding two satellite churches in the towns of Bonneau and St. Stephen, which are thirty to forty minutes away. Reverend Brown struggles to balance fulfilling the respective programming, ceremonial, and visitation needs of all three communities. When she is away, two staff members at Poplar Hill ensure that the community's needs are met. Although the bounty of Reverend Brown's ministry is laudable, the challenges in time and leadership she faces serving several churches suggest that even in cases where women do assume positions of leadership, additional demands of their time, service, and skill pervade.[52]

At St. James Presbyterian, Rev. Carolyn Heyward serves both as the church's "first-lady" and associate pastor, a position she has held since

2001. It is clear that Reverend Carolyn Heyward's position as associate pastor has little to do with her role as Reverend Charles Heyward's wife. Reverend Carolyn has a master of divinity, is ordained within the Presbyterian Church (and has been since 2001), and is well versed not only in biblical studies but is a gifted homiletician in her own right. At the church, she has oversight of the standing ministries of discipleship, fellowship, and service, where her general responsibilities range from preaching and administering the sacraments to visiting sick and shut-in members, to educating new members, to offering leadership to the church's Life Development Institute, which "provides for the ongoing effectual equipping, spiritual nurture, growth and development of all the saints of the St. James family." Outside of the church, Reverend Carolyn has been a moderator for the Racial Ethnic Committee of the Presbyterian Women's Coordinating Team, vice president of the local chapter of the National Black Presbyterian Caucus, and a church representative to the Presbyterian General Assembly, the annual meeting of elected officers within the Presbyterian Church.[53] Her unanimous election to the pastorate suggests that she is highly respected and valued as a church leader. Parishioners greet her with noticeable warmth and enthusiasm, and during services they seem particularly engaged when she stands before the church.

Despite the roles that Reverend Carolyn Heyward and Reverend Brown play within their churches, black men continue to be the most public leaders in the contemporary black church. This visibility is broadly in line with traditional structures within African American denominational churches and with the history of black religious leadership in the lowcountry, both of which privilege black males with the power to impart moral, ethical, and theological knowledge. According to Jacquelyn Grant, "Black women have been invisible in theology because theological scholarship has not been a part of the woman's sphere. . . . If women have no place in theology it becomes the natural prerogative of men to monopolize theological concerns, including those relating specifically to women. Inasmuch as black men have accepted the sexual dualisms of the dominant culture, they presume to speak for black women."[54] For that reason, and given the limited inclusion of women at the leadership level in these churches, it is critical that we examine the religious lives and experiences of Gullah/Geechee women within and beyond the formal institutionalized black church. Moreover, as Weisenfeld and Newman argue, "Scholarship that emphasizes the institution of 'the black church' . . . as the only venue for religious experience and expression and that sees ordained positions within those churches as the primary means of authenticating leadership presents only a partial picture of African-American religious life."[55]

Examination of the modern black church in the South Carolina low-country, like the history of women's participation in the lowcountry praise houses, reveals that Gullah/Geechee women have been present all along and have been facilitating important traditions and changes within the praise house system and the contemporary black church. Women were not kept out of the praise house, nor are they, with few exceptions, currently kept out of church leadership. Despite how women continue to be more prominent in less visible leadership positions, we must also examine the role churches play. Contemporary black churches are the predominant locale in which Gullah/Geechee women live out their faith, and can be a lens through which we come to understand their faith in praxis.

Comparisons of these women's communities, denominational structures, and worship styles reveal that despite geographical differences between their respective churches, numerous similarities also exist. An additional commonality among these women is their staunch religious belief, which is often experientially expressed by their deep faith in the God of Christianity. Having faith is understood to be the same as being religious, and one can only be religious by professing belief in God and the resurrected Jesus Christ, and by acting in ways that reflect this belief. Yenenga considers herself very religious, "a strict believer, sworn believer from waaaaay back." She regularly attends church and tries "to live by some of those rules, you know the rules that were given down long ago." Yenenga is clear, however, that she is not so religious that she "can't understand somebody else's way of living." She suggested, "There're some people that get so religious they can't understand someone else smoking a cigarette or drinking a beer, but I'm not that kind of religious person. Of course I don't indulge now, it's been years ago I used to smoke and took a drink too. But you know because I've passed that now that doesn't mean that I'm so religious that I judge other people you know, but their time will come too when they wanna change their lifestyle." Being religious is thus understood as exemplifying a lifestyle of moderation and being respectful of the way other people choose to live their life. It also means accepting that God will work on others in God's own time.

The women also view being religious as a journey in which one's path is revealed over time. Beatrice considers herself to be "fairly religious," and believes that she is much more religious now than when she was younger. While commenting on the discrepancies between her religiousness as a youth and as an adult she noted, "As I got older I've become more religious in terms of a lot of the stuff I've gone through in my life, I've gotten religious." For Ms. Bea, it is only natural that being religious is a process that unfolds with age. "Some people, they just get more religious when they get older. Other people, they just always religious, it's like they was born dat way." Ruth has also confirmed the progressive quality of the religious journey: "You know we start our process days and days and then we mature along the way, you don't get it all like this, like that [snaps fingers]. It's a journey, you know constant process of growing in Christ, growing in your faith, you know. Things that you probably thought it was important ten, fifteen, even two years ago, maybe today it's not that important, you know because you developed a greater level of understanding, you know, of what is important in life, in people, and accomplish your goals." These women assume, then, that one's religiosity increases as one gets older, experiences more in life, and comes to better understand one's relationship with Christ. This progressive aspect of faith and belief is considered a natural part of one's religious life.

The women of this study are very forthcoming about their faith in God, and view the outward expression of one's faith as a fundamental aspect of being a Christian. This is evident from their heavy use of biblical quotes and religious phrases, and also carries over into the way they respond to other people. When I first met Yenenga in 2003, she greeted me with a warm hug and the comment "God's good." There was an unspoken assumption that my response, if I were Christian, would have been, "All the time."[56] Similarly, every time I met Ms. Bea she would say upon my approach, "Look at the blessed child of God who come here!" These women frequently reference the importance of belief in God, the power of prayer, and the sustaining capacities of faith, and offer attestations of their own faith. As Rosetta Ross suggests, acting on one's faith "means surviving, opposing, and overcoming realities that impede living fully" in all areas of life.[57] Hence, these women's outward expressions are not merely lip service or rote expressions of religious indoctrination; rather, they are a sincere testament of their deep faith, which one can immediately sense in any encounter with them. This profound faith is exemplified by something Yenenga told me: "I know girl He can bring us out of anything, that's the kind of belief I've found. And I know that everything is not gon' be the same, but I always believe I'm gon' make it. As long as I got Him on my side, I will make it and you will too! That's the sort of faith belief that you've got to have. I can't give you mine, you've got to develop yours for yourself. But I can tell you 'bout it and He tells me about that you can just develop your faith." Faith is understood as a gift from God granted in order to sustain believers through hard times. When Faye's youngest son died in 1999, "it was only by the grace of God" that she was able to get through that difficult time. Similarly, Lucinda attributes her long life and good health to God, which she regularly professes, noting, "I've had a lot go on before me, but my faith in God what keep me." For Lucinda, it is her faith that sustains her throughout the challenges that life brings, especially the death of loved ones. Because of its role as a source of strength, faith in God—synonymous with being religious—operates as one of the most important aspects of life for these lowcountry women. This sense of belief in the Christian God as synonymous with an active faith resonates in contemporary sources that examine black women's experiences.

The outward expressiveness of faith demonstrates how the practice of religion and being religious is not solely a Sunday event, nor is one's faith exhibited solely during religious events organized through a particular church. Religious practice for Gullah/Geechee women occurs during the time that anthropologist Marla Frederick describes as "between Sundays," or on an everyday basis. Sundays are the highlight of religious practice and experience for each of these women, but what occurs during the week is equally important from a religious perspective. The periods "between Sundays" help the women maintain an ongoing sense of religious practice, keep them connected to their communities of faith on a daily basis, and, according to Roberta, allow their faith to remain "undergirded" during their day-to-day struggles. Similarly, Roberta's use of prayer beyond the prescribed moments of prayer outlined in the Sunday order of service at Wesley UMC exemplifies her application of faith and belief beyond the schedule and walls of the church. While Yenenga's active role within her church is important to her religious identity, there are also practices that extend beyond her participation within St. James Presbyterian. She prays and meditates frequently, for she believes, "Your prayer life, you don't leave that to the church. When you come home, it's a different thing. Prayer life with a Christian remains a prayer life regardless to where you are." Every morning between 5:30 and 6:00 she prays with eight other women (some who are also from St. James and others who are not) to pray for each other and to "lift [their] prayer concerns for others." From these examples, it is clear that religious practice (also understood as active participation in the church) and outward expression of one's faith beyond the church are of central importance to these women. The salience of faith should not be undervalued, as it is the key to understanding black women's spiritual experiences and how those experiences translate into their theological epistemes.

According to Cheryl Townsend Gilkes, black women's faith functions as a political, cultural, and social strategy, and we must gain greater appreciation for just what a "tremendous force" and powerful change agent their faith has been historically—and continues to be today.[58] These faith stories should thus be viewed as an additional source of African American theological engagement.

While the emphasis on the "everyday struggles of faith" should not be underestimated, ongoing participation in church activities is especially important to their religious experiences as well. Again, being a person of faith is synonymous with being active in a church, whether or not one holds a formal leadership position. Yenenga attends church every Sunday, and Bible study and midday prayer service every Wednesday. She also utilizes her gift of storytelling in the church and occasionally delivers the children's sermon.[59] Moreover, Yenenga serves as an ordained elder at St. James Presbyterian Church, a position she has maintained since 1980.[60] She describes herself as "very active" and does not view this type of participation in the church as exceptional in any way. Ms. Bea also understands her church activity as a normal part of life. In addition to her role as class leader and senior steward (a position she has held for more than twenty years), she volunteers with the church's food bank. The food bank operates every fourth Monday—or more frequently when needed—and serves the lowcountry towns of Mt. Pleasant, Cainhoy, Huger, and McClellanville. When Ms. Bea can afford time away from her basketry duties, she also attends church every Sunday (even if it is not at her home church) and utilizes free time during the week to shop for the nonperishable items to supply the food bank.

Lucille is also very active in her church. In addition to her ties to her home church in Beaufort (Mt. Sinai Baptist), which she visits monthly, Lucille currently attends Poplar Hill Christian Church. She openly admits that she "loves the church" and that she "has no problem going to the house of the Lord." Because of her responsibilities at Poplar Hill, Lucille drives the twenty-five minutes between the church and her home in Moncks Corner at least twice a week. Lucille is president of the missionary board, a position she held from 2006 until 2010, with the responsibility of "[making] sure that the elderly people and the citizens of the church and the community have this and that. The missionary board will visit them if they're sick, give them cards, and run errands for them." During the Christmas holidays, instead of giving the senior citizens presents or money, members of the missionary board cook elaborate dinners and deliver them to the seniors' homes. Annually, each auxiliary at Poplar Hill is required to raise $5,000

for the church budget. To collect their money, the missionary board spon-
sors various trips to flea markets and museums. The highlight of the year is
their One Hundred Angels in White program, when members of the board
sponsor ten young women and men who go around the community collecting money from donors. As the board president, Lucille oversees all of these
activities. Although Lucille works "overtime" and always does "more than
everybody else," during those busy periods of the year, she believes "this is
what I'm called to do."

Ruth and Faye are familiar with being called to the service of the
church and employing multiple skills to navigate within and around male-
dominated structures. Like Yenenga, Ruth is an ordained elder at St. James
Presbyterian Church. She describes herself as someone who has been an
active participant in the church "as far back as [she] could remember." Ruth
spends most of her time at church because there is "something going on
just about five days a week." It was Ruth's affinity for the elderly that initially facilitated her communication with the deceased. She is the appointed
CEO of the church's elder care facility, which offers a variety of services to
senior-citizen members of the church and to the community at large. While
Ruth believes that she has a responsibility to "take time to deal with issues
that affect people's lives," she admits that she is constantly fatigued.[61] Yet
addressing those issues is one of the things she loves, and she does not see
herself stopping anytime soon. Ruth's commitment to serving the needs of
the church is fueled by her role as an ordained elder, but also by her acceptance of her call to preach. Ruth believes that she was "called into ordained
ministry at a young age," which she thought she had resolved by becoming
an elder. She now recognizes, however, that she is "supposed to preach"
and is making efforts to enroll in a Presbyterian-supported seminary.

Although Faye "can preach," she admitted, "God aint call me to preach!"
It was her lifelong participation in leadership positions and service to the
church that she considered to be her calling. Of all the women, Faye's
church activity surpassed even the most conservative expectations for participation in church life. Faye was originally a member of a Baptist church,
and became a member of Wesley UMC when she relocated to Moncks Corner after marriage. After joining the church at the age of seventeen, she held
every single position available to a layperson. These positions included chief
financial officer, chairperson of the board, and Sunday school teacher. Faye
was the first chairperson of children when the Methodist Church banned
segregation and became the United Methodist Church in 1968. She also
served as chair of the Pastor-Parish Relations Committee (PPRC), one of

the most powerful roles within the local church, and chaired the committee on worship and nurture. Faye held two positions within the church at the time of her death: church historian and chairperson of nominations within the United Methodist Women group (she prophetically stated that those would be her final formal positions in the church). As the chair of nominations, she was responsible for ensuring the appropriate leadership positions within the United Methodist Women, including the president, vice president, and treasurer, as well as temporary leaders for various programs.[62] As the church historian, she was responsible for providing an updated history of the church, including all of its committees and subcommittees, and organizing them in the church's archives. She also regularly attended training sessions for her various positions within the United Methodist Church.

Living out her calling did not always prove easy for Faye, and the various difficulties that accompany holding a leadership position within the church were at times overwhelming. These challenges, which came from parishioners as well as difficult pastors, made her limit her positions to a three-year maximum. She explained, "Honey, when you have a leading position in here among Wesley people, if you don't have your closeness to God, people will run you fool! And thank God there's something within holding my rein." Lucinda and Roberta have also experienced this frustration while maintaining leadership positions within the church, and as a result, they have limited their church activity at Wesley UMC to regular attendance at Sunday worship services and Bible study. Lucinda always participated in choirs and in United Methodist Women in the past, but she has stepped down as a formal member of the United Methodist Women, though she plays a more supportive role by attending their sponsored events. She also continues to sing, but only on the senior choir (versus, for example, the combined choir). She attends functions sponsored by other committees and groups within the church but will not commit to becoming an active leader or full-fledged member. "If it ain't the choir," she noted, "I ain't doin' nothin' else!" Roberta used to hold various leadership positions within the church, especially among the United Methodist Women. However, she became too frustrated with the insincerity and insensitivity of the people, and as a result she no longer accepts appointed or elected positions within Wesley UMC. When asked about the challenges of being a leader within the church, she animatedly exclaimed, "[expletive] these rude people in dis church yeh [here], I couldn't put up wid' 'dem myself! I woulda been done slap one of 'dem so long! [laughter] LeRhonda, you laugh, well that's the truth! Faye got patience wit' 'em, but now me, uh-uh!"

Faye's patience is admirable, but it is also indicative of the women's attitudes toward church activity. Being a leader and participant in the church requires a certain kind of patience, yet participating—whether in a leadership position or not—is also treated as normative. As Roberta's comment about Faye suggests, a certain type of deference is given to those who hold positions within the church. On the one hand, this respect is for their particular abilities as leaders and the limited power one attains from serving in a given leadership role. On the other, serving the needs of the church through avid participation in church functions and positions is also viewed as an example of being more religious. More than anything, each woman associates being religious with participating in the activities of the church; they consider one's degree of participation to be an indicator of one's level of religiousness. This view of religious activity as a sign of one's religiosity counters the previously described idea of being respectful of another person's place on the religious journey. It also suggests one of the contradictions in the way these women understand their own religious practice. Religious activity holds such a central place in their lives that their attitudes toward faith in action are foundational to their purpose as human beings and their roles as women.

Gendered Identities

Documenting and analyzing the experiences of the women in this study is one way of gaining a greater understanding of the role gender has played within African American religious practice broadly, and within lowcountry religion specifically. Black women have historically assumed positions as exhorters, elders, evangelists, and deaconesses in various denominations, even before denominational requirements formally granted their ordination. Although it has not been emphasized historically, the role of women within the lowcountry religious community was and continues to be substantial. Consistent with gender patterns within African American church membership generally, lowcountry women constituted the majority in their churches. They were the primary religious instructors and disproportionately served in the capacity of Sunday school teacher.[63] Additionally, though not always formally acknowledged, women were church and praise house leaders and were heralded as sages within the community. It was the actions of female members within the church that had the most lasting impact on the women included in this project. The influence of women directly affected the attitudes that Ruth, Yenenga, Beatrice, Faye, Lucille, Roberta, and Lucinda share about their history of religious practice and their current positions as participants within their respective communities.

For Ruth, the women of St. James were central to her religious and educational development. For many years St. James (like many other lowcountry churches) operated as a parochial school and provided education for blacks who could not attend white schools because of segregation. It was the "center of education on the island because there were no public schools for blacks." In addition to offering Ruth religious and secondary education, St. James was where she learned "how to be a lady." All the teachers of the school were women, and they would pull the younger female students aside and teach them "how to stand up and look and speak," along with explaining "the importance of bathing and you know using your little deodorant and your powder." Ruth credits the women in the church with having a significant effect on her life and her continued participation in St. James Presbyterian after her schooling there ended. As a young adult, she was always with the older women. She was often the only young woman at the women's meetings of the General Assembly, and "carried everybody's luggage because they were too old." Her early initiation into church life by women is a substantial part of her identity as an active member of the church. These women, who instructed Ruth and her peers about how to be "young women of God," had a lasting impact and revealed to Ruth early on her potential as a woman in the world and in the church.[64]

Yenenga also confirmed the significance of women in her life at St. James. Women served as community elders when she joined the church, and it was because of the admonishment of one particular woman, Mrs. Sanders, that Yenenga became a musician.[65] "[Ms. Sanders] knew that I was going to music, and one day she just tried, put me to the piano for Sunday school to play. And that's how I began really playing in church, so you see I've been kind of active doing that all my life." Yenenga noted that the changing roles of women in the church had a direct impact on her religious life. Although there were no church-appointed female elders during the time she was seeking, women were initially ordained as elders at St. James during the late 1950s when she graduated from high school. Yenenga's mother was one of the first female elders in the church. Eventually, more women began to be ordained as elders, and currently "there are more women elders than men." Yenenga admitted that learning about the elders' responsibilities from her mother and seeing other women who actively served the church as elders, Sunday school teachers, and stewardesses made her more aware of women in leadership roles and influenced her decision to become an elder.

The visibility and influence of older women is also prevalent in descriptions provided by Ms. Bea, Faye, and Lucille. Beatrice's church, Greater Goodwill AME, "is still an old-time black church, made of old and young women." At Greater Goodwill, much like in many other predominantly black churches throughout the lowcountry, "the male population ain't too big, especially the young men." Although Beatrice grew up in a home with both her parents, she identifies her religiosity with that of her mother, grandmother, and other women of their respective generations. It was the role of Beatrice's "seekin' mother," Nana, that made Beatrice decide to "always be a part of the church."[66] Similarly, Lucille, Faye, Roberta, and Lucinda each spoke of a powerful presence of women in their churches and readily described the ways that various church secretaries, deaconesses, seekin' mothers, and female evangelists shaped their religious development. Despite these women's influential roles, according to Lucille, the men were most visible and held the highest offices, and "it seemed like the men did most everything." She noted that she learned a great deal about the church from her mother, who was the secretary of Mt. Sinai Baptist church in Beaufort for "as long as [she] could remember—'til death do her part," and also from her aunt, who was the church treasurer. Yet it was when she befriended Evangelist Sumter, a woman Lucille met shortly after she began attending Poplar Hill Church, that her life as a woman of God became so important. She stated, "If it had not been for Evangelist Sumter, I would not be here. I might have even given up on the church. That woman prayed for me and taught me how to pray. She really helped me and helped me see where I should go, what I should do in the church."[67]

Many of the traditional gender roles and positions for black women have persisted into contemporary practices of religion. Despite the large numbers of women and the visibility of female religious leaders within their churches and communities, gender disparity within church leadership continues to be a regular and noticeable occurrence in the lowcountry. As previously noted, women were not always formally acknowledged or appointed as leaders—and if they were, they were not always treated on par with men who held positions that were purportedly equal in status and power. Although she is not completely sure why, Roberta believes that this disparity in treatment and recognition was especially pronounced for lowcountry women. "Women always been headin' up the church, but they wasn't always acknowledged as so. Although we've always worked, it makes some of them [men] uncomfortable . . . makes them feel like they're less than." Faye personally experienced this disparity as a female leader within Wesley UMC.

"I know that there were times where people, mainly men, didn't treat me right or listen to me because I was a woman, even though I had every right to be there. And I would see men who didn't even do as much as me, and oh it would make me so mad! . . . I eventually realized that it didn't have nothin' to do with me; it was them who had the problem. They just didn't know any other way, and I knew God had called me to do what I did, so I just did it." Notwithstanding, everyone within the community knew that the lack of assignment of "formal" responsibilities or an absence of public recognition did not preclude one's call to a particular position or duty within the religious community. Beatrice confirmed this assertion and detailed how everyone in her community and church knew and recognized Nana as a spiritual mother, even though Nana was never granted an elected or appointed "formal" position within the church. For the women in this study, male-dominated leadership within organized denominations has never precluded black churchwomen's deep sense of indispensability to their religious institutions.[68]

Faye's description of the sexism she faced within the church echoes other black women's experiences of leadership within the black church. The well-known early nineteenth-century narratives of Zilpha Elaw, Julia Foote, and Jarena Lee—the first black woman authorized to preach in the African Methodist Episcopal Church—detail the significance of their conversion experiences and also document the resistance, hardships, and ill treatment they faced for aspiring to leadership positions within their churches. In Jarena Lee's case, she experienced a great deal of resistance from the denomination's founder, Richard Allen.[69] In a critique of movements within liberation theology, which espouses freedom for all participants, womanist scholar Jacquelyn Grant chastises black male liberation theologians for perpetuating black women's invisibility and oppression: "[S]ome liberation theologians have acquiesced in one or more oppressive aspects of the liberation struggle itself. Where racism is rejected sexism has been embraced. Where classism is called into question, racism and sexism have been tolerated. And where sexism is repudiated, racism and classism are often ignored."[70] Grant's argument raises particular questions about the ways that black men (especially religious leaders) could be held more accountable in their efforts to speak to and for black women. Her comments affirm yet another reason why, as Weisenfeld and Newman suggest, "the large degree to which personal religious experience, the bonds of communities of faith, and sacred traditions all afforded African-American women access to varieties of power should not be underestimated."[71]

The communal means of getting around the gendered norms that Faye, Roberta, and Beatrice note coincide with the literature about black women's navigation of the black church. Sociologist Cheryl Townsend Gilkes has suggested that older women ("church mothers," in Gilkes's terms) frequently attained communal authority from their roles as moral exemplars and had various levels of power both within and outside of the church because of their personal spiritual experiences. As a result they "held considerable power with *nearly* autonomous and well-organized parallel women's worlds," a feature confirmed in Higginbotham's history of women's groups in the National Baptist Convention and Fredericks's example of black women's activism in rural North Carolina.[72] The strength and power of these seemingly parallel systems—exemplified by Beatrice's description of her Nana's position as "spiritual mother"—further affirm black women's ability to negotiate within and beyond formally established systems of religious practice while simultaneously maintaining a sense of communal authority *and* spiritual autonomy. Gilkes has also suggested that while scholars have gestured to the black church as a social center, they have also failed to integrate women in their analysis of religious agency within the social changes these institutions bring. She posits, "In these accounts, nearly all of the religious leaders have been men and all of the religious women have been followers. There has been relatively little integration of black women's religious agency with the tremendous history of social change generated by women's activism."[73]

This comment about women's exclusion from the narratives of black religious history and activism is certainly true, and this study emerges out of that shortcoming. But these seven women's stories provide only a partial explanation for why black (Protestant) religiosity is continuously expressed through narratives of the roles of Christian denominational participation and their (male) leaders. The fact is that although men are most often the publicly visible representatives, women nevertheless negotiate spaces between hypervisibility and invisibility within the church. According to Evelynn M. Hammonds, black women's bodies are always hypervisible, even when they seem "invisible" because of the ways that they are juxtaposed with the white female body.[74] Hammonds's discussion is tied most explicitly to black women's sexuality as manifest in the nineteenth century. Yet her description of the relationship between hypervisibility and invisibility is particularly relevant to any discussion of black religion because of the ways women have navigated leadership spaces but have been placed in discursive spaces by the literature about Gullah/Geechee religion. Faye's comment that "the women may not be the pastor, but *everybody knows* who really runs the show," explicitly echoes this feature of black women's experience within religion. In other words, although they may be "invisible" because they are not always in the hypervisible position of pastor, their important role within the religious community continues to be seen and recognized by its members. Because these women are familiar with male-dominated systems, they feel empowered to navigate them in ways that provide them with a sense of freedom and agency, and this connects them to a historical memory they value. While this appears to be the case among a small cross-section of southern black women between the ages of fifty and eighty, more information is needed about younger generations of black women (and men) to better understand whether or not ongoing shifts in perceived gender roles have brought about lasting changes in the traditional structures of black denominational churches.

Ascriptions of gender roles within the lowcountry have historically been based upon socially accepted norms of southern gentility, communally held ideals, and standards of religious purity. Generally, women were expected to fulfill the responsibilities associated with the cult of domesticity, and marriage was traditionally viewed as one of the mandatory requirements.[75] The continuation of these ideals today is also not surprising considering the lowcountry's current statistic that nearly half of the population includes members of married households (which is slightly higher than the national average). But these broader trends have particular implications for black women in religious contexts. According to Bettye Collier-Thomas, "one cannot fully understand sexism and gender discrimination in the black community without a careful evaluation and understanding of religious institutional praxis and the internal discourse over the meaning of black manhood and womanhood."[76] The expectation that a woman would be married heavily influenced a woman's relationship with a church. A woman's marital status directly affected her experiences within the religious community and could determine how she was treated, regardless of perceived respect or her formal position within the church. Faye believed that although she had to prove herself as a church leader at Wesley UMC on her own terms, it was always known that her husband was a respected trustee, church member, and citizen of the community at large. This means that even as her own person, she could never get away from her marital status. She stated, "Although my husband had little to nothing to do with me gettin' elected, I was always introduced as the wife of Mr. Terry . . . and they continued to call me Mr. Terry's wife long after my husband stopped going to church."

Church membership became open for women at the time they were ready to "seek"; a woman's marital status directly affected her participation and treatment within the religious community. This was the case at St. James Presbyterian, where Yenenga noted that unmarried women were not always regarded equally even though they dominated the church numerically.

> Now if you joined the church at a early age and then and somehow if you had a baby before you got married, you know that was a kinda shame on you in the church in the time I was comin' up, yeah well and it still is some, somewhere. Well I remember young girls would be in there had a baby they wasn't put out of the church but you were definitely put on the back seat. [Literally the back seat? I asked.] Yeah, the back seat. You were called a "back seat bama" then because you weren't married, you weren't married, you know. . . . And then the funny thing about that I think the kids realized the man, the fella wasn't never a backseater, but always the young lady and I thought then it was so wrong you know, so wrong.[77]

Although the young men who fathered the children were not publicly shamed, having a child out of wedlock was interpreted as sinful behavior for a woman and was deemed inconsistent with the morals of the church. As a result, female members of the church who had children outside of marriage were ostracized and stigmatized.[78] In Moncks Corner, Lucinda experienced the effects of the public shaming personally. "I was workin' on the usher board, never forget it, and I had gotten pregnant. I go back to church think' I'm goin' back and doin' what I been doin.' Honey let me tell you, Mr. S— and them, they made me shame that day!" Everyone knew the father of the child and knew that he was also an active churchgoer and fellow member of the usher board. Yet only Lucinda was forced to give up her position as an usher—an indictment that the male deacons of her church publicly delivered that Sunday when Lucinda attempted to return to her duties.

On such occasions, women were expected to "go back over"—to rededicate themselves to God and to rejoin the church. Women were not the only ones who had to do this. Various transgressions—including stealing, lying, fornication, and adultery—could result in any man or woman having to "go back." Women, however, were disproportionately required to rejoin the church if they had a child out of wedlock, and this could only occur after the sin was publicly denounced, genuine remorse and repentance were demonstrated, and the individual was judged worthy by the deacons and other church leaders. Lucinda was therefore permitted to return to her position as usher and was recognized as a fully active participant in the general activities of the church *after* her baby was born. The process of rededication was extensive and paralleled seeking—the rituals of one's initial journey into church membership. As Faye animatedly recalled, "If you did something you had no business doing, you had to go back. . . . And they don't just go back and say well you know, I come to reaffirm my faith. You got to go back to that altar, go back up there, and go before them deacons, and oh Lord! You got to all over again!" During rededication, one had to undertake an intense period of prayer, much of which was done publicly before the altar. As Roberta described, "You had to get down on your knees at the mourner's bench and plead your case!" Often, one was expected to publicly testify about one's shortcomings, after which the pastor, ministers, and deacons would pray for your deliverance from sin and ask God and the church to forgive you for your transgression. Roberta and Yenenga witnessed these moments, while Lucinda, Ms. Bea, and Faye personally experienced "being shamed." Lucinda and Ms. Bea both had to publicly "go back over" because they became pregnant before they were married. Faye also had to repent for staying away from church for an extended period (approximately two years) when she was a teenager. According to these women, one would not be allowed back into the church without publicly "calling the sin a sin."

Since the advent of the Civil Rights and the Women's Rights movements, perceptions of women's roles in lowcountry culture have undergone significant change. Although women are still expected to serve as primary caretakers of the home and to fulfill the responsibilities of cooking, cleaning, and other traditionally ascribed functions, it is not uncommon for women to work outside or beyond those spheres as well.[79] Yenenga and Ms. Bea are symbolic of this shift, as both provide the majority of their household's income and are self-made entrepreneurs. Similarly, as the only single woman in this study, Ruth embodies this transition in gender roles within lowcountry communities. She has attained a position within St. James Presbyterian that even Yenenga has described as "special." Less than one generation ago, no unmarried woman would have been able to rise to the status, position, and respectability within St. James that Ruth has achieved. Ruth, however, did not view what she has done in the church as exceptional in any way. Rather, she believed that her role within the church is merely "the fulfillment of one part" of what God has called her to do.

Despite the differential treatment of women in lowcountry churches, women have clearly been the predominant constituents of these churches and have served as mediating influences for others who were unable to assume positions of power within the church. This feature challenges the descriptions provided by the earliest textual representations of lowcountry religion. From these women's narratives, it is evident that black women have played and continue to play significant roles as leaders and participants within lowcountry churches. Moreover, these examples confirm that life for women in lowcountry churches paralleled the experiences of women in African American churches throughout the South. As Higginbotham suggests, the preponderance of women ensured that religious life in the lowcountry was in no way an exclusive product of male ministry.[80] The women in this study confirm that they have indeed been active participants in lowcountry religion throughout history. Women in the lowcountry today are utilizing their faith and religious practice to make significant contributions to their communities—both inside and outside the church. Engaging the perspectives of lowcountry women with those of scholarly representations reveals discrepancies in the meaning, function, and purpose of particular traditions. It also illuminates the ways that women have been, and continue to be, significant perpetuators of religious culture throughout the lowcountry.

Culture Keepers

Historically, Gullah/Geechee women have been portrayed as shouters, praise house leaders, and committee participants, as well as singers, community elders, and spiritual mothers. Many of these positions have shifted over time—in name alone, in most cases—to accommodate contemporary sensibilities. Singers and shouters, for example, have given way to worship leaders charged with orchestrating worship service; spiritual mothers are now church mothers or deaconesses; and elders are now literally ordained elders of the church. In one instance, however, there has been a concrete and important change—perhaps in the one position that matters most: Instead of continually being perceived as exhorters or speakers, Gullah/Geechee women are now preachers authorized through ordination to lead churches and to offer the word of God to parishioners. When we compare the historical and contemporary roles that black women in the lowcountry have held in cultivating religious identity and experience, we learn that whether the title of a position has morphed or not, or whether women have even been acknowledged for the ways they have facilitated religious practice or not, lowcountry women have always been shaping Gullah/Geechee religious culture. Women in fact have been the primary caretakers and transmitters of aspects of Gullah/Geechee religious culture and have retained an ongoing position as culture keepers.

This idea is confirmed in a public statement released by St. James Presbyterian Church entitled "Women of St. James in Action":

Women have always played an active role in the life of our Church. They have been actively engaging in ministerial work behind the scenes. During the early era women were not allowed to be visible or out front. But that did not prevent them from taking a vital part in the construction and planning of our first church, they were the invisible backbone. Even during the construction in the bush arbor women were active, for we realize that the finishing touch of women was needed even in that first place of worship. . . . [T]he women of our Church have always been actively involved in positions of leadership. They have exemplified great commitment and leadership on boards, organizations, and committees in the local church, community, Presbytery, Synod and General Assembly levels. And women of St. James are still engaging in mission work in our local community, in the USA and abroad. St. James women have served faithfully and effectively in the church and community as: Officers (Elders, Deacons and Trustees); Church Secretary; Treasurers; Musicians; Preachers; Teachers; Superintendents; Directors; Planners; Organizers; Administrators; Educators; Parish Workers; & etc.[81]

When we learn of these seven women's experiences in the church and in their communities, and we see just how influential women in particular have been to their own spiritual formation, it becomes obvious that Gullah/Geechee women have been important agents in perpetuating the religious traditions of their culture. This is certainly not news, for the ways that women transmit moral, medical, sexual, social, and political knowledge have been well documented. In this study, religion is therefore an essential component of the transmission of culture, and it is a significant part of women's identities. Religion plays a critical role in the lives of Yenenga, Ruth, Beatrice, Faye, Lucinda, Roberta, and Lucille. Each of these women sees religion, religious experience, and religious expression as an indispensable aspect of their sense of self and as vital to their communal engagement. Moreover, these women derive authority from their most intimate religious experiences. Faith thus becomes key not just because of what it expresses in terms of religious ritual, performance, and liturgy, but because of what it means in terms of their ability to enact spiritual and religious change.

This concept of Gullah/Geechee women utilizing religion to enact agency in their lives is especially important. Despite the fact that their lives as black southern women continue to be dominated by social, political, and economic forces that would seem to undermine any agency they might employ, religion becomes a means of expressing a faith that continues to survive despite dire circumstances. Like griots who are generally associated with being the keepers of culture through their storytelling abilities, sharp memory, and profound ability to shape the structure of history, these women and their faith-in-action praxis are also culture keepers. As people whose faith, commitment, and action reflect a deep religious commitment, a dedication to community and to self-actualization, their faith in God and religious practice are not merely evangelical efforts. Rather, faith becomes a means of overcoming their past while living through their present, and helping others to do the same. As Ruth stated, "I know there are things I haven't understood and I still don't understand today, but I also know that I have a responsibility to keep it goin'—that's my job." Faith is thus honored as a "charge to keep" that connects each of these women to her rich past while moving her through her present moment and propelling her toward her future.

CHAPTER 2

Folk Religion

"THE DEVIL'S SPELL"

Old Jake Brown could never be caught
To serve his time, for the trouble he wrought
He killed three men, then took to the wood
And laughed at the posse, which tried all it could
To make him prisoner, and hold him fast;
He scouted its skill, and escaped at last.

So his wife was seized, and compelled to tell
What secret was his? What witch's spell?
"Enty yoh know yoh eayn' ketch Jake?
[Don't you know you ain't gonna catch Jake?]
Him talk we deh Debbil, an' bargain make;
[He talked with the Devil, and a bargain make]
Deh Debbil tell him foh gee um his soul,
[The Devil told him to give him his soul]
Den him gwine keep 'e body whole!"
[Then he can keep his body whole]

'E tell um foh kill a cat w'at's black,
[He told him to kill a cat that's black]
Boil um, an' w'en deh bone seem slack
[Boil it, and when the bone seems slack]
An' softesh like 'till dey fall apa'at—
[And softish like until they fall apart]
Him foh tek deh Catm wid deh libber en' ha'at,

[He was to take the Cat with the liver and heart]
An' go ter deh ribber, een da'ak o' deh moon—
[And go to the river in the dark of the moon]
An' t'row um een but deh Cat wish-bone
[And throw everything in, but the Cat's wishbone . . .]

Gwine float away from all deh res'—
[. . . is gonna float away from all the rest]
Jake mus' ketch um; an' een 'e bres'
[Jake must catch it, and in his breast]
So long's 'e hide deh cat wish-bone,
[So long as he hides the cat wishbone]
Unner mayswell leyum 'lone.
[Everyone might as well leave him alone]
You ain' foh ketch um, dat I know—
[You ain't gonna catch him, that I know—]
Jake an' deh Debbil am frien' foh sho'!
[Jake and the Devil are friends for sure]
—JANE HEYWARD, CA. 1920

> One of my old women was nearly killed the other night by a man who went to her house at dead of night and beat her because she "hagged" him.
> —LAURA TOWNE, 1867

> Nobody 'round here mess with [Ms.] Cinda too much. They know she do the root. I know that's why I don't mess with her too tough.
> —LUCILLE GAILLARD

As described in chapter 1, Gullah/Geechee women have played important roles as spiritual and religious leaders within historical and contemporary religious life. This did not begin, however, with the advent of movements that advanced civil rights and women's rights. Rather, lowcountry women, like African American women throughout history, have always been change agents within black religious communities. As Evelyn Brooks Higginbotham has suggested in *Righteous Discontent* (1993), instead of viewing the black church as the "exclusive product of male charismatic clergy," we must always understand that women had a substantial influence in determining the direction and outcome of black religious expression.[1] This is the case whether or not women were visible in their roles as religious and spiritual leaders.

The idea that black women have had a tremendous, though often unseen, impact upon black religious life—captured in part by my connotation of Gullah/Geechee women as culture keepers—is heightened in recent years as women have become the predominant members in contemporary black churches. A more robust understanding of women's ongoing participation in religious and spiritual leadership among the Gullah/Geechee explicitly challenges the way that we think about African American religions and highlights the importance of examining how Gullah/Geechee women negotiated their roles as spiritual participants and leaders within lowcountry communities. Historically, it is within the roles of conjurers, healers, and root workers that women were prominent, visible religious leaders in the lowcountry. It is also because of these positions, which seamlessly integrated Christian traditions with local folk customs, that talking to the dead became—and continues to be—an important spiritual practice.

Conjure, Voodoo, and Superstition

For Yenenga, Faye, Ruth, Beatrice, Lucille, Roberta, and Lucinda, their current positions as culture keepers are inextricably tied to their Christian faith. Yet we would be remiss if we overlooked the ways that the Christian faith they have inherited has historical connections to and antecedents in local folk traditions. No exploration of Gullah/Geechee religious practice is therefore complete without an extensive discussion of conjure; even the earliest descriptions of lowcountry religion reference the blending of Christianity with local ideas of "superstition." Late nineteenth- and early twentieth-century printed materials—sources for the first generation of scholarship on the Gullah/Geechee—often documented the existence of folk religious practices. In an 1842 pamphlet that taught white Methodist ministers how to introduce southern blacks to Christianity, Charles Colcock Jones asserted, "Intimately connected with their ignorance is their *superstition*. They believe in second-sight, in apparitions, charms, witchcraft, and in akind [sic] of irresistible Satanic influence. The superstitions brought from Africa have not been wholly laid aside."[2] Charles Raymond, one of the first to publish materials about Gullah/Geechee religion, noted in 1863 that lowcountry blacks maintained a "natural" belief in superstition that allowed them to inherently trust in the spiritual power of community-elected deacons and other leaders.[3] An additional description by Leonora Herron in 1895 provides further insight into the general tenor of these "other" folk practices in the South: "The Negro's belief in conjuration and magic is very probably a relic of African days. Though strange and incongruous growths rising from association with the white race, added to and distorted it from time to time, till it became a curious conglomerate of fetichism, divination, quackery, incantation and demonology."[4] For most of these writers, this perceived blending of magic and superstition did not represent "true" Christianity. Rather, it was viewed as an aberrant, idiosyncratic, and distorted version of religion that incorporated remnants of a not-so-distant African past. This religion opposed "right" Christianity, which was presumed distant from identifiable remnants of African theological systems. Most notably described as superstition, fetichism, hoodoo, and conjure, the folk practices of lowcountry inhabitants received great attention from all who documented the ways of the Gullahs.

In the lowcountry, superstitious beliefs among the Gullah/Geechee included descriptions of "platt-eyes" (goblins) and ghosts, for it was assumed among the earliest writings that "the world of the spirits is just as real to the [N]egro as the actual every-day world about us."[5] Of special note is the hag, who, according to Roger Pinckney, is a "particularly troublesome" dual spirit of two types: the total spirit, also known as the "hag hag," and the "slip-skin hag," or a person (usually a female) "who becomes invisible by shedding her skins—pulling it over her head like a sweater—then goes out to wreak havoc after dark."[6] The hag was almost always documented as a witch-woman who would appear when an individual was asleep and "ride" or possess her victim by taking control of his or her body. The person would then be unable to move, yell, scream, or fight, and was completely held at the hag's mercy until released. Although it is unclear why the hag would possess her victims, encounters with the hag were thought to be so frequent that local remedies to thwart her, such as salt packets, incense, and powder, were common. In a statement taken from Miss May Parker by John Bennett, she offered the following description of how to prevent "being hag-ridden": "Instead of placing the shoes in ordinary fashion side by side, tops up and soles down, reverse the position, turn the soles up, and no fiend or witch or sorcerer can step into your shoes and so possess or obsess the owner. Lay also a flannel shirt across the middle of the bed, and on it make broad the sign of the cross; no hag then can trouble the sleepers."[7]

Belief in the continued presence of the arisen dead among lowcountry blacks, especially in the woods, was also ubiquitous. According to S. G. Benjamin, one of the unique "superstitions" of blacks on St. Helena Island was "their belief that if an infant is carried away from a house asleep, its spirit will stay behind, and they will look back toward the house and beckon and urge it to follow with endearing epithets, and to re-enter the body of the sleeping child."[8] Black residents regarded people who were able to see ghosts but were unafraid of them as "born to see evil," a gift that was not exclusive to conjurers and currently manifests as the ability to "talk to the dead." "De devil" was usually described as having the form of a "black dog." Spirits and ghosts could take on the appearance of various living creatures. Platt-eyes were viewed as the spiritual form of the human body that remained present, and at times visible, in the community. As John Bennett described, "Every man has a phantom likeness, separable from his body, able to appear in apparition at a distance, capable of mischief, of metamorphosis, of evil, and continuing to exist and to appear after the death of the owner proper; subject to conjuration and spell, and often possession. This apparitional soul bears likeness to the fleshly body, is its immaterial duplicate, with generally some ominous changes; its grave clothes on, its head in its hands, or revered upon its shoulders."[9] Although Bennett's presentation of a phantom differs from contemporary experiences of talking to the dead—which typically do not include a physical apparition—his assessment of the ongoing belief in the presentation and likeness of the living dead affirms a long history of this practice in the lowcountry.

What is most significant about the historical descriptions of conjure and belief in the living dead in the lowcountry is the extent to which such practices were accepted as widespread and real. In 1878, Benjamin noted, "Obeah worship and a terror of sorcers [sic] still exist with some; but those who were born late enough to gain their impressions of events subsequent to the rebellion may be said to walk on the higher plane of skepticism regarding all such things." Benjamin further remarked that despite the efforts of local teachers to improve the "mental condition of the negroes," the older blacks of St. Helena "still retain[ed] many of their superstitions."[10] According to John Bennett, "in the islands all old people, and most of the young, firmly believe in the root-doctors occult power; they call them hoodoo doctors, conjur-men [sic] and say that 'they gopher' their victims." These conjure-men (also known within the literature as root-doctors and sorcerers) wielded a great deal of power, which locals confirmed. "The conjur-men can poison not only by direct administration of poison internally, but by dropping noxious things alongside of or in the roadway or path along which the victim passes, which exert a noxious or deadly effect upon the passer-by. The great majority are afraid of poison, and fear the root-doctors." While Bennett was convinced that the "more advanced negroes" did not believe in those powers, he acknowledged that, "they do not firmly disbelieve" either.[11] Conjure was not interpreted as an unfounded belief elevated through myth, folklore, and legend, but as plausible a belief system as faith in the resurrected Christ.

In Black Magic, Yvonne Chireau suggests that black American experiences of Christianity and folk religious traditions were the fluid convergence of magic (the beliefs in and interactions with an invisible reality) and religion (the means by which human beings "mediate the sacred realm"). These beliefs reflected a diverse meaning system that African Americans used to form a dynamic "vernacular religion."[12] In her examination of the conjuring tradition and related practices such as voodoo, hoodoo, and root-work, Chireau contends that magic—whether manifest in Protestant Christianity or black folk traditions—was never the antithesis of formal religion, but its own resignified form. Relying on Theophus Smith's phrase "conjuring culture," Chireau verifies the ways black folk healing and medicinal traditions operated in parallel streams with Protestant Christian practice.[13] Conjure thus represented a new system of traditions that met African American spiritual and communal needs.[14]

Chireau's presentation of conjure as a viable religious system within black communities is reflected in the perceived importance of the conjurer among the Gullah/Geechee. These men and women were not viewed simply as significant members of the community because of their medical skills,[15] rather they were considered powerful human beings who bore supernatural gifts. According to Bennett, the locals had a healthy dose of fear and respect,[16] a mixture that was quite common in representations of black southern culture. Lenora Herron confirmed that the conjure doctor "was found in every large Negro community, where though held in fear and horror, his supernatural powers were still implicitly believed in. The source of these powers is ill defined."[17]

The social belief in the power of the conjurer was, and continues to be, a key component in the perpetuation of folk practices in the lowcountry. The conjurer is believed to have two types of power: a supernatural or divine power to heal or "fix" things (in which spells could be used to cure ailments or to cast spells upon others), and a communally perceived power that warranted respect, admiration, and fear from other members within the community. In 1895, Herron reported that faith in the conjurer's power was "implicit," and that "the confidence in their abilities was unbounded. . . . Powers of all kinds are attributed to these doctors. The healing art in various degrees is their gift, and the so-called 'diseases' which they possess exclusive power to cure are, as one of our informers puts it, these: tricks, spells and poisons." Citing an unnamed source, she described how one female conjure-doctor "said she had a special revelation from God, as do all the conjure doctors I have ever heard of."[18] This idea of the perceived supernatural power of conjurers is echoed in one of Jane Heyward's short stories entitled, "The Cunjer Man's Grabe." While passing an African American graveyard on the Sea Islands, Heyward noticed "One of the graves was covered with pieces of old broken glass bottles." When she inquired about the bottles to "a recently bereaved widow who was decorating the resting place of her husband with broken bits of china," the widow stopped what she was doing, guided Heyward away from that particular grave, and reportedly whispered:

> Dat deh Cunjer man grabe, an' him binna punish dis village w'en him been libbin'. E' put spell on my husbin', da's wah mek him dead now! We cubber um up wid deh broken glass, so's ef him try foh come back foh bodder we all some mo', him gwinea git cut up. We done hab 'nough o' him!

> [That's the conjure man's grave, and he used to punish this village while he was alive. He put a spell on my husband, that's what killed him! We covered him [the conjurer] with the broken glass so if he tries to come back to bother us all some more, he's going to get cut. We've already had enough of him!][19]

Similarly, in her poem "The Devil's Spell," Heyward calls upon Mrs. Jake Brown, the conjurer's wife, to explain how after killing three men and being surrounded by a posse, Jake escaped his captors. In Mrs. Brown's description, she reveals information about Jake's seemingly supernatural evasiveness as well as some of the techniques used by Charleston-area conjurers. From the tale we learn that Jake employed one of many practices central to conjure—boiling a dead animal's body (in this case a cat) and keeping one of its sacred and powerful parts (the wishbone) to serve as a protective amulet or charm. The practices of animal sacrifice and the ritualistic uses of the parts to ward off evil are well documented within African American folk traditions and are also associated with "bad roots."[20] We also learn of the ritualistic elements of Jake's spell: that he had to boil the cat; go to the river under the secrecy of darkness; throw the cat's entire body into the river unbound; watch the parts until they rose; and then retrieve the wishbone. Presumably, once Jake performed this ritual he could not be physically harmed. Jake's perceived conjure power was identified throughout the poem: that he mocked the posse who tried to capture him; that they then pursued his wife, asking specifically what kinds of "secret" or "spell" he employed; that his wife also laughed at their feeble attempts to seize Jake and her assurance that he could not be captured; and that the only way Jake could have maintained such control and dominance given the circumstances was to have made a bargain with "the Devil." From these descriptions we see that community members, like the conjurers themselves, believed that the supernatural power of these men and women was divine.

In addition to wielding a uniquely perceived influence among lowcountry African Americans, conjurers occupied a distinct physical place within the community. They retained special spaces where those seeking the aid of the conjurer could visit—often the conjurer's own home. Also known as an "obi-hut," the home of the conjurer was a place of mystery and fear, but was also respected as a sacred realm of immense spiritual power. John Bennett described a home he visited in an undisclosed part of Charleston:

A little, dwarfish house of cane, stakes, room-grass, lianas, indiarub-ber[21] vine and clay, bleached to whiteness; roofed with a palmetto thatch tied down along the roof with canes.

On a mound of earth at the door were balls of clay, red, yellow and white. There were three fetiches of feathers and cadavers of small beasts, and rags, hanging here, which it is understood, attracted favorably spirits and prevented the worshipers from evil influences and craft of the devil.

The house, or hut, was generally in the shape of a small square cabin with wattle walls daubed with a stucco of mud, perhaps touched with white-wash, and covered inside and at the lintels of the doorway with streaks of red and black, rude figures of men and brutes, man and woman with their distinctive sexes italicised, serpents and the tortoise, both of which still are held in superstitious and dread.

A smell hung around the place which has been described as a mis-ture of putrid onions, rancid butter and billy-goat very powerful and very offensive; eh harper acid of the yellow people, somewhat like caprylic acid.

The hut contained the stock-in-trade of the voudou-man.

Pets and calabashes full of grease of various unctuousness and fetid savours in one the skull of a small beast.

At the end of the hut was a heap of odd skulls, and skillets of vario sorts, dog, cow, squirrels, skunk, alligator, fowls, skins of snakes, in bunches, mingled with bunches of long leaves, palmetto and bullbay, still harsh and glossy, with the shells of land-tortoises, and a pile of partly calcined bones. Horribly strange and ugly. Darkness fallen, the negroes came slipping in as midnight approached.

Bennett observed numerous meetings of "witch doctors," including a "strange voudou dance" held at the home of a male conjurer.

There was an orchestra of instruments near the dark end of the hut, consisting of three men beating upon gumbies, cypress-root drums knee; the two witch doctors voudou-men danced in a most fantastic manner, mumping and twisting their bodies into impossible shapes. Now and then the men would leap to their feet, and dance wildly about the priests, singing furiously, with insistent rhythm which grew maddening to the nerves, with the steady beat of the drums. The doctor began some loud babbling, the meaning of which could not be certain. This went on for a long while. From time to time the people answered him in chorus, or joined him. The hollow voice of the witch-doctor resounded curiously through the woods in the silence an incantation. They seemed possessed with an indescribable fury; the excitement was extreme; they leaped forward frantically.[22]

This substantiated belief in the conjurer and his/her perceived powers—which was communally reinforced by the appearance of their homes and the contents therein—demonstrates that fulfilling the socioreligious needs of enslaved and free blacks in the lowcountry was not a job relegated to preachers and deacons. Healers and conjurers served multiple purposes within Gullah/Geechee communities, and while those who maintained these roles may or may not have been recognized by whites, they were thoroughly respected and often feared among African Americans. According to historian Sharla Fett, the medicinal traditions embodied by conjurers, herbalists, and root-doctors functioned as a "sacred foundation" within black communities that operated alongside and in direct opposition to the medical therapies of the planter class.[23] To Fett, African American healing traditions derive from African diasporic traditions, reflect the pervasiveness of African philosophies and therapies, and demonstrate the openness of black health cultures to the processes of cross-cultural exchange. In this tradition, the Gullah/Geechee established a unique system of ritual conjure practice that was distinct from the white beliefs.

The prevalence and active role of hoodoo, superstition, and conjure among lowcountry blacks is unmistakable and echoes similar widespread practices among southern blacks. Whether identified by nineteenth- and twentieth-century writers as superstition, voodoo, hoodoo, or conjure, it is clear that women and men readily functioned as leaders in these traditions. There was a direct relationship between the role of the conjurer and the role of conjure itself within black communities. The term "conjure" referred to both the leaders within the community who performed healing and medicinal acts on behalf of its black members, as well as the distinct, fluid system of practice. Reports among the Gullah/Geechee therefore characterized conjure as (1) *African* in nature or remnant; (2) *secretive*; (3) *supernatural*; (4) *retributional* for vengeance or to redress wrongs; and (5) *medicinal* to heal those already conjured and also those with illnesses unrelated to conjure. These practices provided diagnosis, healing, and justice to the Gullah/Geechee in a system that often denied them such privileges. As Tracey Hucks aptly suggests, "Conjure, hoodoo, and voodoo functioned as religious systems that informed the complex ways in which African Americans explicated supernatural phenomena, accessed dynamic entities of power, and dispensed spiritual prescriptions."[24] Conjuring traditions operated alongside and at times replaced the "institutionalized" religious beliefs passed on from missionaries and planters who sought to convert blacks to Christianity. Conjure was thus a way for lowcountry blacks to maintain cultural memories of their African pasts while incorporating realities of their present existence. The superstition, fetishism, conjure, and voodoo described by these writers were folk religious practices. They were not only characterized by particular beliefs; they were culturally instated, complex, fluid systems of thought. As a system, conjure identified a problem, offered a solution, and noted success or redress by witnesses throughout lowcountry communities.

Modern Manifestations of Folk Religion

Even today, Gullah/Geechee women's understandings of faith include an ongoing engagement with folk religious customs such as conjure, hoodoo, and root-work. Despite the overwhelming success of efforts to convert the Gullah/Geechee to Christianity and its emphasis on belief in "the one, true God," alternative, non-Christian systems have not been obliterated. Even as historical records have vividly documented the ongoing existence of Gullah/Geechee folk religious customs, and most notably conjure and voodoo, these traditions have continued to coexist alongside the practice of Christianity. This synergy between folk traditions and formal Christianity is highlighted in Margaret Creel's seminal work, *A Peculiar People: Slave Religion and Community-Culture among the Gullahs*, which has provided the most comprehensive historical overview of Gullah religion to date. According to Creel, the Gullah "Applied an African ontology, adapted Christianity to it, and created a religion that employed spirituality as a means of self-preservation as a vital component of community life."[25] Folk religious practices were thus crucial to the sustenance of the Gullah community, and were a primary means of maintaining spiritual autonomy in their practice of an integrated form of Christianity that synthesized their African traditional practices.

In 1940, local resident and reporter Chalmers Murray published an article titled "Voodoo Gods Yet Alive on Islands," with the subtitle, "names changed and forgotten but they remain in the mind of negroes." According to Murray, "The Gods and Goddesses of the Voodoo Faith are not dead—they have only changed their form. Their names have long been forgotten; their personalities have been merged with the Jewish and Christian prophets and saints as well as with the demons who live in the bowels of the earth and the devil of the Puritans: and they still give comfort to the believers and wreak vengeance on the wicked." Murray based his conclusion on his experience "spending years observing the religious rites of the Edisto negroes and listen[ing] to them expound their theories on mystical subjects."[26] His description illustrates the Gullah/Geechee's morphing of traditional folk religious customs into and combining them with the prevalent faith system of their time: Christianity.

Murray's distinction between the formal religious tradition of Voodoo (with a capital "V") and perceived local practices of voodoo still resonates today, for it is exactly how the women of this study explain their familiarity with folk customs. For Faye, Lucille, Beatrice, Lucinda, Roberta, Ruth, and Yenenga, the formal practice of Voodoo as a religion has given way to belief systems they call voodoo (with a lowercase "v") or "roots." Only Lucinda, for example, has any familiarity with the specific names of Voodoo *loa* (gods), which include Legba, Erzulie, and Ogoun. Yet the perceived powers associated with the loa, and the customs attributed to invoking their power, have remained. To the women in this study, "voodoo," "roots," and "conjure" are synonymous, and refer to how local people do things like "cut their lover's hair and bury it to make them stay committed" (Roberta, Beatrice); "boil a cat, keep its bones, and paint them red to ward off evil" (Lucinda, whose recognition is reminiscent of "The Devil's Spell"); or "bury a sharp object underneath your mattress to deter nightmares" (Beatrice, Ruth, Faye, Lucille, and Yenenga). These particular practices duplicate some of the customs associated with invoking the loa Erzulie, who is, among other things, a goddess of love, or the loa Ogoun, who is the god of power. Although these descriptions are far from exact replications of Voodoo rituals, they signal potential connections and retain an enduring sense of power among believers.

It is significant that each woman admits to participating in these kinds of rituals alongside their Christian practices. This fluidity is exemplified by each woman's recognition of "the hag," who would "ride" people and incapacitate their bodies. Lucille grew up making distinctions between hags and ghosts during her childhood in Beaufort:

> I don't believe in ghosts anymore, I used to when I was much younger. I don't believe in that anymore, but then again, when it come down to the hag, I believe in hags. I know that hag ride me, even today. I can't move at all. It seems like that hag has me straight down—tied me down. I don't know what the hag is—seem like it's what they call poor circulation today, but it's something possessing me. If I lay on my back and fall asleep, it's just like that hag on top of me, just riding me, like something's holding me down. . . . I can open my eyes, but all I can do is open my eyes. I can't get up until that hag release me. While that hag is on me, I can hear people walking 'round the house talking, but I can't do nothing. It's very scary. Very.

Whether interpreted as "superstition" or not, it is clear from Lucille's experience that some people still believe in such beings. When I asked Lucille to clarify what caused her to stop believing in ghosts (versus the hag), she commented with a chuckle: "When you a chile, you just be scared of the things that everyone else is scared of or what you're told to be scared of. But when you see and feel things for yourself, that sho will make a believer outta ya. That's why I stopped believing in ghosts. I aint neva seen 'em or nothin' like that. I feel presence and things like that sometimes, but they aint never been scary. But that hag, I tell you I know first hand how she can be. That's why I tell you she ride me even today. It still happens to me sometimes."[27]

Another prominent practice that exemplifies the sinuous relationship these Christian women have with folk customs is the placement of a blue eye in a discreet location to prevent evil spirits from entering one's home. All seven of the women readily acknowledge this practice as a commonly held belief they share. During a visit to Faye's home, I was summoned to get ice out of the freezer on her front porch. While retrieving the ice I accidentally dropped my pen behind the freezer, and when I reached to grab it, noticed there was a large blue dot painted on a knot on the wooden porch. When I inquired about it, Faye said, "Oh you saw it! How you know 'bout the blue eye girl?" It turned out that she had not initially wanted to move into the home, but when she saw the blue eye, which had been placed there previously by someone else, she immediately felt at ease. She commented, "When I saw that that blue eye was on the porch, I knew all would be well. No hurricane, no storm, no evil, no nothin' would get to me and my family."

Belief in and practice of folk traditions along with Christianity requires navigating a complex, multivalent system of faith. In addition to being known for her particularly distinct physical appearance and persona, Lucinda Pinckney is also recognized as a powerful "root-worker" by local residents in Moncks Corner. Lucinda's homeopathic treatments have reportedly healed people, and strangers come from throughout the low-country to see her. According to Lucille, "Nobody 'round here mess with [Ms.] Cinda too much. They know she do the root. I know that's why I don't mess with her too tough." On a visit to her home, an off-white doublewide trailer propped up on bricks, I did not notice any obvious signs that "root-work" was practiced there. Lucinda raises chickens and sells eggs, which she spends the bulk of her time attending to during the day. The interior of her house, while cluttered with figurines, pictures of her children, and oversized furniture, is neat and clean. You can tell that Lucinda spends a great deal of time cooking, and she uses an astonishing collection of over one hundred bottles, containers, and pots of herbs. Each time I visited there was always something boiling on the stove, which on occasion smelled like food, but most often smelled like a brew of spices and herbs. The scent is the most memorable feature of her house; there was a uniquely unidentifiable odor in the air, sometimes pungent, sometimes spicy, and other times floral. Our time together was almost always interrupted because someone came to the door for a package wrapped in brown paper, sealed in plastic, or placed in a covered dish. These elements, along with Lucinda's familiarity with Voodoo, certainly influence perceptions of her role as a voodoo practitioner. Yet when asked about how others in the community see her as a root-worker, Lucinda's only response was, "I just help people, that's all. I'm good at mixin' up stuff to keep people from being sick, so that's what I do, and God gave me the gift to do it."

At the very least, Lucinda is an herbalist who uses homeopathy to treat ailing community members. She may very well also be a skilled conjurer, for it is not uncommon for practitioners to be secretive out of concern for legal retribution and the risk of being overwhelmed by customers. At the same time, however, there is no doubt that my observations and experiences with Lucinda, coupled with the communally held perception that she is a root-worker, influenced my personal experience of her. During one particularly hot summer afternoon, Lucinda sent me outside to retrieve several items from a nearby storage shed. She specified the items—which included a medium-sized cylindrical container of what looked like salt, a large green bowl of candle wax, and a small glass vial of sulfur—not by name, but by their containers. A description from my field notes reflects my innermost thoughts from that afternoon: "I don't know what the hell Ms. Cinda is doing in that house, but sulfur and wax and salt? What else could she be doing other than some roots with that kind of stuff? This is exactly why folks think she's out here doing the root. I sure hope she hasn't gotten any of my hair." The concern about my hair is explicitly connected to the local belief that I am familiar with: that powerful conjurers can use any intimate item to cast spells upon their host, including and especially locks of hair. My anxiety about Lucinda's power and her ability to "conjure me" (which abated over time but never completely left) affirms the ongoing prevalence not only of the practice of conjure, but in the continuation of its perceived power.

Given the centrality of Christianity in the community and in her life specifically, it is no surprise that even if Lucinda were in fact a root-worker, it would not be blatantly obvious. When I asked Roberta and Faye, Lucinda's fellow church members, about her reputation as a conjurer, they offered intriguing responses. According to Roberta, "That's what folks say, but you can't believe all of that, man Cinda's harmless! Does she believe in things some of us don't, sure, but that don't mean she practice." Faye confirmed local beliefs in Lucinda's role as a practitioner, and also agreed with Roberta that Lucinda is "different." Faye, however, was not as quick to dismiss Lucinda's perceived power within the community. She stated, "I won't say she harmless, but she sure got her own way. And she's powerful in a kind of mysterious way. Folks 'round here don't know what to make of her. She talk her own way, walk her own way, she even sing her own way. She just do her own thing, and being different scare people, ya know." Roberta's and Faye's responses proved interesting in that they neither confirmed nor denied the possibility that Lucinda was a local root practitioner. What was particularly striking, however, was their shrug-of-shoulders attitude about her position: as long as Lucinda believes in God anything else she does is of minimal importance.

There is a clear, though at times contradictory, divide in perceptions among the women in this study regarding the place of voodoo and roots with their Christian faith. Each of the women staunchly identifies Christianity as her primary faith system yet simultaneously adheres to and acknowledges the power that continues to be associated with folk practices. Although Yenenga, Ruth, Beatrice, and Lucille see voodoo as generally associated with the old ways, they clearly have a great deal of respect for some aspects of folk practices that are a part of their system. Lucille's fear of the hag, for example, was echoed during conversations with Faye, Lucinda, and Roberta. But Yenenga, Ruth, and Beatrice shrugged off belief in those kinds of apparitions as superstition. Yet they all agreed on the importance of customs like placing sharp objects under the bed or painting a blue eye in an undisclosed location to deter evil spirits. As Lucinda disclosed, "I know evil is real, and that people think these old superstitions and things may give us one way, and faith in God gives us another, but I don't see it that way. It's all about belief in something bigger than you." That these discrepancies can be interpreted as contradictions but are not perceived by these women as contradictions reveals the ongoing place of folk religious customs in their lives.

According to Tracey Hucks, presuming that black women's faith systems are based on "religious coexistence" or "dual and multiple religious allegiances" can help us understand the nuances and contours of their religious experience and expression. In her examination of African-derived practices in New Orleans and New York City, Hucks warns against narrow formulations of black, female religious identities:

> Throughout their history in the United States, African American women have sustained open and fluid boundaries regarding religion and have been active agents in shaping their own religious meaning. Thus, scholarly studies that attempt to circumscribe and to assign rigid religious identities to African American women often eclipse the ways in which black religious communities have historically fashioned religious orthodoxy and praxis reflecting their immediate needs. . . . [B]lack women's religious identities include complex dimensions of the supernatural world that often allow for multiple religious traditions to coexist within their lives.[28]

Hucks's notion of dual and multiple religious alliances becomes especially useful when considering how Faye, Lucinda, Lucille, Beatrice, Ruth, Roberta, and Yenenga determine the place of folk practices in their lives and communities. Whether presented as a recent encounter with the hag, as Lucille Gaillard experienced; belief in the power of the blue eye, as Faye Terry affirmed; or questions about Lucinda Pinckney's actual role as a local root-worker, it is clear that these complex systems of folk practices cannot simply be written off as a part of history that is no longer embraced. Rather, when placed together, these materials provide a broad and extensive overview of the religious practices, rituals, and experiences of lowcountry African Americans. Most significantly, they affirm the dynamic processes of cultural appropriation that is such a dominant feature of Gullah/Geechee religious practice. These fluid understandings support the idea, as Weisenfeld and Newman suggest, that historically, "[w]hile African-American women have exhibited profound devotion to particular denominational or other religious structures that have, in turn benefited from their energy and talents, many African-American women, whether out of necessity or choice, have also demonstrated a flexibility in their religiosity."[29] In short, religious practice and religious identity among these women is not as straightforward as a simple acceptance and understanding of their explicitly Christian praxis. One must also take into account the ways that folk religious customs continue to hold present sway among Gullah/Geechee women in ways that are similar to and distinct from the way their significance is documented in history.

The Few Named—The Many Unnamed

Lucinda's perceived role as a conjurer, root-worker, or healer in Moncks Corner suggests the continuity of women's esteemed positions within folk traditions. Interestingly, although there are numerous historical sources that specifically identify women as powerful, influential leaders within folk traditions like conjure, women were seldom named or identified as leaders within the more formally recognized religious traditions and denominations of the South Carolina lowcountry. The images of black women presented by Charles Raymond, dialect recitalist Jane Heyward, and Charleston resident John Bennett are representative of the depictions of women in the literature from 1863 to 1950. According to Charles Raymond, "A leading trait in the American negro, reared under the influences of Southern slavery, is that he is *intensely religious*."[30] His assessment of the deep religiosity of African Americans, marked most notably by their emotionalism, permeated his characterizations of Gullah/Geechee women. Raymond had a slave named "Aunt Sarah" whom he described as "one of the most sensible, reliable, and obedient servants" he had ever had. Yet Sarah was given to ecstatic trances she called "mazes." These spiritual "attacks" occurred on three different occasions in a two-year period and resulted in Sarah becoming so entranced that she was unable to move or speak coherently—an action reminiscent of possession by the hag. In Raymond's initial encounter of the mazes, Sarah burst into Raymond's bedroom and startled him and his wife awake.

> [Sarah's] eyes, expanded and glassy, seemed wildly starting from their sockets; and her hands were spread out before her as if deprecating the approach of some fearful vision. . . . After standing thus a moment with arms extended, and every muscle strained to a statue-like rigidity, she suddenly uttered a shriek, and turning slowly around fell prone upon the floor; arms still outspread, and eyes retaining their glassy, wild, vacant expression. Then succeeded most dreadful groans, the intervals between which were filled with desponding, heart-rendering ejaculations. "O Lord, I'm damned! O master, I'm in hell! O Jesus do save me! I'm in hell! I'm IN HELL! O Jesus, do save me! . . . And thus for half an hour she continued, bathed in a cold sweat, and with pulse scarcely perceptible, until at last her agony ceased from utter prostration. Then, in a half-bewildered state, she rose and went to her cabin, leaving impressed upon our minds vivid imagery a scene so full of horror and utter abjectness that the morning dawned before we again lost consciousness in slumber.[31]

Raymond described Sarah's additional mazes, which were similar in structure and resulted in Sarah requesting salvation or expressing deliverance from her sins. In the months following Sarah's initial maze, Raymond's wife attempted "to instruct her fully in the true nature of repentance, convictions, and the method of pardon through an atoning Saviour." He admitted, however, that Sarah did not find these lessons especially useful and explained to her mistress that there was a difference between how white and black people experienced religion. Sarah's distinction did not make Raymond more aware of differences between the ways that whites and blacks interpreted their religious experiences; rather, he concluded that Sarah "didn't seem to like religion much that was not at all in the line of her emotions." He further decried Sarah's experience as "a peculiar form of religious sensibility."[32] Sarah was eventually relieved from these trances, but only after attending an unspecified camp meeting after which she professed to be delivered from her sins and a fully converted Christian.

Raymond found these events striking because of the startling way they occurred, but more so because Sarah could not provide an "intelligible account of her feelings, nor of their antecedents, and could show no logical connection between her thoughts, ideas, or emotions, and the transcendental state into which she was thrown." Raymond acknowledged that Sarah "connected the facts of her condition with the expression in some form of religious susceptibility."[33] Yet he negatively interpreted Sarah and her experiences of religious trance as emotional, unintelligible, irrational, and peculiar, a conclusion that was based upon the following presumption: "No doubt their ideas upon many subjects are to themselves clearly defined, and could be clearly expressed to others had they any true conception of the form and meaning of words. But, with their super-sensuous temperaments, and entire ignorance of written language, it is not strange that they should be captivated with words containing certain sounds, and then, upon occasions which seem to them appropriate, repeat the words which have impressed them pleasingly, without the most remote conception of their meaning."[34]

Contemporary evaluations of Sarah's mazes reveal, as Jason Young suggests, that Sarah was operating under arguably African-derived (and explicitly Kongolese) conversion practices. Robert Simpson has concluded that Sarah's trances are examples of how shouting traditions were used within enslaved communities to facilitate religious conversion. To Simpson, Sarah's mazes demonstrate how the experience of shouting functioned both as a communal and individual experience and confirm how contact with fellow slaves, rather than the efforts of white planters and missionaries, more frequently resulted in conversion.[35] Yet Raymond's assessment of Sarah's experiences reveals an additional characterization of lowcountry women: that they were unable to rationalize or articulate their religious experience in meaningful ways. Gullah/Geechee women thus became examples of how black residents enjoyed the sounds of words without a full or adequate understanding of their meaning—a feature that stands in stark contrast to depictions of their powerful positioning within black folk traditions such as conjure.

Further characterizations of Gullah/Geechee women as unintelligible human beings are also found in a narrative from Jane Heyward's collection. One of the most frequently recounted tales given during Heyward's dialect recitals was a story entitled "Babble Babble." As a preface to the narrative, Heyward stated: "The negroes are noted for their love of unusual words, and for their delight in oratory of all kinds, when open air speech making is going on among the whites it is always an assured fact, that the audience will taper off into a fringe of black faces if sufficient notice is given." She then continued with the following description:

In South Carolina on one such occasion, and where the whites had journeyed from a considerable distance in order to dedicate a monument, which had been recently erected, with the purpose in mind of keeping alive some patriotic event; there was in the outskirts of the crowd a particularly fervent old Mauma, [as] is the custom in the rural churches she would comment audibly on remarks which particularly pleased her by their sound, even when not understanding their import.

One of the Orators of the day was particularly long-winded, and he had chosen to illustrate a point by using Tennyson's Brook.[36] When he came to the words "Men may come, and men may go, but I go on forever," the audience were convulsed by laughter to hear the old woman ejaculate loudly, "Das deh trut'—Das deh trut' Maussa, Das wah you is do!!!" The Speaker seemed not to hear, but continued. "I babble, babble as I go." "Yes Lord," called out the delighted auditor, "Das deh trut' you talk Maussa, you sho is Babble, Babble as you go—Yes Sah Lord." The audience were so in sympathy with this freely expressed opinion, that it found difficulty in concealing its mirth.[37]

Heyward's "humorous" narrative of the nondescript "fervent old Mauma" confirms how writers like Heyward used women to affirm the assumed inherent irrationality and emotionalism of lowcountry blacks. It exemplifies the ways that these writers dismissed interpretations of religion that differed from their own. In particular, this story notes the call-and-response tradition that has historically been and continues to be a significant part of African American religious experience. It also denotes the oral, emotive expressions that often characterize black religion. Jane Heyward's comment, "[as] is the custom in the rural churches she would comment audibly on remarks which particularly pleased her by their sound, even when not understanding their import," reveals that Heyward, like many other authors in the late nineteenth and early twentieth centuries, was herself unable to understand how lowcountry African Americans interpreted the meaning and expression of their religion for themselves.

Gullah/Geechee women were also incorporated into early sources when they demonstrated the ways that the Gullah danced, shouted, and sang. Rather than noting the importance of women as worship leaders or facilitators of a specific, distinct type of spiritual expression, John Bennett consistently used and relied upon unnamed, nondescript female informants to validate his claims of religious emotionalisms and primitivism among the Gullah/Geechee. In a description of women's participation in a shouting ritual, Bennett noted:

There was a woman in the center of the circle trying to throw herself into a hysteric trance. Every now and then the people sang in chorus with her wild chanting. She could not entrance herself. She sank back into the circle; another took her place; in the midst of the most vociferous singing that could be emitted by human throat. In a few moments, she failing, gave place to a third, a little, brown woman. The singing redoubled in fury. The excitement had become very great. The people were dripping with perspiration; they shouted madly [sic]; they seemed to be out of their sense entirely. The pitch of their voices was so high, and their voices so hoarse that their words were inarticulate, unrecognizable, their dialect so obscure. The woman began to tremble, her hands to twitch convulsively, her face was contorted; her eyes rolled up until only the yellow whites were remained visible; suddenly her bosom swelled with a great inspiration or gasp, her limbs straightened out, her body became rigid, and she fell with a crash. The wildest excitement possessed the people. She was allowed to lie where she fell; she lay upon her back as she fell; insensible; she looked as if she had died in an epileptic seizure. A catalepsy.

Bennett also detailed women's participation in a "voudou dance" ceremony, where "they began to make all kinds of contortions, and set up a wild howl of barbarous song."[38] These rich descriptions provide us with previously undisclosed information on women's roles as spiritual agents who were able to be possessed and to facilitate possession. Bennett's fascination with Gullah/Geechee religious expression is nonetheless marked by his failure to recognize women's roles as the transmitters of spiritual and ecstatic trance.

Bennett kept record of the role of Gullah/Geechee women during periods of mourning. When someone became ill or died, lowcountry blacks would hold a "sittin' up," a formal gathering where members of the community would offer their support by sitting with the gravely ill and their families until the person passed away, and then they would remain with the family after the person died. Yenenga has described the sittin' up as an ongoing, normative practice in lowcountry culture: "Of course when there's a death you know we still gather at whoever's in the family's house that that person had died." I have personally witnessed numerous sittin' ups in the lowcountry, during the deaths of relatives and community members, and after Faye Terry's death, where members of the community, especially the church, went to Faye's home and remained there to reminisce about her and offer comfort to her family until very late into the evening. This occurred every night from the day that she passed away until the day of her funeral. Historically, during periods of bereavement the cessation of work was granted when feasible, so members of the community could "watch for the dead." According to Roberta, the role of women in the lowcountry during the mourning process has historically been and continues to be crucial, for in addition to cooking elaborate meals to sustain the bereaving family and their guests, the women "rally around the family and help them cope."

Although contemporary readings of Bennett's notations account for women's important roles in communal mourning practices, we are reminded that for Bennett, women's participation largely served an emotive purpose: "Negro women can apparently weep at will; they will cry together within five minutes of a certain time of day, or mourning occasions, when a few moments before they were calmly going about their common occupation, laughing and chattering light-heartedly. With mournful cries and wails which cover sham sorrow rather than express real grief."[39] John Bennett's questioning of these mourning rituals overshadows the significance of black women's social networks, the historical and social circumstances of the Jim Crow era during which black women genuinely were able to "weep at will," and the importance of ritualized performance and catharsis within religious expression. His refutation of the authenticity of Gullah/Geechee women's grief denied the very systems that led to the type of mourning these women experienced.

The descriptions provided by Bennett, Heyward, and Raymond are valuable because they capture the details of shouting ceremonies, women's social networks, and communal mourning customs, and for how they document Gullah/Geechee women's roles in facilitating these practices. They also illustrate the attitudes of first-generation writers toward lowcountry religion and the women who practiced it, and as such, are problematic because of the ways they negatively characterized lowcountry religious practices, interpret spirit possession and shouting as senseless, minimize human agency, and diminish the significance of women's roles. Historians and scholars of religion alike have examined the invisibility of women within historical texts. Feminist historians have long contested the absence of black women's narratives, experiences, and names within historical sources. They have also raised salient questions for what that historical absence has meant and offered creative strategies for constructing women's narratives from texts. Similarly, within religious studies, treatment of women's invisibility has been largely focused on two fronts: the omission of named women within the biblical text, and the absence of documentation of women's roles in histories of religion.[40] These scholarly efforts suggest that despite the contradictory and at times troubling ways Gullah/Geechee women have historically been depicted, we can utilize these sources to uncover important facts about their experiences.

(Re)Positioning Gullah/Geechee Women

Prior to the twentieth century, women were historically proscribed from being preachers or deacons and were seldom considered for key leadership positions within the Baptist and Methodist denominations. Gullah/Geechee women were identified as the primary perpetuators of religious traditions beyond the walls of the institutional (Protestant) church. Some of the earliest descriptions about Gullah/Geechee women's significance in lowcountry religious life have been provided by Laura Towne (1820–1901), a missionary, educator, and cofounder of Penn School (1862), the first school for freed blacks in the lowcountry. It remains open today as Penn Center, a National Historic Landmark on St. Helena Island dedicated to the preservation of Sea Island culture. As part of the Port Royal Experiment, Towne envisioned her role on St. Helena Island to be that of a missionary. As such, she, Ellen Murray, and other leaders of Penn School (including Charlotte Forten) taught the newly emancipated blacks of St. Helena, with an emphasis on character development, self-discipline, citizenship, and service. According to historian Michael Wolfe, they also incorporated the broad ideals of American Protestant religion, namely the "agenda of progress, patriotism, and citizenship" to "convert the 'savage' slaves into good Protestant Christians and productive United States Citizens."[41] As a local resident, Towne fostered significant relationships with various black residents, including Maum Katie, an elder within the community whom she frequently visited. Towne's journal from 1864 provides the following narrative:

> I went to-day to see Maum Katie, an old African woman, who remembers worshipping her own gods in Africa, but who has been nearly a century in this country. She is very bright and talkative, and is a great "spiritual mother," a fortune-teller, or rather prophetess, and a woman of tremendous influence over her spiritual children. I am going to cultivate her acquaintance. I have been sending her medicine for a year nearly, and she

"hangs up on top of me," refusing all medicine but mine. I never saw her till to-day, and she lives not a stone's throw off, so you may guess how hurried I am. . . . Mother Katie has a strange history and is over a hundred years old, but bright mentally as if she were but forty. She is blind and suffers horribly with her eyes.[42]

Towne's record reminds the reader of the forced importation of enslaved Africans during the transatlantic slave trade, and its lasting impact upon the social, epistemological, and religious construction of lowcountry communities. Although Katie had lived in the United States for nearly a century, she was not identified as Negro or Gullah/Geechee, but as African. This suggests that Maum Katie's African identity and her "strange history" continued to have bearing on her life on St. Helena Island.

A closer look at this passage reveals even more substantial information about lowcountry religion and women's roles within it. That Maum Katie "remembers worshipping her own gods in Africa" affirms the syncretic nature of Gullah/Geechee religiosity and its fluid incorporation of African, African-derived, and folk traditions with Protestant Christianity. Albert Raboteau has suggested that during the antebellum period southern blacks quite readily "put down new roots in new soil," or that they developed new, hybrid traditions that merged African and American belief systems. Margaret Creel posits that this feature created dynamic trends of African provenance, Christianity, and a New World collective consciousness that were integrated into lowcountry religiosity.[43] Although Towne does not indicate whether Maum Katie specifically remembered her gods by name or continued to worship them as she remembered them, we can presume that Maum Katie incorporated her previous religious identity into her life within the lowcountry. We know this because Towne referenced Katie's African gods as "her own," which signals an intimacy with "her" gods and a distancing from (though not a lack of familiarity with) the gods present in the Americas. As Yvonne Chireau has suggested, "While Africans [in America] were unable to replicate their religious institutions, they usually created new, sometimes clandestine traditions that served their collective needs. Although they transformed the older religions, Africans maintained their ancient spiritual moorings while in America."[44]

Towne's account of Maum Katie is also striking because of what it reveals about Katie's communal responsibilities. Katie holds three interrelated yet distinct roles on St. Helena Island: spiritual mother, fortune-teller or prophetess, and woman of great influence over her "spiritual" children. In the role of spiritual mother (and a "great" one no less), Katie would have been acknowledged as having profound wisdom and the ability to impart her insight upon community members. That she was so advanced in age would have further solidified her communal role as a sage. As a fortune-teller or visionary, she would have been highly respected for her gift of foresight. An arguably spiritual or metaphysical ability within Afro-diasporic cultures, having the gift to "see," or perceive phenomena or events that are indiscernible to others, is often reputed to accompany blindness and would have also warranted Maum Katie great respect from community members.[45] In addition, Towne's use of quotation marks around the term "spiritual mother" suggests that she employed the term as it was used within the community. The persons to whom Maum Katie imparted her wisdom and foresight would have been considered her "spiritual children" no matter their literal age or parentage. As her children, they would have likely relied upon her role as their spiritual mother, and returned to her for advice and assistance. The three monikers Towne attributes to Maum Katie thus reveal the different forms of spiritual power she held, and confirm the various yet esteemed religious roles some Gullah/Geechee women held.

Lowcountry women were also noted for their distinct abilities as conjurers. According to John Bennett, conjure women were readily present in Gullah/Geechee communities and wielded much power to "fix" both whites and blacks in the community.[46] Laura Towne also provided an in-depth description of a conjure woman named Mom Charlotte, whose perceived abilities as a conjurer led to her being physically abused. "One of my old women was nearly killed the other night by a man who went to her house at dead of night and beat her because she 'hagged' him. He came as soon as he heard I had arrived, to beg my pardon and say he would do so no more. But I could not convince him that 'Mom Charlotte' did not go every night to his house and 'hag' him, or that he ought not defend himself by beating her to make her stay away. The poor thing could not walk half the distance."[47] From Towne's portrayal we learn that the man who accosted Mom Charlotte beat her because he believed that she was "hagging" him daily. That Mom Charlotte is described as an "old woman" suggests that she may have been a seasoned practitioner. What is especially revelatory about Towne's depiction is what it suggests about Gullah/Geechee women's roles as spiritual practitioners within their communities. That the man who violently abused her could not be convinced that Mom Charlotte was not in fact "hagging him," that he felt the need to defend himself, and that he nearly killed her as a result of his belief indicates that whether or not she was actually a conjurer, people thought Mom Charlotte had tremendous spiritual power. Undoubtedly, women like Mom Charlotte and Maum Katie were critical to the perpetuation of folk religious practices within the community. Their examples also reflect the fluid merging of local and folk religious customs.

From these historical descriptions provided by women, we learn a great deal about women's historical roles in Gullah/Geechee religious life. In addition to the diaries of Laura Towne, the work of Charlotte Forten has supplied one of the earliest descriptions of religion among Sea Islanders.[48] She was the first African American woman to document the religious traditions of the Gullah, and the first woman of color to publish materials about her experiences on the Sea Islands.[49] Newspaper advertisements and posthumously published diaries, like those of Laura Towne and Charlotte Forten, are no longer the only accounts we have to understand the historical significance of women's roles in Gullah/Geechee religion. Yet they continue to be important because they provide considerable information about what black women in the lowcountry did, how they acted, and what they said. As a result, we can reread these histories to glean a more comprehensive understanding of Gullah/Geechee women's religiosity, and to better interpret the modern dynamics of religious identity, ritual, and custom in the lowcountry. When we place these sources alongside more contemporary examinations of Gullah/Geechee religious practice, they provide a lens through which to view Gullah/Geechee women's current participation in lowcountry religious culture and offer a perspective on how women's roles may have shifted over time.

Soulless Bodies/Bodiless Souls

One of the reasons that conjure, voodoo, and superstition have remained such prominent features of Gullah/Geechee religiosity is partially because folk customs were so prevalent and presumably powerful. A second and equally significant reason is that introducing lowcountry blacks to Christianity was not largely favored or supported by whites in South Carolina before the 1830s.[50] Slave owners were unwilling to allow their slaves to attend church meetings or be baptized, as they feared that their baptism would require that the enslaved be manumitted; many planters did not want the plantation's operating schedule interrupted for the slave to receive instruction; and slaveholders were concerned about the egalitarian implications of Christianity. According to the Christian Apostle Paul, "There is neither Jew nor Greek, there is neither bond nor free, there is nether male nor female: for ye are all one in Christ Jesus."[51] Moreover, Baptist plant-ers—who dominated the lowcountry—maintained great faith in Calvinistic ideals and supported the enslavement of blacks as preordained by God and as a means of eradicating the utter depravity and sinfulness of humanity. In sum, before the 1830s slaveholders viewed the conversion of slaves as anti-thetical to their economic interests and to the divine order, and exerted little to no effort to catechize the enslaved.

The actions of blacks in the South did not advance the cause for religious instruction. The foiled Denmark Vesey conspiracy of 1822 in Charleston and the insurrection of Nat Turner in Southampton, Virginia (1831), had far-reaching effects, preceded only in legal, social, and economic ramifica-tions by the Stono Rebellion of 1739.[52] Both Vesey and Turner, who were described as associated with the Methodist and Baptist denominations, respectively, utilized their interpretations of Christianity to speak against the enslavement of blacks, to refute the Christianity of the planter class, and to justify their planned revolts. In addition, each of the revolts had the assis-tance of community conjure-men, who were generally perceived by whites as illegitimate leaders who based their pseudoreligious practices on fear and superstition.[53] These factors confirmed and fueled the planters' fears that if blacks were allowed to gather in groups, they would be more apt to rebel for their freedom. They also validated white perceptions that blacks were incapable of "rightly" understanding religion and supported the ide-ology that offering religion to blacks was a hopeless cause.

Despite these ideals and events, efforts to introduce lowcountry blacks to Christianity increased in the 1830s.[54] At a speech given before the Agri-cultural Society of South Carolina, Charles Cotesworth Pinckney of the Episcopal Church insisted upon the religious instruction of "Negroes." "This address went through two or more editions and was extensively cir-culated and with the happiest effects."[55] At the same time, the South Caro-lina conference of the Methodist Episcopal Church began to advocate the instruction of slaves and to missionize slaves in the lowcountry. In 1832, local ministers across denominations formed the Association for the Reli-gious Instruction of the Negroes. Methodist minister, founder of the Meth-odist Missionary Society of South Carolina, and slave owner William Capers published A Catechism for the Use of Methodist Missions, a step-by-step guide for missionaries that showed them how to Christianize slaves through the teaching of prayers and hymns, the Ten Commandments, and the Apostles' Creed. This text was distributed and used by "all the missionaries" of the Methodist Episcopal Church. By the end of 1833, the Missionary Society of the South Carolina Conference of the Methodist Church reported, "the missions were generally in flourishing circumstances." It was also during this time that religious newspapers such as the *Charleston Observer, The Gospel Messenger* (Episcopal), and the *Southern Christian Advocate* (Methodist) publicly supported the Christianization of slaves and made this idea readily available to a larger, mass audience.[56] By 1845, religious instruction of blacks was the primary focus of nearly every clergy member in South Carolina.[57]

Support of the catechization of blacks was furthered by the publication of *The Religious Instruction of the Negroes in the United States* by Charles Colcock Jones (1804–1863), a Georgia-born Presbyterian minister and planter who devoted his life to the cause of missionizing blacks in the South. In his overview of the history of religious instruction in America, Jones detailed the superior qualities of the white *master* and the white *race*, particularly in the areas of religion and culture. He juxtaposed white superiority with the "degraded moral character . . . ignorance, vulgarity, improvidence, irreligion, and vice" of blacks. Jones called for religious instruction of blacks en masse, as a means of solidifying and embracing the innate and God-given superiority (and responsibility) of whites, and to eradicate the intellectual, moral, and religious degradation of blacks. He captured the tenor of white planter and missionary ideals in South Carolina, arguing that the purpose of religious instruction was to improve the black personality, to "equal, if not greatly excel" the Negro "in majesty of intellect, elegance of manners, purity of morals and ardor of piety," and to have them "become the very *beau ideal* of character, the admiration of the world."[58] Jones's admonishments reflect the ideologies that led to the increased Christianization of the enslaved in the 1830s. He vehemently advocated the idea that whites were *by their nature* created to dominate the lesser, darker peoples of the world; that it was their responsibility to introduce the enslaved to the right and true teachings of Christianity; and that God had providentially ordained slavery. Jones also confirmed the widespread notion that blacks were innately and uniquely religious, and that their distinctive, deeply instilled emotionalism could be used to the advantage of missionaries.[59] These sentiments were perpetuated within each denomination, and local bishops, ministers, and missionaries created and distributed catechism guides.[60] This led to the formation of specific organizations within individual denominations and to the development of a formalized system of instruction, marked by the creation of manuals, teaching guides, tracts, literature, and techniques to advance the religious cause of blacks.

Whether directed at children or adults, the missionizing efforts of

South Carolina's churches before the 1860s utilized religious instruction to emphasize submission, duty, and obedience to maintain social control, exert divinely ordained privilege, and sustain plantation management.[61] Relying on such biblical texts as the "Curse of Ham" (Genesis 9:18–27), Paul's admonishment to the Colossian church that servants should "obey their masters" (Colossians 3:22), and the example of the obedient bondsman in the book of Philemon, missionaries believed it was their moral and religious responsibility to "correct the condition" of blacks, especially their reliance on conjure, voodoo, hoodoo, and fetishism.[62] In sum, white missionaries used religion, with rare exception, to affirm the inferiority of blacks and to defend the supremacy of whites and the social order as established by white slaveholders. The mass Christianization of the 1830s and 1840s "was an honest effort to win souls through the process of conversion common to all men and at the same time an effort to have the slave element of the population fit into a definite niche in the social order."[63] At the heart of these efforts were the sentiments of white missionaries toward blacks: an amalgamation of religious, political, racial, and economic interests— marked most poignantly by their distinction between what Riggins Earl Jr. has called "black soulless bodies" and "bodiless souls."[64]

Earl has argued that the body-soul dichotomy that permeated the religious, social, and economic ideologies of the planter class was the main problem with the religious instruction offered to southern enslaved blacks. According to Earl, the structure of plantation religion was guided by the belief among planters, missionaries, and preachers in two, antithetical "ideal types" of blacks.[65] The first category, the soulless body, or naturalist type, supported the idea that "slaves of African descent, unlike their white masters, were absolutely void of souls." In this way, slave owners and missionaries reduced the enslaved to mere bodies and utilized the Bible to legitimate their attitudes toward the enslaved.[66] Thus, enslaving African bodies for economic interests posed no moral, ethical, or religious dilemma among slaveholders. They viewed Africans as soulless and believed that enslaving the African body held no spiritual or moral significance and that their external blackness indicated the internal depravity of their souls.[67] The second category, the "bodiless soul" or Christian-master type, maintained the view that Africans were indeed created with souls. Ministers and plantation owners thus believed it was their Christian duty to convert the enslaved to save them from their heathenish, primitive selves while satisfying the laws of God.[68] These missionaries and slave owners cared about the immortal soul of the slave but had no interest in changing their mortal condition.

This was the pervading ideology from 1830 until emancipation. According to Earl, the perpetuation of these two ideals "constituted the core theological and ethical problem of slavery."[69]

Religious instruction as facilitated by southern whites put them in a difficult and at times contradictory position. It affirmed the importance of religion and acknowledged the spiritual self of blacks, but simultaneously confirmed black inferiority and taught them that their enslavement was compatible with Christian faith. According to church historian Thomas V. Peterson, "On the one hand, they believed that the African was a descendant of Adam and ought to be converted to Christianity, thus implying that a common brotherhood existed among men. On the other hand, they believed that the Negro was greatly inferior to the Caucasian and should be subordinate, thereby undercutting the notion of common descent."[70] This contradiction did not go unnoticed by blacks, who, despite the attempts of white planters, missionaries, and preachers to shape their beliefs to ensure obedience and submission, were selective in their internalization of the religion they were taught. While many slaves accepted Christianity, they simultaneously appropriated what they interpreted as valid, and rejected what they did not. South Carolina missionaries and planters who entered the lowcountry continuously noted blacks' "peculiar" appropriations of Christianity and documented their frustrations about how the Gullah continued to believe in conjure and fetishism despite instruction to the contrary. Charles Raymond noted in 1863, "In all instances which I remember to have noticed . . . I have found among the religious slaves of the South traces, more or less distinct, of a blending of superstitions and fetishism, modifying their impressions of Christianity."[71]

Blacks, though enslaved, operated as active agents in their introduction to, conversion to, and appropriation of Christianity. They constructed and reconstructed for themselves visions of God that at times included—but often extended beyond—their masters' understandings and practices of Christianity.[72] It therefore makes perfect sense that the enslaved interpreted religion in ways that planters and missionaries did not understand, for they constructed their religion out of their own narratives, histories, memories, and experiences, which included their African heritage, and were thus inherently different from the heritage of their masters.[73] Songs, testimonies, and folk stories (especially trickster narratives) were among numerous counterresponses of the enslaved to their bondage.

All of the published and unpublished sources included in this chapter bear the influence of the soulless body–bodiless soul religious ideologies that permeated the lowcountry. Jane Heyward (1864–1939) grew up on Stewarton Plantation in St. John's Parish (Charleston County), which was a slaveholding rice plantation. Her father Edwin Dubose (1825–1865) built a chapel on the plantation and allowed Episcopalian ministers to preach to and confirm "eleven colored persons" on April 12, 1863, and sixteen blacks on April 11, 1864, "some of them from other plantations."[74] Charlotte Forten went to the Sea Islands as part of the Port Royal Experiment, a "social experiment" created under the auspices of the Port Royal Relief Association of Philadelphia for the purpose of preparing recently released slaves for their role as free blacks in America. This preparation included teaching blacks how to read and write as well as instructing them on how to become better Christians.[75] Charles Raymond described the conversion of enslaved blacks to Christianity as an opportunity for positive change, but noted the limitations of that change because of the inherent peculiarities of their very being (e.g., their blackness).[76]

This account of religious instruction therefore cannot be separated from the content of the nineteenth- and early twentieth-century sources on Gullah/Geechee religion or from the contemporary manifestations of black religiosity in the lowcountry. Knowledge of this history contextualizes the preponderance of negative tones, viewpoints, and statements present in the descriptions of Gullah religion and spirituality. In short, many of the attitudes these authors held toward Africans and African Americans reflected the same ideologies perpetuated throughout the South during missionizing efforts. Knowing how Christianity was introduced to the Gullah/Geechee is also critical for understanding how religion among blacks of the lowcountry has historically been depicted and how religious customs have changed today. The history of Christianization in the lowcountry reveals the significant ways that religious practice, religious traditions, and religious leadership in the lowcountry were understood and interpreted by those who documented it in writing, especially in comparison to those who continue to live with the implications of these depictions.

Religious Autonomy

Gullah/Geechee religion has always been a syncretic appropriation of Christianity and traditional folk customs. Given this background, the relative geographic isolation of lowcountry black communities, and their black majority, Gullah/Geechee religion has also been enacted with varying levels of autonomy. To the Gullah/Geechee, religious autonomy meant navigating a fluid socioreligious sphere that included men as deacons and preachers but also women as conjurers and folk healers. Local practitioners (conjurers, root-workers, midwives, and the like) and formally appointed African American leaders (deacons and preachers) wielded a great deal of socioreligious power. They were highly respected, viewed as religious exemplars, and treated as moral authorities. Deacons and preachers, however, had to balance a delicate positioning within multiple communities. In the white church infrastructure, to which they were always in some way connected, they did not have a great deal of *executive* power. Instead, they almost always had to report to white deacons or a white pastor. According to Charles Raymond, the deacon was "the pastor without being a preacher; and [was] also the connecting official link between his colored brethren in the church and their white associates. What the white pastor can never know, concerning the moral and social character of the colored flock, the negro deacon can know; and the pastor depends upon him for advice and knowledge concerning the wants and weaknesses of his slave brethren."[77] If, for example, a deacon recommended the removal of a particular member from the church due to religious depravity, it did not occur simply at his admonishment. Despite his substantial role within the black community, the deacon's authority was limited in the world of whites.

These legally and socially sanctioned limitations on religious affairs did not obliterate religious autonomy among enslaved and free blacks. Blacks in South Carolina were generally not allowed to gather without a white person present between 1739 and 1865. Those prohibitions certainly did not mean that they did not gather; the documented presence of hush harbors and other secret places where the enslaved met during the antebellum period to practice their religious traditions affirms their continuous efforts to express their religiosity on their own terms.[78] The creation of meeting-houses also afforded them different religious freedoms, as they were able to practice religion both with and without white oversight. This was particularly affected by geographic location, as there was not much distance between many of the small islands and inland areas. Blacks' ability to travel was determined by their having the time and permission to travel and by finding transportation. Despite these challenges, lowcountry residents met and were often familiar with each other, a feature that disrupts notions of Gullah/Geechee "isolation" that are commonly assumed in writings about lowcountry blacks. Members of the various islands, for example, would come "from across the creek" and share in the lives of other black communities.[79] This communal or translocal interrelatedness was further facilitated in the lowcountry in 1861. Ten thousand slaves were left virtually without the presence of whites when slave masters fled inland at the impending Union attack of Port Royal Sound (the inlet between Phillips Island and Hilton Head). These slaves officially became free citizens of the United States on July 17, 1862, "when the U.S. Congress determined that all slaves who belonged to rebels presently behind Union lines were free."[80] Yet the religious autonomy of the lowcountry blacks was not dependent on their free or enslaved status. Despite religious, geographic, and legal sanctions, African Americans in the lowcountry had always maintained their own religious practices, rituals, and systems.

The absence of white ministers, planters, and overseers and the facilitation of religious services by African Americans also led to religious autonomy among the "black majority" in the lowcountry. In Methodist churches, blacks became subject to—and entitled to—many of the same regulations as whites and could therefore serve as class leaders and exhorters. Among Baptists, which were the most predominant in number in the lowcountry (and blacks constituted a majority), blacks functioned as exhorters or preachers and deacons; they also led prayers, visited the sick, buried the dead, and occasionally performed marriage ceremonies.[81] On the occasions that white ministers were not present, elderly blacks (usually men) led the religious services of the church/praise house. In the elections of deacons, Charles Raymond was aware of "hundreds of such meetings" where deacons were elected "without even one white person being present." He further described: "In the agricultural districts, and upon the plantations where there are large communities of negroes surrounded by other similar communities, and wholly removed from any disturbing influences, the social and religious character of the slaves are developed freely and without restraint. Here only will you find the full exhibition of the peculiar virtues and vices of their characters as modified by the influences of religion."[82]

Many lowcountry black women and men were enabled to worship freely and without restraint. In one description Laura Towne recounted: "We had such a funny time at church to-day. There was no white minister, and two elders preached and one prayed . . . ."[83] The Gullah/Geechee preached, prayed, led their own services, and appropriated and employed their pluralistic Christian religious sensibilities and folk religious practices in their own sense of time. On the first occasion that Charlotte Forten attended the Baptist church on St. Helena, she noted, "The people came in slowly. They have no way of telling the time. Yet, by eleven o'clock, they had all assembled and the services began."[84] In his description of the announcement of

Saturday evening church service, which usually took place by the ringing of the church bell, Raymond inquired, "Who ever saw a negro hurry himself to be in season for any thing, unless somebody was constantly shouting for him? And it at last came to be generally understood that the time when the services should commence was to be determined by the assembling of the congregations, and not by the ringing of the bell."[85] Scholars of African diaspora religions contend that Western notions of time are limited in their appropriation to African diasporic cultures. The Western concept of time is linear and operates on a past, present, and future continuum. According to John S. Mbiti, this construct is inconsequential and foreign to many African diasporic cultures, where time is understood as *potential time* and *actual time*.

> Time is simply a composition of events which have occurred, those which are taking place now and those which are immediately to occur. What has not taken place or what has no likelihood of an immediate occurrence falls in the category of "No-time." What is certain to occur, or what falls within the rhythm of natural phenomena, is in the category of inevitable or potential time. . . . *Actual time* is therefore what is present and what is past. It moves "backward" rather than "forward"; and people set their minds not on future things, but chiefly on what has taken place.[86]

This understanding of time, which is similar to McKoy's "diaspora temporality," suggests that black diasporic cultures are shaped by a flux between linear time as constructed in the West, and cyclical time as conceived in African and diaspora cultures. As lowcountry residents were African descendants, it is no surprise that this fluid understanding of time permeated Gullah/Geechee culture. That fact that enslaved and freed African American communities of the lowcountry had some sense of freedom in determining how and when they would worship is most significant. Again, the ability of black communities to interpret and practice religion despite limitations imposed by whites reflects their ingenuity and creativity. While directly affected by the culture of which they were a part, lowcountry blacks had their own say in how they utilized religion.

As Margaret Creel has suggested, it should have come as no surprise to missionaries that "tightly knit communities of African-Americans still clinging to patterns of social behavior and modes of worship, largely a mystery to whites, having developed through African cultural convergence," were found throughout the lowcountry. She has emphasized that the Gullah maintained spiritual autonomy in their practice of Christianity and argued that trends of African provenance were adapted and integrated into their belief systems and folk practices. To Creel, the primacy of religion among the Gullah/Geechee was a direct result of the African spiritual beliefs and cosmologies of the BaKongo and other Bantu-speaking areas, for it guided Gullah religious interaction with Christianity. She posited, "To believe Gullahs totally accepted the Christian posture suggests that they did not struggle against the cultural domination that masters imposed through religion."[87]

Lowcountry blacks thus merged the Christianity they received from missionaries with religious ideals derived from their histories as African diasporic communities. Margaret Creel has noted that among the Gullahs, "Christianity and traditional African religion combined to provide them with an ideology of freedom, and a noble, mystical explanation for their existence as a people."[88] From her perspective, those who categorized Gullah religion as a predominately white or simplistic form of Christianity failed to recognize how they constructed their own religious identities. While this in no way meant that the religion of lowcountry blacks was entirely or exclusively African, it did mean that traditional African cosmologies in adaptive forms were present in lowcountry religion. To Creel, an Afro-Christian religious synthesis offered Gullah communities their collective consciousness as people of faith and aided their abilities to maintain spiritual autonomy. Similarly, Michael Wolfe has examined the religious practices of St. Helena to demonstrate how diverse traditions from folk religion, Southern evangelical Christianity, and traditional African practices merged to form one living faith community. Lowcountry residents' appropriations of "new meanings" to "old rituals" led Wolfe to conclude, "Culturally speaking, in the early 1800s, slaves in the United States ceased to be Africans and became African Americans. Similar rites existed between the two but the meanings had all changed."[89]

To understand black religious autonomy among the Gullah/Geechee it is important to recognize that religious freedom also meant the incorporation of African and African-derived traditions. This cannot be underestimated. "It must be remembered that the negroes of the South are far from a homogenous body, they are not, and never were; they were Africans, many strains; widely different. There are on Southern plantations representatives of well-nigh numbered tribes."[90] All who observed and documented lowcountry religion noted this African preponderance. It also led Charles Raymond to conclude that the distinctive aspects of African American religion were influenced by the presence of African and African-based traditions. "Religion does not obliterate the constitutional peculiarities of a man, or do away with the force of habit or training. It indeed changes a man by implanting new affections, and imparting new motives and hopes, but without impairing the individuality of the person. The life of the negro slave in America is a peculiar one; and hence Christianity in him must manifest itself in many respects in a peculiar manner."[91] These descriptions of the "peculiarity" of religious practices in the lowcountry demonstrate how religion among blacks in North America between 1860 and 1910 fall under the larger rubric of the existence of African and African-derived religious traditions, which led to the development of African American religion.[92] Although there were minor attempts to Christianize enslaved blacks, such as the creation of the Society for the Propagation of the Gospel in Foreign Parts (1801), efforts to introduce enslaved blacks to Christianity were individualistic and localized. In addition, while Christianity and Islam were alive and well before the transatlantic slave trade, historians and religious scholars have noted that the majority of the Africans imported into the Americas adhered to indigenous worldviews, cultures, and systems of belief. That Africans were continually being imported (albeit illegally) into the Charleston area well after the transatlantic trade was banned in 1808 also sustained the continuous acculturation of Afro-diasporic traditions. Moreover, an understanding of the nature of the transatlantic trade is compelling. Africans were deported en masse from various western, central, and coastal locales. Most often, they were not directly transported to North American harbors, but stopped in numerous trading posts throughout the Caribbean to exchange and acquire new "cargo." In sum, the presence of African and Caribbean worldviews, practices, symbols, beliefs, religions, and other elements of culture have always been prevalent in the history of lowcountry blacks.

One can therefore imagine the religio-cultural melting pots that were the enslaved plantation communities of lowcountry South Carolina. Although the sources documenting the existence of these multiple elements of culture before the nineteenth century are scant, this does not mean that they did not exist or were not actively shaping culture. It is clear that the religious practices among lowcountry blacks were not exclusively Christian, although by 1910 the Christian component of black religion was particularly noticeable. Culture does not occur in a vacuum, nor can it simply be obliterated because of the life-altering experiences of the middle passage, enslavement, the plantation system, the threat of continuous relocation, and Reconstruction. Therefore, whether directly identifiable with a particular African (or Caribbean) ethnic group or not, the presence of African and African-derived religious traditions is not merely a possibility, but a fact. The existence of varied, non-

Christian folk religious traditions including conjure and hoodoo confirm the cultural viscosity that has always been a feature of lowcountry religion.

Contemporary Configurations of Religious Freedom

Joining the history of religious autonomy together with spiritual dynamism in Gullah/Geechee culture offers a more comprehensive way of understanding the importance of communally constructed religious practices in the lowcountry. In *Rituals of Resistance*, Jason Young explores identifiable links between the religious practices of west-central Africans (Kongolese) and the Gullah/Geechee of South Carolina and Georgia. Young's analysis, which falls within the third generation of scholarship on Gullah/Geechee culture, suggests that folk traditions exhibited in the lowcountry (such as belief in the hag) should not be thought of solely as conjure practices specific to the lowcountry; instead, they should be viewed as conjure practices that exemplify folk religious traditions within the African Atlantic religious complex. His emphasis on the historical exigencies of the slave trade reveals that the spiritual power attributed to Kongolese political leaders parallels that afforded formally and informally to appointed religious leaders (including conjurers and root-workers) within the lowcountry. Young's comparison of these two regions and their ethnic groups is important because it leads him to conclude that religion functioned as a primary means of resistance to the system of slavery and also as the ideological underpinning that supported slavery: namely, perceived black inferiority. The spirituality of the enslaved—which was mediated through complicated systems of accommodation of and adaptation to a myriad of religious practices, experiences, and rituals—was instrumental to how they dealt with, survived, and literally resisted the brutalities of slavery.

It is the context of resistance, and the ways folk traditions continued as an integral part of black interpretations of synthesized Christian and folk religious practices, that is most salient here. Through Young's historicized presentation of connections between the Kongolese and Gullah/Geechee, we can see the ways that religion continues to be a primary means of resistance. The Gullah/Geechee, like many local black Atlantic communities, "proved adept at resolving and amending Christian doctrine with dogma in line with their own cosmological conceptions and with the immediacy of their own condition."[93] Today, although bonded to denominational requirements, black religious expression in the lowcountry continues to be constructed around conceptions of creative appropriation and spiritual autonomy. For Yenenga, religious autonomy is synonymous with living out her calling as a church participant and storyteller in whatever way she deems fit. Similarly, living a life that is committed to the church and augmented by the connections she has to the elderly and senior members of her community further links Ruth's faith as a Christian woman with her understanding of the importance of communal connection within and beyond the church. For Beatrice and Lucille, the work they do in their respective church communities and with their hands (Lucille as a seamstress and Beatrice as a basket weaver), and their shared belief that they are called to the work they do, also suggests an organic and seamless incorporation of folk and Christian practice.

Faye, Lucinda, and Roberta have suggested that it is their ability to be their true "spiritual selves" that ensures they still attend church. Faye once said, "The work I do ties me to it [the church], but I wouldn't continue to come here week to week if I didn't feel like I couldn't praise God the way I wanted to. If that was missing, I'da been done gone." Her sentiment of being able to express herself freely also seems important to Roberta, who recognizes the importance of being a part of the United Methodist Church, but values having the ability to "praise and pray and shout as [she] want[s] to." She further described, "Sometimes when we go to these district-wide meetings with them other churches, you can tell they praise all reserved because of how they clap. But we get into it, into the music, the message, the feeling . . . I promise you, if we had to just do what they do, you wouldn't see me in this church." As someone who utilizes skills to help others that some may interpret as functioning outside of "traditional" Christian practice, Lucinda also recognizes the significance of religious freedom. She sees her ability to treat a range of illnesses through her "concoctions" (as she often calls them) as a "gift from God." When asked whether or not her lifestyle outside of the church conflicts with what she sees as being a part of church she replied, "Oh, not at all. You know sometimes, especially as ya get older, you come ta see the ways in which God has something in store for you. Just for you. Not anyone else, and nobody else is even gonna be able ta understand what you and God got goin' on. Not the preacha or the deacon or your friends or even ya husband. I know what I'm good at. I know what gift I got. I sing, and I mix 'em [herbs] up. I don't care if they don't understand that in the church, and especially if it's the preacha. . . . [She pauses and snickers.] But I tell ya one thing LeRhonda, they sho' understand when they get sick an' can't nobody else help 'em but me." These responses suggest that contemporary notions of religious autonomy are therefore synonymous with being able to worship, pray, sing, shout, practice, and live their faith in whatever way these women deem appropriate for their own lives.

The comfort with which the women in this study navigate their identities as Christian women and believers in and practitioners of localized folk customs suggests that the fluid appropriation of African diasporic and Christian traditions continues to be an important feature of Gullah/Geechee religion and culture. I have previously suggested that the Gullah/Geechee acceptance of folk customs alongside a predominantly Christian faith system lends to reading Gullah/Geechee religious practices as distinct. The ways Yenenga, Lucille, Faye, Ruth, Lucinda, Roberta, and Beatrice fluidly appropriate their Christian faith while maintaining varied degrees of belief in and adherence to traditions such as conjure, and in a way that does not disrupt their theological commitments, affirms this unique quality among Gullah/Geechee women. As we will see, talking to the dead exemplifies this synergy of folk religion and Christian theological practice, and remains an integral part of Gullah/Geechee religion.

CHAPTER 3

"Ah Tulk to de Dead All de Time"

The notion that other worlds are attempting to communicate with this world is widespread. . . . This is nothing new to the sea coast negroes. They always have believed in supernatural beings and strange lands and seem to possess the ability to converse with the dead.
—CHALMERS S. MURRAY

Lowcountry blacks have consistently professed belief in seeing and communicating with the dead, which is affirmed in Yenenga Wheeler's exclamation about the frequency with which she talks to the dead.[1] This claim is also confirmed by the ongoing prevalence of folk customs such as belief in the hag, belief in the ongoing existence of "apparitions," and conviction in a fluid cosmology that accepts death (and the dead) as a natural transition of human life. As South Carolina native and scholar Janie Moore has noted, "The Sea Islanders have the concept of the 'living dead'—not so named, but they believe in a continued relationship between the dead and the living."[2] Metaphorically, talking to the dead provides a convenient conceptual frame for understanding a complex practice within lowcountry culture. It is important to note, however, that talking to the dead is not a metaphor for Lucille, Roberta, Faye, Lucinda, Beatrice, Ruth, and Yenenga. Talking to the dead is as literal to these women as their belief in God. It is an essential aspect of their very existence as human beings, as African Americans, and as Christian women of faith.

Talking to the dead most often occurs in two types of practices. The first are customs traditionally interpreted as religious, which include prayer, seekin' (a process of gaining church membership), shouting or experiencing ecstatic spiritual moments, and sacred music traditions. The second category includes cultural activities that may not be typically understood as religious: storytelling, sweetgrass basketry, dreaming, and the concept of remembering.[3] While some of these activities may not be considered "religious" in a traditional sense, these activities—which are at the center of these women's lives—are tightly interwoven by religious imagery and concepts. Although worship services and other activities that are usually construed as religious facilitate talking to the dead more frequently than others, talking to the dead is not confined to a specific time or space. The practices associated with talking to the dead are not limited to the walls of any church, are not always affiliated with religious organizations or groups, and are not enacted to facilitate ecstatic experience. Whether described as "religious" or "cultural," all of these practices are understood as religious because these women interpret them as such.

As lived and experienced by these women, talking to the dead challenges traditional definitions of the terms "talking" and "dead" and ruptures normative translations of these words. The term "dead" in the noun or adjective form refers to an inanimate object, something that is inactive, lifeless, or silent, or something that at some point was alive but is no longer.[4] To these women, the dead are not interpreted as inactive or silent but as consistently present. Thus, while "dead" alludes to one's physical absence, the ongoing spiritual presence of the deceased is treated as normative and functional. In other words, in the lowcountry, the deceased, though physically transitioned, are very much alive. Similarly, the verb "talk" references communication by speech or spoken word. Talking, as employed by these women, initially occurs by sensing or feeling a deceased person's presence. Once that presence is acknowledged or interpreted as "among us," one can then communicate with the deceased. During this exchange, one listens to what the deceased has to say or tells the deceased about one's concerns, needs, or hopes. Talking, however, is most often silent because the deceased or the living person may not literally "say" anything; rather, talking to the dead is a spiritual experience where connections are made with the deceased, and the presence of the dead reveals more than words. It is through this four-tiered process—openness, acknowledgment, acceptance, and communication—that these women connect to those who are gone yet still remain.

Talking to the dead should not be confused with forms of ancestral veneration that occur in numerous religious traditions. The living dead as perceived among these women are not worshipped or enshrined. Nor are these spirits or presences acknowledged as deities; to these women, God—as embodied in Jesus Christ and manifest through the Holy Ghost—is the only professed divine being. Similarly, while talking to the dead is a literal connection to spiritual presences that may become evident in the physical presence of a deceased person, it is not the same as a belief in ghosts, or the physical manifestation of a deceased person's spirit. Usually, these women do not literally see the dead. Rather, they feel the dead physically, which gives the women a distinct sense of peace. Talking to the dead, though related in the sense that it is a connection with spirits, should not be interpreted as the expression of a haunting or the presence of evil spirits such as the hag; rather, it has a positive connotation and is not characterized by fear or dread. Additionally, unlike a *literal* presence of the dead in living communities, as Toni Morrison's *Beloved* depicts, talking to the dead represents a vivid *spiritual* connection that lowcountry women have with those who have passed on. Talking to the dead affirms these women's deep spiritual faith and how their faith results in connections to the divine and spirit realms. To talk to the dead, for these women, is indicative of their positions as powerful spiritual leaders and as culture keepers who maintain and perpetuate religious practice among the Gullah/Geechee.

"When de Dead Speak, I Listen"

Lucinda has lived in Moncks Corner her entire life. Although she grew up as a "child of the Baptist Church," she has spent her adult life as a member of Wesley UMC. Lucinda describes her connection with the dead as "something that always been part of me," and attributes her association to the fact that she has outlived many of her closest family members. Lucinda recounts feeling the presence of her younger sister, who tragically died when Lucinda was fifteen. She also has a distinct relationship with her mother, who passed away shortly after Lucinda turned twenty. For Ms. Cinda, the notion of being connected to the dead is "a natural thing" that has "been a part of [her] life so long [she] couldn't imagine it not being a part of [her] life." Lucinda's close connections with the dead are as longstanding as her relationship to the church and the God of Christianity.

Lucinda's association with the church is intimately connected to her relationships with Roberta and Faye. Unlike Lucinda, Roberta did not always live in Moncks Corner but relocated the twenty-minute drive from St. Stephen's when she got married at the age of eighteen. She now lives nearly a stone's throw away from Wesley UMC. With her husband, Thomas, she has raised three children, three grandchildren, and one great-grandson. Now eighty-two years of age, Roberta has grown more accustomed to receiving care. She has had some difficulty walking since a car accident severely damaged her hip thirty years ago, yet she manages to "walk every day, sometimes two or three miles." It was during one of these walks that Roberta first experienced an intimate connection with the dead. While recuperating from the accident, Roberta began to pray intensely for healing. What she found was not that her hip completely healed, but that she experienced periods of intense peace that were also accompanied by "a presence." This presence was not God, Jesus Christ, or the Holy Spirit, but the spirit of someone she felt she knew. She has continued communicating with the same peace-giving presence to this day.

The distinct feeling of a spiritual presence beyond that of the Holy Spirit was also familiar to Faye Terry. Fondly known as "Grammae" by her family, which consists of her daughter, four grandchildren, and eight great-grandchildren, Faye described her life as "full of hope in the midst of a lot of tragedy." Like her friend and fellow choir member, Lucinda, she outlived her husband, as well as two of her four younger siblings and two of her three children. Faye recognized that she had an intense connection with deceased family members, including her mother, husband, and sister. Although she was hesitant to acknowledge that she "talked to the dead," she admitted that there was something distinct about her connection with the dead, especially as she was immediately able to distinguish the presence of her mother's spirit from that of her husband or sister. Their arrival, which varied in occurrence, instilled peace in Faye and "help[ed] to calm [her] spirit." The recognition of a calming presence connected Faye and Roberta, who became "very close friends" upon meeting. Although they never spoke openly about their shared connections with the dead prior to their conversations with me, their inclusion in this project helped them to recognize yet another commonality.

Like Lucinda, Faye, and Roberta, Lucille and Ruth share the recognition that the deceased are active participants in the world of the living. For Lucille prayer facilitates that sense of presence, but so does her belief in that which is not always tangible and does not always warrant explanation. For the past twenty years, Lucille has worked and lived in Beaufort, Cross, and Moncks Corner and has maintained membership in various churches in these areas. She grew up in Beaufort with her mother, father, and six brothers and sisters. She attended two churches, Mt. Sinai Baptist Church in downtown Beaufort and New Hope Christian Church in the town of Burton.[5] Mt. Sinai was the church her mother grew up in and the church she and her siblings joined when they were young; New Hope Christian was her father's church. So instead of giving up membership at either church, the family maintained a shared membership between the two. Every second and fourth Sunday until Lucille left home at the age of seventeen by way of marriage, she and her siblings would attend her father's church.

Lucille's dual church membership opened up the realm of possibility for her belief in things "beyond this world" at a very young age because both churches actively articulated the presence of spirits. At Mt. Sinai, the Spirit was explained as the presence of the Christian God in metaphysical form, also known as the Holy Spirit or Holy Ghost. At New Hope, the Spirit was also explained as the Holy Ghost, and there was an emphasis placed on spirit possession by the Holy Ghost, which would lead to shouting and other ecstatic experiences such as speaking in tongues. At New Hope, however, the spirit (lowercase "s") was also articulated as the "cloud of witnesses," the spirits of family and community members who had passed away but who remained metaphysically present.[6] As Lucille described, "From very early on, I just knew the spirits was with me." The active incorporation of belief in spirits that do not possess people and were not treated as deities helped Lucille accept and believe in the presence of the living dead at an early age. Now at the age of fifty-nine, Lucille continues to acknowledge their existence.

Ruth Kelly also recognized the presence of the dead as a young adult. Ruth was always cared for and surrounded by older women, which gave her a sense of maturity that made her wise beyond her years and facilitated her ability to talk to the dead. "I stayed with those old people and those older people in the congregation and hung with them and grabbed on to their, you know, skirt tails." Ruth recognized, however, that when those elderly women died, she did not feel as if they were completely gone. The presence of these women remained with her not only in her memory but also "in her spirit." Now at fifty-five years of age, Ruth believes that her intimate connection to older generations led to her having a strong, early belief in the deceased: "I knew that I believed when I was young." The relationships Ruth established with the living directly influenced her ability to talk to the dead.

For these women, listening is an important aspect of talking to the dead, and the most common way that listening occurs for them is through music, dreams, and prayer. Lucinda frequently hears the dead speak through music. She dreams of music at least three times a week and awakens during the night with songs on her mind that she does not remember ever singing. Once she is awake, she is able to recall the tunes and immediately accepts that her mother has communicated with her through a dream and given her a song. Similarly, Lucille and Ruth believe that music makes a connection with the dead possible.[7] On most occasions, however, the women feel the deceased in their dreams. Both Faye and Lucinda recount talking to the dead while they sleep. Faye's husband Richard, who died from lung cancer in 2003, visits her often: "My husband comes to me sometimes and he just sits with me. I can just feel him, you know, and it comforts me." Lucinda dreams frequently of her mother and will immediately wake up after encountering her in a dream. "I don't see her. I hardly ever see her, but I know she there. I can feel her. Sometimes she tell me what to do." In this form of communication, a loved one who has passed on talks through a dream and offers comfort and direction to the dreamer, or admonishes her to act or live in a particular way. As Faye and Lucinda have described, the dead may be physically visible in a dream, usually as the human form in which the women last saw them alive, but are most often present as invisible spirits who do not literally speak.

Prayer is an additional way in which the women openly listen to and communicate with the dead. Faye and Ruth also participate in "prayer trees," where they call other women of their respective churches or communities and pray for them. Praying is believed to facilitate communicating with the living and the dead. During these times of focused meditation, personal reflection, and silence, one is understood as being open to the movement of the spiritual realm. One is also believed to have the ability to hear the dead speak more clearly than during other moments when one's listening capacity is hindered by the busyness of life. It is through prayer, especially prayer for others, that Roberta senses the dead. Something "just happens" when she prays for the sick and other members of her family whom she recognizes as "standing in the need of prayer." Difficult to capture with words, the listening-speaking exchange common to the practice of talking to the dead is encapsulated by Roberta's exclamation, "I don't know how to explain it, but I jus' know when de dead speak, and they speak you know, I listen!"

Talking to the Dead as Religio-Cultural Practice

At the age of seventy-seven, Yenenga Wheeler openly acknowledges her connection with the dead, stating that she is "too old to lie 'bout such things." She is proud of her heritage as a lowcountry resident and speaks fondly of times when "things didn't move so fast." Her role as a professional storyteller is a significant part of her life, and for the past twenty years she has become formally recognized throughout the lowcountry as the "Gullah

Storyteller." Although she acknowledges that she had always "been kind of good at storytelling," her participation in a 1992 mission trip to South Africa sponsored by St. James Presbyterian ignited her professional commitment to storytelling. During the trip, she recounted the numerous stories she knew to others. Upon returning to South Carolina, one of the members of the church asked her to participate in a local arts festival. The event went so well that she continued to receive calls, and has made a career of it.[8] Storytelling is her "God-given purpose" in life, her primary occupation, and also the principal means by which she is connected to those who have gone before her.

Yenenga's use of storytelling serves five purposes: (1) it functions as a history lesson that recounts relationships between southern blacks and whites in the segregated South; (2) it gives Yenenga the opportunity to educate younger generations about the issues and concerns that were relevant to previous generations—thereby connecting the living and the dead; (3) it provides her with the ability to connect to what she interprets as an African-derived practice in the tradition of the *griot*; (4) it allows her the chance to describe the longstanding prominence of Gullah/Geechee religious customs; and (5) it grants Yenenga the literal opportunity to talk to the dead. In the broadest sense, Yenenga's stories demonstrate the interrelatedness between blacks and whites and reminds lowcountry people—especially black youth—of their history and the significance of their collective heritage. Drawing from a storytelling form that she calls "Gullah humorous stories" or "plantation-type stories," Yenenga utilizes a witty call-and-response style that invites the hearers to actively participate in the narratives by repeating a host of phrases. She connects the intertwining histories of *buckra* and African Americans, while recounting the narratives in a way that emphasizes the beauty and subtlety of the Gullah language. In one untitled story, Yenenga recounts the following tale in the Gullah dialect:

> [This is] one of da old one my daddy used ta always tell me, "don't forget ta tell this story." It's a black man goin' ta Charleston to work because at that time they would catch the ferryboat to go from James Island to Charleston, and my great gran—my grandaddy they tell me he was a rudder, a person who was a rudder drove the ferry back and forth. So anyway, this old man goes, young man, well, he up in age goes to Charleston to do some work over there, and he was downtown puttin' in those cobblestone bricks downtown in the streets and make sure the grass was out ya now and it would get a little more money than I probly could feel.

So Buckra comes ta Charleston, they been comin' a long time to visit down yeh, an the old man was taught when he left home, "mine ya manners, 'aint nuttin' ta talk you keep mout' shut, you don't know nuttin, ya know." So he remembered that. The old man once he was downtown workin', Buckra come ta Charleston and you know we was always raised to say good mornin', good evenin', give respect. Well, Buckra come to Charleston an' he see da old black man and he 'aint say nuttin' to 'im. All he say, [imitates a gruff male voice] "hey looka here, so can ya tell me where's The Battery?" The black man look up say "battry?" [sic], say yes sir dem chern [children] got battry in dem car he say, "but I 'aint got none and I 'aint know where dat be." Buckra man look at him again an' say, [again imitates a gruff male voice] "Well looka here, so can you tell me where's the Custom House?" The old black man say "Custom House?" say "I 'aint got nuttin' but a boat house out on James Island and I 'aint know where dat be neidda!" So he look at him one more time an say "looka here, you oughta know this, do you know where's the jailhouse?" Black man say, "looka yeh now, I 'aint never been deh, I 'aint tryin fah go deh, so I neva gone be deh, I don't know." Well by this time the white man was out and done with this old black man! So he look at the old black guy one more time an' say, "looka here," he say "you don't know nothin' eh?" Well the old black man look down the street so and look back an' look at him an' say, "I know one thing, I 'aint los!"

This story seems as straightforward as its plot but is a powerful reminder of the importance of talking to the dead for Yenenga. In this story, a visiting white man asks an elderly black man for directions to very common landmarks in downtown Charleston, including The Battery (a popular promenade and defensive seawall) and the Custom House. The black man in the story feigns innocence, as he recalls being instructed to "keep his mouth shut" when it comes to talking to whites. The white man becomes exasperated by the black man's limited knowledge, especially when he asks for directions to the jail, a place he presumes the black man "oughta know." In the end, the black man demonstrates he is in fact much more knowledgeable than the white man because he is self-aware enough to recognize that he knows where he is. A closer look at this story, however, reveals a host of elements that confirm the historical dynamics of race relations in the South Carolina lowcountry. From the tale we learn perceptions of white privilege (the white man was disrespectful toward the more senior black man, whom he presumed lacked common sense), differences in class status (the black man worked as a "rudder" and street mason), and the rules of engagement local blacks were taught about their interactions with whites ("mind your manners, there's nothing to talk about, you keep your mouth shut, and you don't know anything").

Yenenga subsequently offered the following analysis of her story: "So I think we was smart in a roundabout way so he didn't have to tell him 'bout knowing where those places was, and I figure he probably knew, but he showed no respect to him to say anything, so he didn't give any information. And by him askin' him all dem questions black man knew he was lost. He went on about his business and did his work, and that was the end of that story!" To Yenenga, the emphasis on the black man's being smarter than the white man who was lost indicates the importance that, contrary to the viewpoint of whites, lowcountry blacks were indeed fully capable of intellectual thought and common sense. This part of the story, which echoes the format of a parable or lesson, would be reinforced to Yenenga's hearers.

Yenenga's use of storytelling in this way—as a heuristic device—is commonplace to the role of griots in many west and central African contexts, and also stands in a long tradition of Gullah/Geechee folklore, exemplified in the previously cited work of Jane Heyward and many other publications.[9] It is also in keeping with the custom of women's oral history and storytelling as demonstrated in the memoirs *Lemon Swamp and Other Places* by Mamie Garvin Fields; *God, Dr. Buzzard, and the Bolito Man: A Saltwater Geechee Talks about Life on Sapelo Island, Georgia* by Cornelia Walker Bailey; and a recent contribution from Genevieve W. Chandler entitled *Coming Through: Voices of a South Carolina Gullah Community from WPA Oral Histories*. Yenenga's use of storytelling also affirms Joseph Holloway's assessment that for the Gullah/Geechee, "the oral tradition is a crucial element of culture, a means of retaining and passing on history from one generation to the next."[10] She provides all who hear her tales with an active history lesson and teaches them about the Gullah language by using words such as "buckra" and asking people to guess what it means. She views this as especially important to the children because "a lot of children hear them words, and don't know what it is." In her eyes, although young people live within the lowcountry culture, they are unaware of what it means to be called Gullah and show little appreciation for it. In this way, Yenenga sees her stories as a means of "bridging the gap" between the past and present.

Yenenga's stories also confirm her relationship to Christianity and speak to the larger religiosity of lowcountry African Americans. Many of her stories depict aspects of lowcountry religion. In one of her favorite tales, "Reb

Lost His Hat," a story that recounts the promiscuity of a local black minister, she comments, "Ah like fuh talk 'bout dem church! Oh, we can pray and sing, you know we high-spirited people." Similarly in "White Folks Never Thought Black Folk Went to Heaven," Yenenga narrates how a recently deceased white woman struggled with the idea that black folks would be alongside her in heaven and argued with God that black folks could not wear white robes or a halo "because they comin' up 'yeh wit' all dem afros." In addition to contesting racial discrimination, Yenenga's story characterizes religion as a racially inclusive space where all are welcome, in contrast to the racially segregated earth.

On the most intimate and spiritual level, however, Yenenga views her craft as a direct connection to her heritage as a descendent of slaves and to her deceased family members. The stories she recites are those she learned from her father and paternal grandparents, and she makes every effort to tell the stories in the same form, tempo, and style as they were told to her, with little modification, while at the same time ensuring that her personality "comes through." Yenenga believes that these folktales "permanently became a part of her" through her relationship with her father, who reiterated and expanded the stories in her presence. Delivering stories to an audience consistently connects her "back to her roots from childhood all the way back to slavery." When I asked, for example, why she felt it necessary to begin her untitled story about the lost white man with an indication that her father taught her this story and that he emphasized the importance of not forgetting it, Yenenga replied, in a somewhat exasperated manner, "oh chile, to tell this story is to tell his story, is to talk to him, my father."

Storytelling thus reflects Yenenga's God-given ability to retain and recall narratives, but it also explicitly and directly connects her to ancestors. Yenenga described to me what happens to her when she tells stories: "Ya know I'm tellin' these stories and the kids is laughin' and enjoyin' themselves, but it's like something else comes over me, ya know? I know I'm talkin' to them and they are talkin' through me, tellin' me what to say to the people. When dat happens, I know I'm callin' on all the African griots and mah grandma and grandpa and mah daddy, all of them who taught me how to tell stories. . . . It's an amazing feelin'." In Yenenga's description, the phrase "I know I'm talkin' to them and they are talkin' through me" reflects how storytelling extends beyond an artistic or oral activity. It is practice that facilitates an explicitly spiritual link to the dead. For Yenenga, storytelling is simultaneously a profession, a means of promoting community, an example of the rich history and pervasive use of folktales in lowcountry culture, and

a form of documenting the ongoing importance of religion to the Gullah/
Geechee. Storytelling, however, also functions as a means of talking to the
dead and is a direct connection to her past. A "cloud of witnesses" guide
Yenenga's past and talk to her as she tells their stories to others. Yenenga's
use of storytelling affirms how in the lowcountry history is often orally documented rather than written, and that relationships with the deceased can
be established through varied forms.

Yenenga is not the only one who uses a religio-cultural practice to talk
to the dead. For Beatrice Dixon, at sixty-eight years of age, the craft of basket making allows her to embrace her relationship with the dead. Sweetgrass basketry dominates Ms. Bea's life and is a cultural activity that has significant spiritual meaning. In *Sweetgrass Baskets and the Gullah Tradition*, Joyce
Coakley notes, "The unique art of sweetgrass basket making was brought to
the South Carolina Lowcountry in the late seventeenth century by enslaved
West Africans who found palmetto leaves and grasses similar to those used
in their native Africa." These grasses include sea grass, mada (palmetto
tree leaves), and bulrush. She also characterizes sweetgrass basketry as a
simultaneous labor of love and of intention, for it is an artisan's craft that is
passed down from generation to generation.

> Not only was [sweetgrass basketry] a traditional craft passed on, but the
> making of baskets afforded the opportunity for older relatives to share
> lore, family traditions, and historical events as recorded by their enslaved
> relatives. As many as three generations could be seen working for five to
> six hours daily on a porch or under a shade tree in summer and around a
> fireplace or wood-burning stove in winter. For those with family stands,
> a mother was accompanied by a daughter daily during the summer and
> sometimes Saturdays during the school season. Elders talked and chil-
> dren listened as fingers worked the grass.[11]

Sweetgrass basketry is indeed a painstaking, laborious, and delicate art.
Basketry is also a daylong occupation (weather permitting), and during
peak tourist periods between March and August can also require working
seven days a week. It is not uncommon for the tourist season to produce
enough income for Ms. Bea and her family to "rest easy for a little while."
Ms. Bea's basket stand is located at a prime site in downtown Charleston,
minutes away from the City Market and the Old Slave Mart. Beatrice's relationship with the deceased is readily accessed through her craft of making sweetgrass baskets, which provides her with a direct connection to the
woman who taught it to her at the age of six: her grandmother.[12] She views

her grandmother, whom she affectionately calls "Nana," as "one of the best basket makers of Mt. Pleasant." Any discussion of her craft leads to a fond and vivid recollection of the woman who gave her "such a special gift." In addition to teaching Ms. Bea how to weave baskets, Nana encouraged Beatrice to be unafraid of the dead. "Nana always was talkin' to herself, and when I would ask her who she was talkin' to, she would tell me, 'I'm talkin' to my people.' People thought she was crazy and used to be scared of her, you know, but I never did." Her grandmother also encouraged her to expect the dead to be present among the living. "My Nana would always say, 'after I'm dead and gone, when you see clouds, expect to see me,' and I did— I still do." To date, Beatrice "stands still when it is cloudy to see if Nana will come." Although Nana passed away when she was seventeen, Ms. Bea speaks about her in the present tense and believes that Nana is still with her. "I know she's wit' me. She stays wit' me and guides my hands. . . . Nana knows me and knows when to show up. She's wit' me so much that it's like she just a part of me. I can talk to her about anything and most times I don't even have to say nothin'. I can't really explain it, you know. I just know she's here, she's just here." In this way, the connection Ms. Bea maintains with her deceased grandmother is as significant to her understanding of faith and religious practice as her participation as a class leader at Greater Goodwill AME Church. Her ongoing communication with her Nana does not at all conflict with her Christian practice.

It is this ongoing communication between the dead and the living, marked most noticeably by the belief that the dead are "here," that unites the experiences of these seven women. Yenenga and Ms. Bea's religio-cultural practices of storytelling and basketry are crafts that facilitate an explicit exchange between the living and the dead, and they use their crafts to recall and connect to their dead loved ones, who, in addition to having taught them their crafts, continue to be an active part of their lives. Though the dead are not ritualistically summoned, their presence may be requested through an inquiry much like the one Beatrice uses when she asks her deceased grandmother to "guide [her] hands" while making baskets, or felt in the way Yenenga's recollection of her father's instructions allows him "to talk through her." Ruth's intense connection with the elderly, especially those she was close to during her youth, attests to her belief in the spirits of the deceased, and she is clear that their presence remains with her. For Ruth and Roberta, praying, an act that is simultaneously religious, because it invokes a spiritual connection, and communal, as it puts the needs of others before one's own, becomes the religio-cultural practice that ties them to the living and the dead. Similarly, Lucinda frequently hears her dead mother speak through music, and when she dreams of music that she does not previously remember encountering, she makes every effort to teach others the song and, on occasion, to have her choir sing the songs she has heard. Faye recognized that she had an intense connection with deceased family members, including her mother, husband, and sister. She admitted that there was something distinct about her connection with the dead, especially as she was immediately able to distinguish the presence of her mother's spirit from that of her husband or sister. Their arrival, which varied in occurrence, instilled peace in Faye, which she noted "helped to calm [her] spirit." In every case, the loss of loved ones and other traumatic events have led to each of the women's increased belief in the presence of the dead who, while transitioned from the physical realm of existence, are still among the living.

From these examples, it is clear that there is no single espoused formula for how one communicates with the dead. Talking to the dead is generally a private experience that affirms spiritual authenticity, but it is also a well-known practice that communities, particularly of women, share with their friends and families. Although communication between the dead and the living occurs with some variation, it is evident that for all of these women belief in the presence of the living dead has direct religious, spiritual, and cultural significance—and it is as real to them as their belief in God. Gullah/Geechee women's ability to talk to the dead affirms their status as culture keepers—significant contributors to the maintenance and sustenance of a dynamic religious culture within the lowcountry—and it reflects their role as spiritual leaders within their communities. Admittedly, their ability to talk to the dead is not the sole reason why they are important players. These seven women hold formal positions (as church musician, minister, committee chairperson, elder, etc.) and informal ones (as prayer group leader, music group member, conjurer, etc.) within their churches and communities. Talking to the dead, however, becomes a significant trope that affirms their identity as culture keepers. Talking to the dead surpasses denominationalism, exceeds the limits of geography, and speaks to the broad use of the custom as a spiritual practice. Most important, talking to the dead confirms a longstanding, local spiritual practice reminiscent of and connected to the prominent role Gullah/Geechee women have played as elders, folk practitioners, and spiritual mothers—positions that were cultivated through the process of seeking membership in a church.

Seekin'

Each of the women fondly recalled the personal significance of the seeking tradition in their lives. Seeking—which the women called "seekin'" or "seekin' ya soul salvation"—is the former ritual process by which numerous African Americans of the South Carolina lowcountry became members of local churches. Patricia Guthrie, Margaret Creel, and Michael Wolfe have suggested that what eventually became the seeking rituals that the women of this study experienced were introduced to lowcountry blacks in the 1830s when Methodist missionaries instructed slaves to become members of local churches.[13] Seekers were placed "on trial" and missionaries taught them how to pray and to memorize popular scriptures. After successfully completing this trial period, which lasted as long as the leaders deemed the process necessary, the seekers were prepared for water baptism, after which they were welcomed as full members of a church. "At meetings with slaves, after preaching and teaching, the Methodists would then inquire if anyone would like to come forward and 'seek Jesus.' Those who professed such a desire would then go 'on trial' and remain in this limbo status until the missionary deemed them ready for baptism. Probationers, or 'seekers of religion' were required by Methodists to know the Creed, Sacraments, and Lord's Prayer, and they were not 'eligible for baptism until they had learned them understandingly.'"[14]

Viewed as an experience everyone had to go through to fully participate in the life of the Christian church community, seeking involved instruction as organized by religious sects. This ritual included praying, experiencing visions, and having dreams. One would lie prostrate, literally, in an effort to "seek God's face," or to discern God's will for one's life. Seeking also entailed an intense period of prayer and fasting during which the seeker was understood to be in a closer relationship with God because he or she was uninhibited by external influences. During seeking, as Yenenga noted, one would "be under a heavy prayer meeting now, lotta singing, lotta praying was done for you. You'd really learn how to do that too . . . you kind of got into that habit of that prayer." Seeking is another means by which the Gullah/Geechee ritualistically practiced talking to the dead, for it explicitly invited seekers to communicate with ancestors.

Seeking is a historical derivative of two church membership practices that arose during the Christian mission efforts that began in the 1830s: experience meetings and "catching sense." Experience meeting was the term *given by planters* to the process by which blacks expressed their intent to become a member of a church. Planters called these moments "experience meetings" because it was the time when blacks publicly expressed their conversion to Christianity and a communal desire to become a member of the local church or praise house. According to Charles Raymond, these meetings were "usually held as preparatory to the [N]egro's 'joining the church' upon a public profession of religion." Historically, African American conversion to Christianity in the lowcountry was characterized by a four-tiered process: an increased awareness of the heaviness or pressures of daily life; an intense sense of conviction about sin; a sense of relief from these pressures; and a desire on the part of the converted to live a burden-free life. For the duration of this process, blacks would go out "into de field" and "to de yard" to pray, and then would "stop in de fence corner," to try to relieve a sense of "heaviness." Oftentimes, however, they would only feel worse and would not experience relief until a vision or dream revealed to them how to alleviate their sins or the heaviness of life. Relief also came during the dream or vision when they were taken up into "hebben" to personally see God.[15] Throughout the experience meetings, converts would share their particular story publicly. At the end of the narrative, the planter or minister would ask the candidates (male or female) if they thought they were converted, to which they would always reply yes.

Black lowcountry residents on St. Helena Island and surrounding areas called this experience "catching sense." Patricia Guthrie has extensively examined the meanings of church membership on plantations from the antebellum to the post–Civil War era. In her text *Catching Sense: African American Community on a South Carolina Sea Island*, Guthrie notes that the practice of "catching sense" bore particular meaning because of the ways that it connected members within and beyond the plantation.[16]

> The ties established with a community where a person catches sense remain forever. Should a member fall sick, his/her plantation members are there to offer assistance, whether it was in the form of money or labor or simply to sit and provide company and compassion. Even those who leave the community do not sever the ties of belonging. This is seen especially among women who, when they marry, leave the community where they belong. Though removed through marriage, women return to their home plantations for weddings, burials, and to comfort the sick and bereaved.[17]

Catching sense forged unifying bonds of socioreligious identity, for it was under the guise of church membership that enslaved and free blacks would most frequently gather at a given plantation praise house. The effects of these bonds were long lasting. Church membership was significant to black community members because it functioned as a means of creating community and belonging (the privileges of praise house membership were generally "instantly conveyed") during times when kinship ties were continuously shifting. While the ongoing and unpredictable effects of the plantation economy—especially the processes of interstate and interplantation trading—were particularly disruptive and detrimental to maintaining familial connections, African Americans of St. Helena utilized religious membership to create long-lasting ties. "During slavery, even when people were sold to another plantation, they still belonged to the people they grew up with and with whom they had learned about the meaning of life and the social meaning of relationships." The catch-sense system, which grew directly out of enslavement, was a way to formally create community and allow individuals a rightful place within that community. While catching sense facilitated a feeling of belonging based on the geographic limits of the plantations, praise house membership, which was "open to all plantation residents who [were] members of the church congregation connected to that praise house," often meant more to the community than physical borders.[18] This was especially the case since many plantations lacked markers signaling where the boundaries of one plantation ended and another began.

Experience meetings and catching sense were therefore significant not simply because of the singing, praying, testifying, reciting of scripture, reading of the Bible, and conversion experiences but because they demonstrated how "belonging to the community and being acceptable to God [were] almost synonymous."[19] According to Creel, seeking eventually became characterized by four features: the renouncement of all social and worldly pleasures; the maintenance of night vigils and journeys into the wilderness, where one would experience visions and spiritual travel; the declaration of a satisfactory emotional experience and readiness for church membership; and the pronouncement of one's freedom from malice or ill-will toward another.[20] These features derived from the instructions of white missionaries and from lowcountry interpretations of the probationary rituals, and their use ensured that white planters and missionaries came to believe that Christianity could be used to improve the moral condition of lowcountry blacks. Charles Raymond noted, "That the negro is made better by even such a change no one can doubt. That his religion is to him a source of unceasing comfort and support none can deny." More than a means of garnering white approval or for appropriating the Christian ideals of conviction, pardon, and regeneration, however, these rituals were a way for African American members of lowcountry communities to express "their own descriptions of their emotions when under the influence of religious truths and spiritual operations."[21] These processes thus served multiple purposes for lowcountry blacks. They likely appeased white planter and missionary efforts to convert blacks to Christianity. Participation was also one way for African Americans to publicly acknowledge a personal sense of religious conviction. Experience meetings or catching sense served as public examples of an intimate religious or spiritual experience and stood as the public attestation of their individual commitment. These conversion customs gave attendees a way to express their individual interest in becoming a member of a particular subsect within the community. Moreover, they established community ties through an acquired understanding of religious and communal responsibility.

What seeking shares with experience meetings and catching sense is the emphasis on professing a "satisfactory" spiritual experience in order to become a member of a church. Seeking differs, however, from experience meetings and catching sense because of the explicit role of elders in overseeing and determining the outcome of the process, its treatment as a rite of passage for teenaged and adolescent youth,[22] and the fact that candidates did not have to petition a particular church, as their membership was determined by the outcome of their seeking process and at the behest of the elders who guided them through the practice. Seeking was distinct because it involved the incorporation of the youth into the church or praise house without the involvement of planters or white ministers. The women of this study experienced seeking as a celebration of their formal entry into the church at a young age. Faye seeked at the age of ten or eleven, and she knew it was the beginning of her spiritual journey. When her mother informed her that it was time for her to seek, she was not at all surprised; in fact she was excited because she knew, "by the time you twelve years old, they [adult community members] expected you to be able to confess your beliefs and to join the church." To Faye, her formal "initiation" into the church was an important aspect of seeking. What was most important, however, was the recognition that her spiritual journey, which began with seeking, would unfold over her lifetime. Seeking was also important because of how it was instrumental in shaping the belief in God that these women currently maintain.

None of the women could articulate the origin of the seeking beyond Yenenga's claim that "this is what we've always done." Roberta, Beatrice,

Lucille, Lucinda, Ruth, Yenenga, and Faye verified that seeking lasted a varied length of time, involved a probationary period of instruction where individuals would isolate themselves during an intense period of prayer, and resulted in the outcome of church membership. The women also noted that the renouncement of worldly pleasures, which occurred during the period of prayer and meditation, directly affected one's ability to discern God's will. Going into the woods at night, spending time in solitude, and waiting for the appearance of visions and dreams ensured, as Ruth pointed out, "You didn't have no distractions." Moreover, none of the women identified with the idea that one was required to declare oneself free from ill will toward others while seeking; rather, seeking, while communal, was also very individualized. According to Beatrice, "When you seeked, you 'aint have time to think about nobody else—it was just you and God."

Seeking simultaneously operated as an individual and communal process, and all of the practices surrounding the seeking tradition revealed information about which church a young person should join. Most often, a small group of youth between the ages of ten and fifteen would begin to seek together. According to the women and the scholarship on the seeking tradition, these groups ranged from three to ten. Lucille described, "When I got ready to seek my Papa [grandfather] came to the house, came to my house and told me what to do. . . . After my Papa told me what to do, then that's when I started seekin'. But I wasn't the only one seekin'." While under the care of a group of elders from the community, the youths were eventually guided through their prayers and dreams individually. At the end of the process, each seeker was called on one by one to stand before a group of elders and reveal what they dreamed or envisioned. In Lucille's case, which seems to be somewhat of an anomaly, "Papa," Lucille's grandfather, was called because he was the superintendent of the Sunday school and the elder who guided her and the five others through the process. As the superintendent, Papa informed the pastor of Mt. Sinai Baptist Church that Lucille and the other children were ready to seek. In this case, rather than a group of elders facilitating the seeking process, Papa was the one who guided them.

Generally, seekers of a respective group did not necessarily join the same church, as it was the elders who determined one's readiness as well as their church destination. The role of community elders—women and men—during seeking was particularly noteworthy because the seeker went to the elder for instruction. As Lawton suggested, "The spiritual teacher is the intermediary between the seeker and the organized religious group. It is essentially upon their recommendation that the seeker is permitted to become a member of a church."[23] These leaders, who truly operated more like spiritual parents, guided the participants through the seeking process. Beatrice's grandmother, Nana, was also a well-known "seekin' mother" in Mt. Pleasant and directed numerous seekers, including Beatrice, through seeking activities. As Yenenga described, it was only the "old people" who could tell if you were ready or could place you in a particular church.

The women's narratives reveal that *tarrying* was an essential component of seeking. Tarrying took place when elders informed seekers that they had to endure the seeking process a while longer before they could become members. Ruth recalled, "As we were seekin' we would tell them [the elders] our dreams. And they would say, 'okay, you doing good, keep tarrying, keep tarrying.' That means just keep going, keep going you know, laying before the Lord. The Pentecostal church would probably call it tarrying, well I guess it's the same process because you're waiting for the Lord's direction and you're listening, ya know, and He is to speak to you in that still small voice through dreams or visions." Samuel Lawton documented that seekers were at times instructed to "go pray and come back."[24] His assessment confirmed how the spiritual leaders determined one's readiness but did not focus on the lengthy period of returning to intense prayer—a key aspect of tarrying. To "go pray and come back" suggests the elders expected seekers to leave and pray for an unspecified, though presumably brief time before returning to them for assessment.

Going to pray and then returning, which the women understand as tarrying, could lengthen the seeking process by days or weeks, as it was up to the "seekin' mother or father" to determine one's readiness for church membership. If the seeking elder(s) did not feel that the vision clearly revealed the seeker's church destination or did not indicate that the seeker was intensely focusing on establishing a relationship with God (which was most often determined by fasting, prayer, the memorization of scriptures, etc.), the elder would then tell the seeker to tarry, to continue praying, reading scripture, or fasting. Often, this resulted in ongoing or recurring communication with the deceased as the lengthened process of going into the woods, intense fasting, and prayer heightened the seeker's ability to talk to the dead. Again, without the support and permission of the elders, a seeker would not be presented before the deacons or the church, she would not be baptized, nor would she be welcomed into the church as a full member. Ruth and Lucille were personally encouraged to tarry during their seeking process. Ruth believes that tarrying lengthened her seeking process by at least five days. Lucille noted, "When I thought I was ready, Papa would come and tell me, 'you're not ready, just tarry longer.'" The objective of tarrying was to ensure the seeker's readiness and to guarantee to the best of the elder's ability that the seeker was not faking a genuine experience with and connection to God.

There was some variation among the women and writers about the role of the African American leaders during the seeking process. According to written sources, these leaders became an integral part of the custom once missionaries converted enough lowcountry blacks to Christianity and praise houses were built. They were organized into two distinct groups—black elders and spiritual parents. The elders were typically appointed by a church or selected by white planters. The spiritual parents, who were perceived to be more powerful and wise among community members, functioned as interpreters of dreams and visions and served in the capacity of healers. In an effort to identify specific African cultural continuities, Creel compared seeking leaders to the diviners and spiritual parents of traditional African cultures, specifically the leaders of Poro and Sande secret societies.[25] To Creel, going out into the woods to pray among the Gullah was comparable to what the initiates of these African societies did when they went into the bush to relate to nameless ancestral spirits that inhabited streams, rivers, and trees, and then shared their conversations with a spiritual parent who interpreted the encounter. My interlocutors, however, interchangeably referred to the women and men who guided them through the seeking tradition as "elders," "spiritual parents," "seekin' mothers," and "seekin' fathers." According to Lucinda, who "seeked her religion" in 1934 at the age of twelve, there were no distinct groups among the leaders. Similarly, Lucille indicated that differentiation between groups of elders was unnecessary because "seekin' united seekers to the seekin' mothers and fathers and to the church." As referenced by the women, the leaders were not appointed by any church organization or by whites (the category Creel has called "black elders") but were recognized within the black community as sages. Furthermore, they did not collectively belong to any one denomination. Again, the purpose of the elders and the seeking process in general was to promote church membership but also to connect the seekers to the community of faith.

Seeking was a ritualized form of spiritual guidance by community leaders that took place beyond the walls of the denominational church and was initiated by a cross-section within the community rather than any single church body. Elders, who were selected from within the community, were equally made up of women and men, were respected for being spiritually wise, and did not belong to any single denomination. The purpose of this group of elders was to facilitate the process of church membership and religio-spiritual intimacy. Their objective was not to send an individual to the place they wanted him or her to go, or for that matter, to send one to the church their parents attended. As Lawton notes, "It is the spiritual teacher to whom the seeker relates his visions of dreams, and the seeker's activity is governed by the spiritual teacher's interpretations of the experience. Both spiritual guide or teacher and seeker claim independent revelation from the Spirit concerning their pupil-teacher relationship. The spiritual teacher claims thus to have a standard of 'password' which the particular seeker to be instructed must attain."[26] One had to successfully reveal a dream or vision that an elder could interpret as meaningful in order to become a member of a given church. According to Lucille, "They waited until you had a particular kind of dream before telling you. They did that 'cause if you prayed every night like you was supposed to, then the Lord would reveal the dream to you."

The elders utilized their interpretations to inform seekers "that their sins were forgiven, that they [were] true believers or that they are saved," according to Lawton.[27] As Lucinda described, the elders also tested seekers: "You got to tell them 'bout your dream and everything, they just don't baptize you! You go through a procedure. They question you about certain things, you know, they call you in there it's just the officers, elders—they have kind of like a conference in there. You don't go before de whole church then, they talk to you separately. Then if you ready, you get baptized with the others. That's the way it happened with me now, they [got] the consent from the church." The role of the elder was critical. In addition to teaching seekers the various activities of the process, interpreting one's dream, and determining one's readiness, they were responsible for introducing younger generations to the religious practices of the community and for presenting the seekers to the larger religious community. The powerful leadership position of the elder as exhibited during seeking demonstrates their larger importance within lowcountry religious communities. From extensive research of missionary sources, slave narratives, spirituals, church minutes, and court and plantation documents, Creel notes that the elements of "vision" and "travel" within the seeking process link Gullah religion to the Poro and Sande secret society traditions, and reflect the importance of folk religious practices that sustained their communal identity.[28]

Ruth began seeking when she was thirteen years old, and she and five other youth met every Tuesday and Thursday in a small hair salon on James

Island. She could not recall exactly how long it took her to seek, but remembered that it "took weeks and weeks and weeks." Seeking was a time when you had to "personally lay before the Lord and discern what body you had to join."[29] According to Ruth, one could not watch television, talk on the telephone, or listen to the radio while seeking; rather, the seeker was required to pray and read the Bible frequently. A member of the last group to seek their membership into St. James Presbyterian, she described seeking as the process in which one would "go out in the wilderness, find a spot to pray to God so that you would be shown what church body you were supposed to be a part of." There were prescribed activities that included learning The Lord's Prayer, Psalm 23, and select hymns and gospel songs. Seeking was a very serious step in one's life, a "process you shouldn't take lightly."

To the women, seeking was a distinct and unique experience. According to Roberta, "Seekin' was a whole 'nother thing in and of itself! . . . It was so special, it was different than anything you'd ever experience." Although they all learned some of the prayers and songs they knew from regular church attendance, they also noted that elders taught seekers things that were revealed only while seeking. Yenenga explained, "The songs and prayers and stuff you learned when you seeked was different than anything else you learned. They never taught you how to pray like that in Sunday school!" Yenenga, who joined St. James Presbyterian Church at the age of twelve, was proud to point out how she "seeked her religion." "When I was a little girl and went in to join the church, we had to seek and that meant you had to go to the prayer meeting house at least twice a week and it was in each community there was a praise house and you would go to the prayer meeting with your parents . . . and they would pray for you and then when you said you were ready to join church they would instruct you about seeking." She described seeking as "getting up late in the night or when everybody else was asleep" and going "outside your house to pray among the bushes . . . and even you would go out sometimes before daybreak." She also noted, "You'd go out . . . to pray, and you would stay out to pray without realizing that anything around you would bother you, that nothing would bother you while you were there." When I asked her if it scared her to go out at night alone she commented, "well if it did and you ran, you sho wasn't ready to join church!" She later admitted, "That [going into the woods] was a test not to be afraid."

Going into the wilderness was a critical part of the seeking experience. When Ms. Bea seeked into Greater Goodwill AME at fourteen, she "went into the woods to the stump [of a tree]" and prayed every night for three weeks. She also prayed every morning between five and six o'clock, at noon, and at six o'clock in the evening. She explained that going into the woods was so important because, "You had to go find God. You had to go call Jesus by His name at night, on your own, in the dark. It was the only way to find God." Faye also "seeked her religion," but she did not literally go out into the woods to pray: "Going in the wilderness and seeking wasn't like goin' out here—people thought it was goin' out in the woods, but it wasn't necessary goin' out in the woods, but it was getting along with your church leaders and elders and mothers and deacons and things and prayer service and you know. And lettin' them lead you into, you know, into the church." Like Faye, Lucille did not literally go out into the woods. Instead, she followed her mother's instructions during her seekin' process. Lucille's mother encouraged her to "just pray" alone in her bedroom instead of "going out into the woods for half a day." Lucille recalled that her mother was concerned for her safety and did not want her eleven-year-old daughter "goin' out into the woods at all time of night." Thus, for Lucille, other than to bathe and relieve herself, she did not leave her bedroom—not even for chores or to eat during the seven days that she seeked. When it was time for dinner, which was a time when everyone in her house ate together, she "couldn't come out." Instead, her parents "brought the food and stuff inside the room."

The dream or vision one experienced while seeking was particularly significant because it determined one's readiness (or lack thereof), and established what church one would belong to. "When you saw someone in the dream, they [the elders] could place you to whatever church you were going to go to." What one saw or experienced during the dream varied. According to Lawton, it was not uncommon for seekers to see various supernatural beings, human, animals, animate and inanimate objects.[30] Yenenga has confirmed the presence of various beings during the seeking process: "Ya might see, maybe a vision you would think of Christ or imagine in ya mind. Or there were a lot of times old people I can remember, what kinda horse did you see or did you ride, what direction you were going in? Say for instance if I was living in an area and I was walking and seeking and praying and going towards that Presbyterian church side, you maybe just be walking or something. And then they could kind of pick that up you know in your dream." Not everyone had the same dream or vision. After a period of intense prayer where she "really had to buckle down and pray, pray, pray," Lucille dreamed of being baptized. She recalled, "I saw myself being baptized. It seemed like the Lord was speaking to me in my dreams, and I got baptized in the water and when I got up out of the water, I was praising the Lord. When I told my grandfather the dream that Friday morning, he said, 'You're ready.'" Faye saw signs of things she could not explain. She never saw human beings, but she saw Jesus and events that would eventually come to pass. "I remembered that I was in my bed upstairs praying, meditating, and the vision I had was of what I had been told Jesus look like . . . he was black, white, Indian, and everything . . . I can't explain what happened. I just know there was a change in my thinking, in my actions." More than anything, the transformative power of that dream remained with her throughout her life.

Ruth also referenced the lasting power of the dream during the seeking experience, though her dream did not occur in the way that it did for the other women. Ruth never felt that she had the type of dream she was supposed to have. On the evening she and the other youth were scheduled to tell the elders what they had dreamed to determine if they were ready, Ruth told her mother that she was sick. She decided to feign illness because she "didn't have this dream that I, that everybody expected me to have." Getting out of the process was not easy, however. When she did not show up at the salon, the elders went to her house and asked her, "Do you believe you ready?" Ruth did not know how to respond because she "thought it was up to them, you know, to decide." She told them that she believed she was ready, but that she did not have the dream. To her surprise, the elders responded, "As long as you believe, you ready." Despite their acceptance, Ruth continued to feel unsure of her successful completion of the process.

That same evening, however, Ruth went to sleep and experienced the dream that indicated to her that she was ready to be a genuine member of the church and religious community of James Island.

> I had a dream that I was in a field, standing in a field of some type flow-
> ers—lilies or some type flower—and a stairway came from the heavens
> down, and I began crying 'cause the spirit come. And all of a sudden there
> was a huge, and I remember to this day, a *brown* hand, not a white hand,
> not of my family or anybody, but a *huge* brown hand that came down the
> stairway out of the sky. And I reached up and it grabbed holda me, you
> know, and I woke up. And to me that was my dream. After I was done
> with the process, to let me know I accep' you, you know, you're worthy.

The feeling that God accepted her has remained with Ruth, and since then she has never questioned or doubted her worth as "one of God's daughters." When asked why having the dream was so important to her, she replied, "I believed that's what I needed because the elderly people said that. . . . To a child that was so important because it was important to the older people."

Ruth's response indicates just how significant validation by the elders was in the seeking process and, in particular, how crucial to determining one's preparedness for church membership.

The emphasis placed on experiencing dreams and visions during the seeking process was also significant because it encouraged seekers to talk to the dead. It was during the seeking process, where these women "called on the name of Jesus," that they also sought the support of deceased family and community members to become affiliates of local Baptist, United Methodist, Presbyterian, and African Methodist Episcopal churches. The dreams and visions these women experienced while seeking often connected the seeker to an ancestor.[31] During her seeking process Yenenga dreamed about her great-great-grandmother and other deceased members of St. James. "I often saw ancestors you know. One night I dreamt about my great-great-granny who was in conversation with me and I told that to them [the elders] and they said 'oh yeah.'" One night shortly after the encounter with her grandmother, she had a conversation with a woman she recognized but could not place by name. When she described the woman to the elders guiding her seeking process, they confirmed that it was one of the members of the local Presbyterian Church who had passed away before Yenenga was born. In this way, talking to the dead has given Yenenga a way of rereading her history, as it has explicitly informed how Yenenga interpreted her personal commitment to the church and her family's history with the church. Although Yenenga always accepted that her connection to St. James was an outcome of the seeking process, the recognition that many of her family members (including the great-great grandmother she dreamt of but had never met) had deep ties to the Presbyterian Church has helped her to see herself as "destined" to be part of the Presbyterian Church. Yenenga believes that it was "God's will and the help of my ancestors" who guided her toward lifelong membership at St. James Presbyterian.

Although none of the other women personally encountered familiar ancestors in their dreams, they readily acknowledged the frequency of seeing the deceased during the seeking process. Faye noted that her younger sister saw their great-grandmother during her seeking process. Ruth's father saw a deceased community leader who attended the local Baptist church, while her mother saw someone from the Presbyterian Church and ended up becoming a member there. Seeking was one of the clearest examples of talking to the dead, for it was through the occurrences of dreams and visions that these women connected to the deceased by way of religious encounter.

Baptism and full admission into a church marked the end of seeking rituals, and seekers were baptized as individuals or as a group. Lucille, for example, revealed her dream to the elders of Mt. Sinai Baptist church by herself but was baptized with six other seekers. Baptism was among the most memorable aspects of the seeking process. Faye commented, "It felt so good to be in your white [dress]—it's a feeling you can't hardly describe. You know you made it in there, and you stick with it." Coming to the end of the process also instilled excitement in the seeker. Yenenga echoed, "You would get ready because you were going to get a white dress you see. You definitely was gonna join church in white." Dressing in white demarcated one's spiritual purity. Yenenga equated dressing in white with being purified, "somehow a virgin." She also experienced getting ready for baptism as one of the most memorable aspects of her seeking process. She exclaimed, "It was all I remember, gyal you feel so good! All in white to join church on a particular Sunday."

In addition to its being the only way one could join a church, seeking reflected the communal value of church membership, instilled discipline and moral value in the younger generation, and helped the youth to develop an intimate, personal relationship with God. This is reflected in Lucille's description of the personal significance of seeking. "It was very important because from what my parents taught us during that time back then, you know, they said that's the only way you can get close to Christ, by seekin', prayin', you know every day to Him, so you get close to him like that." It was important to Lucille that she did exactly what her parents and other members of the community wanted her to do. She further noted, "You know, seekin' and trying to get into the church and doin' the right thing, you know, that's how I was taught. So back then it was very important that we did that, we had to do that." Seeking therefore had special meaning to those who experienced it as individuals but also bore great communal significance.

Genuine, heartfelt belief in God was certainly encouraged by the elders, but it was (along with church membership) also an intended outcome of the seeking process. Intense periods of prayer and solitude were built into the seeking process, and the seekers were taught how and what to pray, and to go out into the wilderness so that they could "get close to" God. This was yet another indication why the seeking process varied in duration from group to group and person to person. Roberta has suggested that group and individual adaptation was meant to ensure that one genuinely believed in God, a process that "wasn't cookie cutter" for everyone. "Even though we was all seekin' at the same time, that didn't mean everyone believed the same way or even really believed. That's why we had to take our time." Roberta vividly recalled the moment that she truly began to believe in God, and offered the following description of that night: "How I seek my religion to God? Get down, a bench, get down on my knees, and call on Jesus! Gyal that thang had me so bad I can [re] 'member that night. That thang had me so bad I couldn't go to school the next day. I was so holstered down, I remember that, now! Yes sir! You get down on your knees and you call on him. Jesus, Jesus, Jesus, Jesus!" Lucinda noted that calling on the name of Jesus was central to her own seeking and that it was only with the elders' awareness of your belief that you would be welcomed into the church. She said, "When I came through that wilderness thing, I believed in Jesus enough to confess my beliefs! I knew what I believed now, I knew that I believed in Jesus Christ, you know, crucified, dead, and 'risen again, I believed in that! And then I was baptized by water."[32] An intense connection with the God of Christianity through Jesus Christ was therefore a central characteristic of seeking.

Ruth has suggested that seeking, which culminated in baptism and church membership, was only the first stage of "true conversion." For her, seeking marked the beginning of your "spiritual journey—a constant growing in Christ and growing in your faith." Seeking was therefore interpreted as an individual's first baptism. The second baptism, which was the sign of "true conversion" or salvation, was baptism of the Holy Spirit. Faye recognized at an early age that there was a distinction between seeking, which meant learning how to pray, being baptized with water, and becoming a member of a church, and salvation. While recounting the intensity of prayer during seeking she exclaimed, "Just 'cause you seek don't always mean you saved!" She further described:

> I'm telling you, I had confessed my beliefs, was baptized—and there aint nothin' like a baptism now, that does something to you too—but that was not when the Spirit, that was not when I was saved with the Spirit. . . . It must have been from four or five years later [after seeking and joining the church] before I was baptized with the Holy Spirit, that's a different, that's a different situation. Yeah, I confessed my beliefs, and I did believe it, but honey, when that other one comes, you don't need no tarry or nobody to, honey, it can come by yourself!

Salvation, denoted by baptism by the Holy Spirit, therefore came after seeking, and could take years to occur. For Ruth and Faye, seeking was the foundation of their faith journeys and ensured that one began an intimate, spiritual connection with God. Seeking, however, did not ensure salvation, which could only come from the baptism of the Holy Spirit and heartfelt belief in God. One's ability to receive a second baptism was directly influenced by the nature of one's belief in God, which began during seeking.

Seeking was a process that shaped, formed, and affected these women's religious development. It facilitated an individual, spiritual connection to communal, ancestral, and divine presences through a set of organized religious practices. The seeking experience, which was shared with others who endured the seeking process, also harvested deep communal ties, as seekers were, as Roberta described, "bonded for life" with those with whom they had "a wilderness experience." Seeking had a special meaning to those who navigated it, for it allowed young Gullah/Geechee women a means of intimately connecting to God's presence, a connection that, once established, would "get a hold of you and stay with you throughout your life" as Ruth explained. Hence, while seeking was a process by which they joined churches, it was most memorable to these women as the means by which they developed an intimate relationship with the God of Christianity. Seeking was therefore not merely an event that began with communally established rituals and ended with church membership. Seeking was an integral part of their spiritual development and formation because it symbolized the beginning of their lifelong relationship with God. Seeking made a direct relationship with God possible—a relationship that continues to bear meaning in their lives today. Seeking, although no longer practiced, remains a significant part of their lives, for Beatrice, Lucille, Lucinda, Roberta, Ruth, and Yenenga continue to sing and teach the songs and prayers they learned when they "seeked" their religion.

Whatever its origins, it is clear that seeking was an example of low-country blacks' pluralistic religious sensibilities. It was established with a structure that missionaries introduced, and merged with ritualistic appropriations that Africans and Americans brought to bear on the experience. Margaret Creel and Jason Young have suggested that the Gullah combined intricate initiation ceremonies transmitted from their West African identities and merged them with critical reflection on Christian theological ideas about sin and God to create their own religion. By their own accounts, low-country women explicitly recognized seeking as a process that simultaneously connected them to God, their faith, and their ancestors. Seeking linked these women to the spiritual leaders who facilitated their process, and in so doing, fostered relationships with elders that had the potential to be sustained long after the elders' deaths. For example, Yenenga, Lucille, and Beatrice continued to communicate with their spiritual parents long after they died. Because of the ways dreams and wilderness experiences fostered a direct connection to ancestral spirits, seeking was among the most pivotal experiences that facilitated talking to the dead. This custom was affirmed among individuals and within the community at large, and made seeking one of the earliest ways that each of these women became comfortable with the practice of talking to the dead. The importance of these multiple modes of connection—between the divine, the living, and the dead—is not merely an example of African-Christian syncretism for lowcountry residents and should not be minimized. Rather, it is yet another example of the distinctive means by which lowcountry residents appropriated their faith and illustrates the prevalence of talking to the dead in lowcountry culture.

Talking to the Dead as Normative Practice

Whether through seeking rituals, personal connections with the deceased, dreams, belief in nondivine spiritual presences, storytelling, basketry, or prayer, these lowcountry women perceive talking to the dead as a normative practice. This is the case whether or not the practice occurs under the auspices of a church-sanctioned activity. There are several salient features of lowcountry religio-culture that support the practice of talking to the dead. The first is the strong Trinitarian emphasis espoused from lowcountry pulpits, during Bible study, and over the course of religious meetings that the women in this study frequently attend. Pastors, ministers, and evangelists alike have consistently emphasized and encouraged church members to establish an ongoing connection with the Holy Spirit. These religious leaders also focus on the human aspects of the Trinity and have characterized God, Christ, and the Holy Spirit as spiritual entities personally accessible to anyone who believes. During a worship service at St. James Presbyterian, for example, Reverend Charles Heyward delivered a sermon entitled "The Third Person of the Trinity." During the sermon, he described the Holy Spirit as "a ghost that you should not be afraid of . . . a person that speaks and acts."[33] This ascription of human qualities to the divine, which has made belief in spirits accessible to many African Americans, has helped lowcountry blacks remain open to the possibility of connections with the spirit world.

The practice of talking to the dead is also commonplace because of how the tradition has been collectively passed on by activities such as seeking, storytelling, and sweetgrass basketry—customs that are heavily influenced by African-based and African-derived worldviews. Numerous west and central African cultures believe that the worlds of the deceased and the living are continuous. As African religious scholar John Mbiti notes, "The spiritual world of African peoples is very densely populated with spiritual beings, spirits and the living-dead. Their insight of spiritual realities, whether absolute or apparent, is extremely sharp. To understand their religious ethos and philosophical perception it is essential to consider their concepts of the spiritual world in addition to concepts of God."[34] The pervasive influence of African cultures on lowcountry worldviews—especially the impact of these worldviews on local religious practices—should not be underestimated. Belief in the authority and wisdom of elders and spiritual parents, the frequent occurrence of dreams and visions, the entrance of a seeker into the wilderness to "find God," and the connections made with ancestors are features of the seeking tradition that parallel African traditional and African-derived religions including Yoruba, Santería, and Vodoun. As these practices were widely and frequently performed among lowcountry blacks, acceptance of the worldviews supporting them was transmitted. This meant that communication with ancestral and divine spirits was generally accepted by black inhabitants of the lowcountry along with the behaviors, rituals, practices, songs, and traditions that welcomed interactions between the living and the dead.[35] Yet these traditions and their broader acceptance are shifting. Though no longer actively practiced in the lowcountry, that each of the seven women who sought their religion now play such substantial roles as religious leaders in their respective communities and also actively talk to the dead is no mere coincidence. Ironically, however, none of the seven women's children were introduced to the church by way of seeking. Faye and Lucille's daughters, for example, were quite surprised to learn that their mothers seeked into church membership. This speaks to the impact of changes in the traditions, including a diminished sense of connection with the deceased, among younger generations.[36]

Third, talking to the dead is such a pervasive practice because of the fluid ways in which it has been interpreted and applied. Historically, lowcountry blacks believed in the continued presence of the dead, which was demonstrated in their beliefs in platt-eyes, hags, and individuals who are "born to see evil." These beliefs are not merely superstitions but are part of a complex religio-cultural system that made and continues to make lowcountry residents open to communication with the dead and to the conjurers who facilitate(d) these connections. While talking to the dead has been a part of lowcountry religious practices—including seeking, shouting, conjure, and voodoo—it has also been a part of cultural traditions including basketry and storytelling. All of these features have led to lowcountry blacks' fluid appropriation of talking to the dead. This flexibility explains why, although the idea of talking to the dead could easily be interpreted as non-Christian or superstitious, the women had no difficulty or reluctance acknowledging the ways they "tulk to de dead." It also helps one understand why none of the women viewed their belief in talking to the dead as antithetical or oppositional to their belief in and practice of Christianity. These sinuous interpretations of belief in communication between the living and the dead have facilitated a variety of practices that support coexistence of the natural and supernatural.

Fourth, talking to the dead has had a lasting influence in individual lives and subsequently on the broader community. When in 2001 Faye Terry made the decision to step down from the office of president of the United Methodist Women, it was her experience of talking to her deceased grandmother that solidified her choice to no longer hold the position. Faye, who had held virtually every position within the United Methodist Church that a layperson could hold, had certainly prayed about the decision, and she had even fasted for several days to gain clarity. Self-identified as a "gifted and born leader," Faye wrestled with the choice to leave the post because she felt that her calling in life was to be a leader. She knew that she "could only do God's work by leading God's people," but recognized that the demands of the job were emotionally, physically, and spiritually taking their toll. Her willingness to serve the God of Jesus Christ faithfully through the service of leadership was in some ways at odds with her personal desires because she simply was miserable in the position. In her heart she wanted to abandon the job, but she simply did not feel at peace. On the night before she made her decision, she dreamt of her grandmother Caroline, who she described as a "loving grandma" and a "stern woman who could pick a switch that would tear you up if you got out of your place." Faye recalled, "I remember seeing her so clearly—more clearly than I had seen her in a long time . . . it was kinda shocking she was so clear! And she just said to me, 'you know what you must do, you know what you must do!' And I cried . . . because I thought the women would think I was givin' up on them. And she just looked at me and patted my hand and smiled. And I knew."

The next morning, Faye called the pastor to inform him of her resignation, and two weeks later, a new president was appointed, the same woman who has successfully held the post since 2001. To Faye's pastor or an outsider, Faye's decision would simply reflect an administrative change, but to Faye, her choice was a direct reflection of the impact of talking to the dead.

When we see the ways that the folk practice of talking to the dead shapes and informs the decisions these women make—decisions that affect their own lives, the lives of their families, and the lives of community members—the importance of the tradition becomes clear. In the broadest sense, talking to the dead influences the relationships these seven women have with the deceased and the living. But talking to the dead is more than that. By connecting with the deceased, the seven women in this study make determinations about the choices they make, the various ways they live out their faith, and how they interact and engage with the people around them who are still alive—choices that have present and future consequences. The act of talking to dead and how it is made manifest through religious practices, music, and the collective act of remembering, contribute to how Gullah/Geechee women become culture keepers in the development and changing of their faith systems. These women's local communities are affected by their decisions to retire from being the church musician in order to tell stories full time (Yenenga), to sing and make healing ointments (Lucinda), to work with the elderly (Ruth), or to completely remove themselves from any position within their churches (Roberta)—and many of these decisions are informed by the process of talking to the dead.

CHAPTER 4

"Sendin' Up My Timbah"

Because of the peculiar situation of the South Carolina islands and the great preponderance of Negroes over whites before and since the civil war, Gullah music has remained almost in its original purity. . . . While the body of the Negro spiritual is drawn from the American environment, their spirit is African.
—MASON CRUM

The music stirs my soul, it touches me real deep.
—ROBERTA LEGARE

A History of Musicality

The musicality of the Gullah and their rich history of religious song traditions were well documented, particularly in the first-generation literature on lowcountry life. When Charlotte Forten arrived on St. Helena on October 28, 1862, she was transported by a crew of black boatmen, whose "rich sonorous tones" filled the short trip with a "sweet, strange and solemn" rendition of "Roll, Jordan, Roll."[1] Similarly, Laura Towne noted the singular use of song when she first came to St. Helena. While the men would row and sing, "Every now and then they shout and change the monotony by several very quick notes, or three or four long-drawn out ones. One man sings a few words and the chorus breaks in, sometimes with a shout or interjectional notes."[2] Music functioned to keep time and rhythm between the rowers, but also operated as a means of communication. As they spoke to each other through song, their singing broke into the stillness of the evening, the sound of the oars in water, and the repetition of the rowing rhythm. From their very first moments in the Sea Islands, Forten and Towne were introduced to the central place of music and song traditions in the lowcountry.

This use of music in rowing demonstrated that music was not isolated to religious meetings among lowcountry blacks, but was very much a part of everyday life. Charlotte Forten described how each day in school the children sang songs of various significance and meaning, including "Marching Along" and "John Brown" as well as spirituals like "Down in the Lonesome Valley." The splendor of the music captured its listeners, as did the powerful way in which it was delivered. Forten was particularly struck by the music. "They sang beautifully in their rich, sweet clear tones, and with that peculiar swaying motion which I have noted before in the older people, and which seems to make their singing all the more effective."[3] In addition to describing the singing as "beautiful" in every reference to the songs they sang, she frequently noted how their singing entranced her and affected her emotional state; upon hearing the music she would at times feel happy, filled with joy, sad, or lonely. Forten believed that "Look upon the Lord" was "The most beautiful of all their shouting tunes. There is something in it that goes to the depths of one's soul."[4] On her first Sunday on St. Helena, she noted that while the sermon was "quite good," she "enjoyed nothing so much as the singing—the wonderful, beautiful singing." She therefore concluded, "There can be no doubt that these people have a great deal of musical talent."[5] Forten was so fascinated by the song traditions of the islanders that she commissioned a song for Penn Center on December of 1862, which they all sang at Christmas and celebratory events.[6] To date, this song is sung during the Summer Investment Program (SIP), an educational and recreation camp held annually for local youth in June.

Forten was among many who came to admire and appreciate the distinct features of lowcountry music.[7] In 1923, a group of twenty white men and women of Charleston began to gather informally in each other's homes "For the purpose of singing negro spirituals. The object of these meetings was merely the pleasure which would be derived from the gatherings, and from singing, and in learning from each other such songs as might not be known to all."[8] This group later became the Society for the Preservation of Spirituals, whose purpose was "[t]he preservation of the Negro Spirituals and Folk Songs, the education of the rising generation in their character and rendition, and the maintenance of a social organization for the pleasure of the members." The society became so popular that it branched out beyond performances in the homes of its members, to offer concerts in Charleston and in southern states including Georgia, but also in New York, Massachusetts, Pennsylvania, and Delaware.[9]

This sacred music's everyday quality was one of its most distinctive features. Although spirituals and religious music were "sanctioned by the church, primarily religious in origin, and always regarded as something sacred, it was nevertheless freely admitted into the duties and pleasure of secular life."[10] Music sustained and helped lowcountry blacks get through their daily work activities. As Melva Costen has suggested, in African American musical expression, "there is no clear line of demarcation between secular and sacred in language and performance; a strong sense of communal togetherness is evoked; existential situations provided the subject for the poetic language; and the common means of transmission are by way of the oral tradition."[11] This everyday quality continues to be a part of the religious music in the lowcountry and is reflected in the narratives of lowcountry women. These women speak of the deep value and meaning of sacred music, as well as how their respective positions as spiritual leaders and devout Christians are explicitly tied to their relationship to music. It is also through music that the seven women in this study continue to talk to the dead.

Singing the Same Song

Every New Year's day, Faye, Lucinda, Roberta, and other members of Wesley UMC gather not at the usual ten o'clock Sunday morning worship time but at noon for the Emancipation Service, a program celebrating Abraham Lincoln's signing of the Emancipation Proclamation in 1863.[12] The service commemorates the legalized freedom of their enslaved ancestors and celebrates their distinct and not too distant past as former slaves. Church members and visitors alike look forward to the sermon, which is delivered by a special guest preacher, and to the intricate repast of lowcountry dishes—fried chicken, hoppin' john, red rice, macaroni and cheese, and collard greens—served in the fellowship hall immediately after the service. The highlight of the program, however, is not the food or the preaching, but the first half hour of the service when the choir sings "old time songs and spirituals."[13] Drawing from the senior membership of the church, the combined choir pays tribute to the songs that were sung in the past—songs that may not be sung often or at all at other times of the year. They sing traditional African American spirituals including "Steal Away," "Fix Me Jesus," and "Swing Low Sweet Chariot," as well as songs that are local to the lowcountry, such as "Pure Religion (You Can't Cross There)," "Doh Me a Lingah," and "When God Calls Me."[14]

That the pinnacle of the service is music is not coincidental. Roberta, Lucinda, and Faye are active members of the senior choir at Wesley UMC, which meets every other Saturday to rehearse. As members, they look forward to singing every first Sunday because it gives them the chance to perform the songs that "the church doesn't usually sing," according to Roberta. In keeping with their positions as "culture keepers," they view their role as the perpetuators of the "old time music," which, according to Lucinda, is important because "we just don't want people to forget the way we used to do it." Lucinda has a special personal connection to the music. She is one of the senior choir's primary soloists and as a lead singer describes her intimate relationship to spirituals and gospel music as one she inherited from her mother. "My mother could really sing, you know, oooh, she could sing! And I get it from her, she's the one who taught me." When Lucinda sings, she frequently calls upon the spirit and memory of her mother during her solo. She also prays to her mother before she sings. This connection, both between her mother and the music, is so powerful that, as she described, "Sometimes I wake up in the middle of the night and those old songs come to me like a dream." It is also one of the clear ways that she talks to the dead, for it is through the music that Lucinda most explicitly connects to her mother.

Lucille and Beatrice also have an intimate, personal connection to music. In addition to her role as president of the missionary board at Poplar Hill Christian Church, Lucille serves as the president of the sanctuary choir, the church's combined adult choir. Her role as president keeps her "busy 'roun the clock." As the church's most active choir, they rehearse every week— a task Lucille has to negotiate with her other position as president of the missionary board. Yet she loves to sing and does not know where she would be without music: "Music is just so important, the singin', the shoutin', it's the music that brings the Spirit. . . . I wouldn't be able to connect with God spiritually without them songs." Ms. Bea (Beatrice) is a member of the senior choir at Greater Goodwill AME, which sings every first Sunday. She is not able, however, to sing as often as she would like because of her basketry and a part-time job, which takes up the bulk of her time during the week and on weekends. When she is able, however, she also devotes her free time to an ensemble called Sister Sister, a group of four women (three are members of Greater Goodwill) who "go 'roun the lowcountry singin' dem old songs and sending out the message of God through music." She also incorporates music, especially "dem old spirituals" into her basket weaving. Although she does not have a radio at her basket stand, she hums and sings spirituals, hymns, and gospel songs to "pass the time" and "keep the rhythm." "There is a rhythm to everything, you know," she said, "but especially to this [basketry]."

The women of St. James Presbyterian are also intimately connected to music. Because of the time demands of her role as elder, Ruth is not an active participant in any of the church choirs. Yet as a part of the church leadership, she is readily aware of the impact of music during worship. "Music really helps the Holy Spirit come. With the music, you feel the process, the transformation process and the moving of the Holy Spirit while you're in worship." She therefore supports the use of music in every aspect of worship and often suggests contemporary gospel songs and hymns to the choir director. Music is a noticeably important part of the worship service at St. James. In addition to the four choir selections that are sung during the service, worship is prefaced with a "medley of praise." The medley incorporates various hymns such as "Great is Thy Faithfulness," and "He is Lord," as well as traditional spirituals including "Down by the Riverside." In addition to being a community storyteller, Yenenga is a lifelong musician. She was the primary pianist and organist at St. James for thirty-five years before retiring in 1995. Although retired from St. James, she continues to play at Wallingford Presbyterian church in downtown Charleston twice a month. While she admits that playing gives her "a little extra income," she really does it because "it's what I love to do, second only to telling the Gullah stories." She listens to music all the time—"when I drive, when I wake up, and before I sleep." Yenenga's love for music also extends into her storytelling as she incorporates narratives that speak to the pervasiveness of religious music in the lowcountry. In one of her short stories "Ouman Chair" (Woman Chair), she describes how a male choir member struggled with being the lone male voice in a choir full of women.

What is particularly noticeable about how the music facilitates communion with the Holy Spirit are the ways that music also makes the practice of talking to the dead possible. Whether creating sweetgrass baskets or singing with Sister Sister, Beatrice sees her use of and access to music as a way to spread the Gospel or to talk to her Nana. Similarly, though Yenenga no longer plays the piano professionally, she always has music "on her mind and in her Spirit" and frequently uses music in her Gullah stories. The use of music thus allows her to access the Holy Spirit or her parents and grandparents, who encouraged her to learn the piano and taught her to tell stories. Lucinda, Lucille, Faye, Ruth, and Roberta also express a similar fluidity between encountering the Holy Spirit and talking to the dead, though they make clear that the two are not synonymous or conflated and that accessing God via the manifestation of the Holy Spirit is the most spiritually important experience. "Getting the Spirit" does not automatically mean that one will communicate with the dead, nor does an encounter with a deceased friend, relative, or loved one directly result in an interaction with the Holy Spirit. Talking to the dead can occur within the same sector of time as the Holy Spirit is encountered, but not simultaneously. Meeting with an ancestor is not synonymous with encountering the Holy Spirit. Rather, the entrance of the Holy Spirit marks a sacred moment when communication with the dead can also occur—provided one is open to the experience. This is most clearly expressed in Lucinda's statement, "There's when the Spirit come, and then there's the other things that happen right after, like when I can see her [her mother]." In this way, the experience of talking to the dead, as facilitated through music, takes on the same four-tiered pattern of talking to the dead in any other context—openness, acknowledgment, acceptance, and communication.

For Ruth, Lucinda, Yenenga, Faye, Roberta, Lucille, and Beatrice, music is at the core of their lives as active church members and as Christian women of faith, and a shared belief in the power of sacred music further unites their experiences.[15] During interviews and observations, music was readily brought up, and almost always initiated by the women. When I would inquire about seeking, for example, they would begin to talk about the songs they remembered or learned during that time. Their active participation in church choirs or local music groups and their consistent use of music to enhance their work reflect how these women actively incorporate and pass on these musical traditions. Throughout my time with them music was a means of accessing their religious experiences. On the companion audio materials, Lucille teaches me how to "properly" incorporate the lowcountry clap on "My Hope is Built II." Similarly, the "Meeting Songs Medley" came out of my time with Yenenga when she recounted the songs that were sung during her seeking process. The practice of music, much like their faith, extends beyond the weekly church services, monthly programs, and annual commemorations into their daily activities. Hence, the everyday quality of lowcountry music that has historically attracted attention to its distinctive music practices continues to be a viable and living aspect of lowcountry religious culture.

There is something special about the expression, instrumentation, and vocalization in lowcountry religious music. The depth of emotion and spirituality that is readily expressed through praising God is evident upon hearing and observing music during worship. When one hears the songs (especially those accompanied by the "lowcountry clap") and ecstatic moments of shouting, the soul-stirring quality is unforgettable. The rhythms, theology, and language of the musical practices in the lowcountry are as distinct as the Gullah dialect. Drawing from a rich history of dynamic creation and appropriation, this unique culture of music currently stands as a largely untapped resource within ethnomusicology and within the study of modern African American music. In this culture, the primacy of music, which for each of these women is a very real, live, and present form of divine manifestation and ancestral connection, reflects how it has successfully sustained its distinct place in the African American sacred music tradition.

Contemporary forms of lowcountry music, though understudied, are key to passing on religious tradition. It is through the hearing and singing of songs that these women readily express their belief in Jesus Christ and, at times, can communicate with the deceased. The collective memory of this music is long lasting, as music is as significant to religious belief, practice, and tradition as participation in church activities and belief in God. The music surrounding this culture is therefore both vocal and functional, for it meets the spiritual needs of the individual, operates as a current mode of communication, and is organized in relation to the liturgy of the church. Lowcountry women and men see sacred or religious music as a means of both celebrating and living out their faith. Music becomes a means of bringing the community together while giving individuals the ability to personally communicate with and express their belief in God. I argue that sacred music styles in the lowcountry are not isolated to the experiences within formal religious contexts but are often employed in everyday life as a means of sustaining one's religious identity. Historically, the Gullah/Geechee incorporated spirituals, and later Christian hymns, to facilitate work (exemplified in Charlotte Forten's description of being transported to St. Helena Island and by Beatrice's use of hymns and sacred songs to aid her basket making). In short, women and men simultaneously see music as functional and faith-based, and there are very few differences in how they make meaning from music.

What is special to the lowcountry, however, are the ways that music also makes possible the practice of talking to the dead—a process that can occur for men and women but is highlighted in this study for the ways it is engaged by women. This music is also a way of sharing and transmitting a collective experience of the past. Lowcountry music practices are thus a form of living memory. They simultaneously draw from a rich cultural past yet bear relevance in the present as contemporary expressions of what is remembered. At the same time it is a lived practice—a way of living out one's faith and the spiritual practice of talking to the dead in the present. This reflects an overlap between sacred and secular spaces and confirms that the evocation of communal existence is very much a part of the daily worlds of Gullah/Geechee women.

Language and Rhythmic Praxis

The significance of music in the lowcountry parallels the use of oral tradition in Gullah/Geechee culture, as the language and style of the oral traditions carry over into its sacred music.[16] Lowcountry music preserves the cultural heritage, reminds the people of "how far we've come by faith," and maintains communal, ancestral, and divine connections.[17] These oral traditions—which share conceptual characteristics with Yenenga's storytelling—include call-and-response, shouting, and creative verbal description of experiences that actively pass on communal traditions. All of the women speak openly about how they continuously draw upon these musical practices, and I witnessed these features during the worship services I attended and the songs I heard sung. These observations revealed, as Guy Johnson suggested, "Isolated areas like the Sea Islands are not areas in which one finds an intensification of African traits in the spirituals, but merely areas which have favored the preservation of spirituals which are elsewhere obsolescent."[18] In "The Religious Life of South Carolina Coastal and Sea Island Negroes" Samuel Lawton argued that spirituals and hymns were the dominant forms of lowcountry religious music, and that hymns were "used more than any other type of musical selection."[19] These two types—spirituals and hymns—are still predominant in lowcountry sacred music, but the music of the contemporary lowcountry differs from songs sung by the enslaved and has expanded to incorporate contemporary gospel music. According to Eileen Southern, songs sung by the enslaved maintained a continuous poetic form that "typically consist[ed] of four-line stanzas alternating within four-line choruses."[20] In contemporary lowcountry music, the numbers of stanzas or verses employed in a song does not always bear the four-line stanza form, and the use of stanzas heavily promotes communal participation. At the same time, the history of hymnody is so rich in the communities that the churches continue to incorporate the linguistic patterns of slave songs and to draw from their rich history of spirituals. In the case of these contemporary lowcountry music forms, it is not the "Africanness" of the music that is of greatest importance, but the current meanings attributed to the music that is significant.

Examining the language present in lowcountry music beyond the antebellum spirituals is critical to understanding the Gullah/Geechee connections with their past. It is also a means of understanding the ways that contemporary communities are adapting their rich musical history to make the music relevant in the present. Like many other African American musical traditions, the sacred music produced in the lowcountry is "the product of an improvisational music consciousness. They were not . . . totally new creations, but were forged out of many preexisting bits of old songs mixed together with snatches of new tunes and lyrics and fit into a fairly traditional but never wholly static metrical pattern."[21] The music today therefore includes colloquial expressions of the Gullah dialect—"my" is pronounced "mah"; "I" is pronounced "Ah"; and "God" becomes "Gawd." This music shares the metrical complexities and rhythmic patterns of the music traditions of the enslaved, but the current appropriation of song styles and instrumentation reflect a revisionist style that uses new lyrics and incorporates new songs that add a distinctively modern element. This has meant that although more contemporary gospel songs are incorporated into the musical repertoire throughout the lowcountry, they are appropriated to fit the lowcountry style of music. An example of this is the song "Call to Christ," as sung by Lucille.

> He said come to the water and stand by my side
> And drink from the fountain you won't be denied
> For I've seen every teardrop that fell from your eyes
> And I rose to tell you for your sins he died

Here, the four-stanza construct characteristic of spirituals is the primary structure of the song, yet there is something new about this music. Lucille is not sure where the song is from, and did not know that the song is actually entitled "For Your Tears I Died," which was originally recorded by Rev. F. C. Barnes and Rev. Janice Brown on their 1984 album "No Tears in Glory."[22] She does know, however, that she heard it being sung at another local church, and she then "took it back to her choir." All of the other women were unfamiliar with the song but expressed appreciation for its "simple beauty." The song means a great deal to Lucille as it "reminds [her] that [she's] saved. It's just so straightforward—Christ knows all my pain, all I have to do is trus' him." It becomes quite clear that although the song traditions of the lowcountry from the past influence the contemporary musical practices, the process of appropriation and change in contemporary music is continuously occurring. This transition parallels the shifts occurring in most evolving communities.

While many of the songs are simple in structure, they are quite complex in tempo and meter, so much so that European forms of musical notation cannot accurately capture the music. Repetition is a profoundly important theme of the music and the stanza and choruses are linked through the recurrence of a refrain. As a result, varying a word or two creates large numbers of stanzas or verses. The basic pulse of the meter is usually maintained by a style of hand clapping distinct from any other forms that use the body to keep beat. Similar to patting the juba, this form of keeping rhythm, the "lowcountry clap," speeds up the tempo from the original pace of the song. The initial clapping pattern is directly on the beat (usually the second and fourth beats of a 4/4 tempo), but an extended, multiple clap eventually works its way into the song (which contributes an additional 3–6 beats within the 4/4 tempo). Although the song may begin in syncopation and a more standard 2–4 clap is usually incorporated with few variants, the song eventually becomes multimetric and cross-rhythmic. It incorporates the use of the hands and feet, and further establishes a polyrhythmic beat within the lyrical transitions of the song.[23] This makes the structure of this music extremely difficult to encapsulate.

As a predominately vocal music, its making involves the interaction of song leaders with the choir and larger congregation, reflecting its individual and communal structure. In particular, call-and-response is one of the most common features. A soloist or leader will sing a verse, which is then repeated by the choir and congregation, who typically respond with the same verse or a corporate refrain. The soloist plays a tremendous role in the song, for with a leap or dramatic shift in his or her voice he or she has the power to "take a song up" or "bring a song down."[24]

This soloist feature is pervasive in African American sacred music forms, and as Bernice Johnson Reagon notes, represented broadly in rural congregational singing in the South.[25] The significant role of the song leader has deep historical roots. For many years after emancipation and before the onset of shape-note singing, African American churches in the lowcountry did not have hymnals and their members did not read written music. It was therefore not uncommon for the lead vocalist to "line" the hymn or song— to sing the line of the song that the congregation would sing next—and the congregation to respond in a form called common meter. This style continues to be a frequent means for song leaders to guide the movement, structure, and corporate performance of a song. An additional distinctive feature of lowcountry music is that unless it is a hymn, the song is rarely sung in unison and the soloist who began the tune may not remain its leader. It is common for others to "pick up" the lead and add their own verses. The song then transfers from person to person until practically everyone has had the chance to lead the song and incorporate their own testimonies. Whether upbeat or slow in timbre, "the personality of the lead singer rings proudly in every note sung."[26] In the song, "Pure Religion," for example, the numerous verses are sung before the refrain, and once the refrain begins, the verses are no longer sung.[27] The leader is key to the movement of the song, as she or he can carry the song on indefinitely with the incorporation of verses.

> Where you goin' ole liar? (yeah!)[28]
> (Where you goin' I say)
> (I'm goin' down tah Jordan, ya can't cross there)
> Where you goin' ole cheatah?
> (Where you goin' I say?)
> (I'm goin' down tah Jordan, an' ya can't cross there)
> Additional Verses
> Where you goin' deceivah / where you goin' ole sinnah
> Where you goin' backstabba / where you goin' adultra
> Where you goin' ole preacha / where you goin' believah
> Where you goin' ole devil / where you goin' ole trickstah
> Refrain
> Oh church said ya must have
> (Pure religion)
> Ya must have
> (soul converted)
> Ya must have
> (Pure religion or ya can't cross there!)
> repeat refrain indefinitely

In "Pure Religion," a congregational song with a leader (versus soloist), the verses are repeated indefinitely, and are sung for as long as the leader chooses. The song moves into the chorus once the leader has determined that the congregation is "ready," which means that the song's tempo has increased and that the congregation is "worked up" in anticipation for the song to transition to its refrain. The refrain or chorus is typically the repeated musical phrase that the song returns to immediately after a verse.

In this case, however, the refrain is sung at the end. This disrupts the tra-ditional verse-chorus format that structures hymns and modern songs and instead exemplifies a contrasting verse-chorus form. The structure also increases audience participation and their anticipation to contribute to the song's progression.

The involvement of the congregation intensifies the movement and tempo of the song. Once the community gets involved, unconventional har-monic blends with traces of blue notes and individual pitches and tones seem to naturally develop alongside tonal modulations and key changes to create a complex, polyphonic melody. This in turn creates hot rhythms with an overlapped refrain and a syncopated back beat clap. It is important to emphasize that individuals might begin to sing the refrain before the leader concludes his or her solo, and that the leader might begin the next solo before the chorus finishes. This phenomenon is most often referred to as overlapping call-and-response patterns.[29] Corporate spontaneity and indi-vidual improvisation often lead to an organic community performance at the onset of any song. Just as the unity of the singing and great beauty of song gave the enslaved a sense of unity and agency, it gives the participants in today's lowcountry church a feeling of power and authority.

Instrumentation often accompanies this music and its use and form is varied. It is common for a soloist to begin a song a cappella and without specific meter, or to begin a song slowly until its tempo increases when the instruments and the congregation join in. The drums, keyboard, guitar, congas, and Hammond B3 organ accentuate the singing from the congre-gation, and their use marks a distinction between contemporary music and the music associated with spirituals. This polyrhythmic addition enhances the power and tempo of the song while giving it a more structured meter. It also pushes the song's progression. It is common practice for the instru-ments to emulate the human voice and at times replace the hand-performed rhythms exemplified by the lowcountry clap. Musicians are also expected to incorporate their own improvisation without overwhelming the vocalists.

These features coalesce in the song "Way By and By," which is led by Lucinda.[30]

Way by and by
(Way by and by)
(We gonna have a good time, way by and by)
(Way by and by, way by and by)
(We gonna have a good time, way by and by)

In the Beulah land
(In the Beulah land)
(We gonna have a good time, way by and by)
Way by and by
(Way by and by)
(We gonna have a good time, way by and by)

As the song progresses, Lucinda incorporates verses, "shoutin' over there,"
"singin' over there," and "preachin' over there." These are experiences that
she and the other choir members are familiar with—moments that occur
often in the here and now. As she dictates, the choir also sings, "meeting Jesus there," and "peace over there." These moments describe experiences that have not yet occurred—moments that represent a life they do
not quite know but long for. Hence they also incorporate having peace in
"Beulah land," a place where, contrary to their current existence, one can
always "have a good time." Lucinda also inserts the verses, "got a mother
over there," and "my father over there," and true to form, the choir replies
"mother over there" and "father over there."

Her personalization of the song is significant, and the tone of her voice
changes as she inserts these phrases, for it is the moment that she is actively
recalling and connecting the memory of her deceased parents. Whenever
she sings this song, she recalls the memory of her parents "who have gone
on before" and vocalizes her anticipation of one day being able to see them
again.

This song is especially notable for its rhythmic transitions. Initially, the
musicians are unable to get the rhythm, and cannot accompany the song as
Lucinda sings at her own pace. The song begins somewhat awkwardly as
the musicians offer accompaniment, only to realize that during those initial moments, the song cannot be accompanied. At the 1:07 mark, the song
transitions dramatically from a slow tempo spiritual that is sung only with
vocal accompaniment to an upbeat song accompanied by the lowcountry
clap and the Hammond B3 organ. Also significant to this song is the trans-
ference of the lead role. The song appears to have ended, but is reinstated or
"picked up" by the musicians. Lucinda is no longer the leader but falls into
the repeated phrase "by and by" with the choir. The male organist begins to
lead the song and takes the song to its end.

The singing of hymns is also a common style in this music, and it is the
hymns that have drawn many to note the unique features of lowcountry
sacred music.

When Blacks began to establish their own churches, they did not discard the sophisticated hymns learned from their experiences in White Christian worship; rather, many of these hymns were adopted and converted into original Black songs. These "made-over" White hymns were the results of diverse influences including: (1) African religious music, (2) the African call-and-response song, (3) European or American religious and secular songs, and (4) various African and Afro-American dialects. And how were they made over? The melodies were often improvised to fit the needs of the Black worship service. On the other hand, many of these melodies were kept intact, but the rhythm and harmonies of those hymns and songs were changed to reflect the Black worship experience.[31]

The versions of "It Is Well with My Soul," "A Charge to Keep I Have," and "My Hope Is Built," are examples of this intricate process of application, transition, and appropriation.[32] These hymns are usually sung in unison by the congregation with hymnals in hand, but are typically lined out and sung in a call-and-response style. When lining a hymn the leader intones the music line by line, and after each verse is given out, guides the congregation in their singing. This is a powerful spiritual statement of community. As Lawrence Levine has suggested, the call-and-response patterns and practice of hymn lining contributes to the music's "overriding antiphonal structure." This leads to a continuous dialogue between the individual and larger congregation, allowing the individual to simultaneously preserve her distinct voice while blending it with the voices of others.[33]

Lucinda, Beatrice, Roberta, and Faye express a personal preference for singing hymns. For Lucinda, when she wakes up in the middle of night, only those "old time songs" help to lull her back to sleep. To Faye, "there is nothing like a good hymn." Lucille, however, finds the contemporary songs more spiritually beneficial and feels like "it's more spiritual here" (at New Hope Christian) than in her home church, Mt. Sinai Baptist in Beaufort, because they sing fewer hymns. Nonetheless, these songs are often the favorites of many of the church members and have a powerful and extraordinary effect on the singers. "Someone always shouts, the women begin to cry, and a deep, solemn religious spirit is immediately established in the church."[34] This mode of expression also frequently leads to the shout, where the leader and chorus alternate rapidly while increasing pitch, while members of the congregation clap, stomp, and dance around them or off by themselves.

As a collection, African American sacred music reflects the ingenuity of a people who "reinterpreted the religion designed to reinforce white supremacy" and applied it to their musical practices.[35] This is especially true of the religious music that has developed in the lowcountry. An examination of the theology of the religious songs in the lowcountry can help us understand its value to the community at large, and further uncover the profound personal meanings it holds for these women.[36] The theology of this music "was formulated out of the context of God's revelation and providence as revealed in the history of an enslaved people."[37] Hence, it always reflects the struggles of communities to survive and to understand the meaning of their struggles in the midst of their faith. This faith is one of belief and inquiry; it echoes the ongoing belief in the manifestation of God, incarnate in the image of Jesus Christ, but also questions the meaning of hardships for a people who continue to struggle as a minority in this country. As William McCain has noted, this theology is therefore "not the theology of the academy or the university, not formalistic theology or the theology of the seminary, but a theology of experience . . . a theology of imagination . . . a theology of grace . . . a theology of survival."[38] The songs these women sing in their homes and at their churches are marked by vivid imagery, metaphorical figures of speech, personification, direct language, and faith in divine deliverance from situations of oppression.[39] These songs also convey the women's deep sense of faith.

The theological themes and images of this music reflect a perpetuation and preservation of communal values. These songs offer all who sing and hear them opportunities to express their faith and to participate in a corporate identity denoted by a shared history as African Americans.

> Oh Operator
> (Operator)
> Gimme long distance
> (long distance)
> Say you got (Jesus on the line)
> Oh Operator
> (Operator)
> Gimme long distance
> (Long distance)
> Say you got (Jesus on the line)
> Call Him up

(Call Him up)
And tell Him
(And tell Him)
(Tell Him what you want)[40]

In "Operator," there is an inversion of the relationship between the believer, God, and Jesus. Rather than Jesus facilitating access to God, which is the traditional construction of the Trinity in Christian theology, Jesus is accessible only through the Operator, God. Roberta describes that in this song, "God is the operator and through him and Jesus, you can speak from your heart, tell them what's going on. . . . It's long distance 'cause it don't always feel like they close when all the stuff of this world is goin' on." The relationship between Jesus and the singer is personal because she can call Jesus and tell him exactly what she needs.

Scholarship on African American religious music suggests that the primary characteristics of its theology is its inclusion of imagery that denotes African Americans as a chosen people, the incorporation of biblical figures, and its focus on the other world, or heaven. Although many of these features still exist in lowcountry religious music, the theology of the music has shifted. Contrary to scholars who argue that the theological imagery of these songs is mostly that of the chosen people, the images in the contemporary music are those of deliverance and rest. As LeRoy Moore Jr. suggests about the spirituals, this contemporary music, which is the foremost expression of religion, is "not essentially escapist in the sense of either an other-worldly release or a this-worldly relief. It may be either or both, but it is primarily self-affirming. It is a music of being at home with one's self."[41] This negotiation of other-worldly features and self-affirmation theme is evident in traditional spirituals like "Rest for the Weary."

Now tell me how far am I from heavun?
Tell me how far am I from de shore?
Dere'll be rest for de weary
And dere'll be rest for me

In this song, which is sung in harmonic unison by the congregation, the theme of heaven and deliverance from the worries, cares, and concerns of this world dominate. Rest is the desired goal, and the singers acknowledge that true rest will only come in heaven. This song also reflects the personalization of the lyrical text. The self-affirmation is clear—rest is available not only for others who are weary from the pains of this world but also for *me*. This personalization is present in other songs as well, including "Sit Down Servant." Heavily drawing upon the practice of overlapping call-and-response patterns, the believer is understood as the faithful servant, one who will be granted rest.

> Oh sit down servant (sit down)
> Sit down servant (oh sit down)
> Sit down servant (sit down!)
> Sit down an' rest a lil' while
> *Verse*
> I know ya tired (sit down)
> I know ya tired (oh sit down)
> I know ya tired (sit down!)
> Sit down an' rest a lil' while[42]

Deliverance from the harsh realities of this world takes the form of resting. The song suggests that one has come a long way and deserves rest, an allusion to the toils, tribulations, joys, and sorrows acquired on the journey of life. At the same time, however, the theme of rest and deliverance looks slightly different in this song. Whereas the language in "Rest for the Weary" alludes to eternal rest, in this song rest is available for all servants now, not only in heaven. Thus, there is an eternal and temporal element in their understanding of deliverance.

One of the major differences between the music surrounding the slave culture and the contemporary music stemming from the lowcountry is the use of biblical themes. Although songs like "We Are Climbing Jacob's Ladder" continue to be sung, the theology of most songs incorporating biblical imagery has shifted from the incorporation of prominent biblical characters and places such as Daniel, Ezekiel, Moses, Jonah, and Jericho, to a primarily Christ-centric or theocentric focus.[43]

"DOH ME A LINGAH"	"KNEEL AT DA CROSS"[44]
Doh me a lingah (doh me a fall)	Oh chil'ren kneel (at da cross)
Doh me a lingah (doh me a fall)	At da cross (kneel at da cross)
God can (save a sinful man)	Chil'ren kneel (at da cross)
God can (save a sinful man)	At da cross (kneel at da cross)
Oh God can	Chil'ren kneel (at da cross)
(Save a sinful man!)	Oh! (Jesus will meet you dere!)

In these songs the concepts of sin and salvation are straightforward. The first indicates that although one may linger ("doh me a lingah") by acquiescing to the ways of the world, God can save the sinner, despite his or her shortcomings ("doh me a fall"). The second suggests that the cross is the place where Jesus will meet you. "Kneel at Da Cross" calls all of God's children to kneel before God and make their requests known. Hence, we see how the music greatly emphasizes the theme of salvation. We are also given images of a personal God who will come to the supplicant in her or his time of need. Thus God and Christ are not remote and abstract deities of the past, but an intimate, immediate, and personal Godhead of the here and now.

An additional song that Faye, Roberta, Lucinda, and Lucille fondly recall is the Negro spiritual "Couldn't Hear Nobody Pray,"[45] which Faye and Lucinda learned while seeking.

Oh I
(Couldn't hear nobody pray)
Oh, Lord
(Couldn't hear nobody pray)
Oh Lord
(Way down yonder by myself)
(Couldn't hear nobody pray)[46]

The focal point of the song is prayer and reflection upon the intimate solitude that prayer facilitates, which was at the heart of the isolation achieved during the seeking process. While seeking, the emphasis was on a direct connection with God without the disturbance or effect of external influences. Though seekin' is no longer practiced, the fundamental idea of the process—the development of a personal relationship with God—is exemplified in additional verses inserted by the lead vocalist, including "on my knees" and "on the altar." No longer relying on images of a chosen people, African Americans in the lowcountry have transitioned to an emphasis on the God who is present and personally accessible. The music has become personally applicable, where motifs of right relationship and holy living operate alongside images of heaven and deliverance. These themes, which are commonplace in this music, reflect an ongoing theological appropriation of experience and belief.

These songs, which all of these women sing, have sung, and are at the very least familiar with, are a part of their lives within and beyond the walls of the church. Beatrice, for example, frequently sings "Rest for the Weary" on the long days outside at her post two blocks away from the City Market, especially the days when her "hands grow tired." These songs also mean a great deal to the women and are the tunes that they call upon to reaffirm their faith, to help them through difficult times, and to remind them of the God who has brought them "this far by faith." For these women, music is an intimate part of their lives and they dynamically incorporate and pass on these musical traditions. They each actively participate in church choirs or local music groups and use music consistently to enhance their work. The practice of music, much like their faith, extends beyond the weekly church services, monthly programs, and annual commemorations into their daily activities. Hence, the distinct rhythms and everyday quality of lowcountry music that have historically attracted attention to the Gullah/Geechee communities continue to be part of the religious music.

It is important to understand how these songs simultaneously connect the women to their past and their present. All cultures have some concept of time, although it may be defined and used differently. Essentially, time is a mechanism of control, "the coordinating principle that orders human life in all societies,"[47] individually and collectively. This understanding of time holds true for the Gullah/Geechee as well because it is grounded in the experience and lived memory of the people. Yet it is a form of religious expression that permeates their sacred music practices. In this way, time in lowcountry culture reflects Joseph Adjaye's argument that "time throughout the black experience has provided the fundamental beat to which the rhythm of that experience has responded."[48] As I have previously explained, western conceptions of linear time do not always accurately capture the way time works among the Gullah/Geechee, which John Mbiti distinguishes as potential time and actual time, and Sheila McKoy describes as "diaspora temporality." This is in no way intended to suggest that the Gullah/Geechee implicitly incorporate an identifiably "African" sense of time. Rather, to understand the ways that time in lowcountry sacred music takes on a cyclical and linear quality—best exemplified in the use of the lowcountry clap and the repetition of verses that literally push a song forward to invoke the Spirit—is to recognize that their use of music is more likely an ongoing connection between black diasporic cultures. The interconnectedness of rhythmic practices and theological motifs, along with the use of the features to suspend and push time by connecting with past traditions, present experiences, and God, denotes a spiritual bond that is simultaneously ancestral, communal, and divine.

It is this nuanced understanding of time and its layered use in lowcountry music that stands as a contemporary connection between the Gullah/Geechee and their African and Caribbean heritage. In comparing time in

Gullah/Geechee culture to that of African traditions, Joseph Holloway suggests that lowcountry understandings of time pattern those of African tribal and communal traditions:

> Time in the African sense is no mere abstraction that has taken form in a linear progression; rather, time remained circular and episodic, told and retold, based on great events that occurred in a living historical past. This circular pattern of time is realized in such natural phenomena as birth, aging, and death; African time continues after death, because time is circular and not linear. Ancestors could be reborn back into the community of the living, or they could simply dwell in the world of ancestral spirits. For Africans, time is both sacred and profane, dividing the human world into sacred and nonsacred time, the temporal and eternal. This concept of time differs from the European in that with the latter, time is linear and life ends with death.[49]

For the Gullah/Geechee, this cyclical concept of time demonstrates a continual link with their ancestors and God, and is readily identifiable in the call-and-response, pause, and repetitive style of sacred music. Music thus also functions as a means of "tulking to de dead." The meter, rhythms, tempo, and accents of the songs seem to take control of time. Often it seems that time is suspended in this music, especially when a break in vocalization and instrumentation occurs and the only sound heard is that of the hands clapping and feet stomping. Additionally, the song style causes a sense of pause, and one is often so "caught up" in the moment of the music that it is quite easy to lose track of time. These traditions and styles also push time ahead. The use of the clap and instrumentation move the beat forward, which in turn leads to the speeding up of the music itself. This occurs almost every time a song is sung, for most begin slowly and then change to a very rapid pace. The language and rhythmic practices of this music spatially extend the world of the community upward, while extending it temporally backward. This suggests that the music, similar to the presence of God—the subject of the music—is not confined to any time or place.

Sendin' Up My Timbah

Performance of the song, "Sending Up My Timber"[50] is a key example of how the meaning, language, rhythmic practices, creative appropriation, theology, use of time, and spirit of lowcountry religious music coalesce and result in talking to the dead.

I dreamed, that I dreamed
Of my heavenly home
I'm goin' up dere one day
May be mornin', night or noon
I don't know just how soon, I am
Refrain
Sendin' up my timbah (every day)

Theologically, this song addresses the relationship between the believer and God with an emphasis on right relationship. The timbah, or timber, is the material God is using to make the mansion in heaven, and the materials it is built with are determined by what one does before reaching heaven. Faye characterized the song in the following way: "So as God is buildin' the mansion, you're doin' what it takes down here, everything you can here on earth to ensure your mansion." In other words, what one gets "up there" is contingent upon what one does "down here," especially what one sends up there from down here. Although none are certain of when or if they will reach the heavenly home, all are encouraged to send up their timber through works, prayer, and right-living while on earth. The theological language of the musical text creates space for individual and communal participation and interpretation. Faith, patience, and optimism are set alongside themes of weariness, burden, the heaviness of the earthly life, and deliverance from those pressures.

The feeling this song transmits is the direct result of a music that unites spirituality, personal expression, faith, and hope. Something visceral occurs with this song in particular. It begins with a slow drawl, a nearly atemporal, arrhythmic pattern that is without instrumental accompaniment. Hence, the Hammond B-3 organ follows suit only by playing the major chords at the end of each musical phrase. As soon as the song begins, people are clapping and crying out, "alright!"; "yes!"; "yeah, yeah!" It is initially difficult to chart the music because Lucinda establishes the tempo by singing at her own pace. The choir, which Roberta and Faye are a part of, accompanies her with harmonic humming that pushes the song forward yet has the effect of lulling the song so that the hearer cannot help but anticipate its continuation. This reflects how the leader begins with an opening phrase and the congregation joins in. The tonality of Lucinda's voice is matched by a vocabulary of sliding words common to the Gullah dialect: "day" becomes "day-ay-ay," "noon" becomes "nooooon-ahhh." The choir, consisting of ten women and two men, stops humming and joins her in a blended harmony to sing, "Sendin' up my timbah every day." The tempo then immediately changes, prefaced by Lucinda's falsetto, "oh yes I'm . . ." and a more pronounced and distinctive rhythmic beat begins, distinguished by the lowcountry clap, and the drummer enters. The song is then changed from a seemingly mournful spiritual to a fast-paced, all-out celebratory song.

They sing the refrain "sendin' up my timbah" fifteen times, and the fifteenth time transitions to the next series, or "round." Every round of fifteen is broken into a pair of phrases, with each set marked by a chord progression. The last pair is different from the other repetitions of "sendin' up my timbah," and the choir adds, "sendin' up my timbah every day." With each round, the tempo and volume increase. In the entire song, the refrain is sung eight times. Meanwhile, within the second round Lucinda improvises an original verse, "when I join, with my friends who have gone before me," which sounds more like, "when ah joyyyyyyn-ah, wit mah frie-ie-anddd, who have goooooo-naaaaah before-aaaah."[51] As the song continues into its fifth round, the fourth repetition of the refrain, a high-pitched scream erupts from Lucinda—the Spirit has come, and the moment becomes recognized as spirit possession and "shouting." By the seventh round, more members of the choir, led by Lucinda, are screaming and jumping up and down. Several members of the choir have literally fallen away and are no longer standing. The refrain is barely discernable, and the lyrics that can be heard come from a distance, indicating that the congregation has become the choir and is carrying the song's refrain. The organ and drums also move the tempo and push the song to a rapid, climactic end where only they can be heard, along with the pastor shouting, "Send it up! Send it up!" Even after the song has ended, members of the choir and congregation are offering praise to God through claps and shouts of their approval—"Amen!"; "Yes Lord!"; "Thank ya God!"; "Hallelujah!"

Different sounds become more prominent at various moments in the song, many of which, though the rhythm is ongoing, evoke a feeling of atemporality. The continuous repetition of the refrain with the increased tempo gives the music circular sense. The incorporation of ecstatic moments, marked most noticeably by instrumental and vocal breaks in the music, is especially important. At the same time Lucinda begins to shout, the drummer stops playing the snare and cymbals, and utilizes the bass drum only—an effect that offers a pause in the music. This break makes the music feel as if it has suspended time, which also coincides with the entrance of the Holy Spirit. The manifestation of this suspension and connection is multilayered. The drummer crashes on the cymbals to signal the repetition of the refrain (2:09, 2:30, 2:50, 5:00, etc.), but crashes *and* breaks at "high" moments of the song, where the presence of the Spirit is audibly noted through the shouting and screaming of the choir and audience (4:02, 4:41, 5:17, etc.). He also crashes and breaks immediately before and immediately after these moments throughout the song. As the lead vocalist, Lucinda also contributes to the song's sense of atemporality. Although she improvises the solo, she only modifies the lead by slightly altering the words and phrases (e.g., "I'm sendin'" versus "oh yes I'm sendin'"). That is, until she audibly cries out, which to her is "when you know the Spirit hit me." Even though she eventually is no longer able to lead the song as she is so "caught up in de spirit," the moments where she "shouts" and fades out as the song's vocalist are almost always accompanied by her return to the lead, as if she never stopped singing (5:05). Though the song has not literally stopped as the musicians are continuing to play and the choir and congregation sing, her falling away makes the song feel as if it is suspended.

Lucinda's performance of "Sendin' Up My Timbah" exemplifies how one's ability to talk to the dead confirms one's spiritual authority. In addition to being a prominent local conjure woman who describes herself as "good at mixin' up stuff to keep people from being sick," Lucinda is an amazingly skilled vocalist whose musical ability and deep spirituality often invoke the entrance of the Holy Spirit as well as the presence of her deceased mother. When she stands up to lead a song like "Sendin' Up My Timbah" in her church, Lucinda stands before the community as a gifted vocalist, a potent herbalist and voodoo practitioner, and someone who is perceived to be a spiritual powerhouse because she can easily and frequently invoke the Holy Spirit *and* converse with the dead. Whether she "gets the Holy Ghost" (the physical manifestation of the entrance of the Holy Spirit, a kind of spirit possession) or experiences her mother's presence while singing, the community (in this case, her church) recognizes her experiences as legitimate and authentic spiritual experiences. Lucinda thus becomes spiritually potent in part because of her ability to talk to the dead. Having this ability suggests a spiritual maturity and wisdom beyond one's years and therefore affords a great deal of respect. Lucinda's role as a conjurer and culture keeper further influences the respect she receives, and music is one of the most important ways in which she passes on the tradition of talking to the dead to her family and community.

Music, Dancing, and the Shout

Singing during worship can produce the physical manifestation of God, also known as the entrance of the Spirit, or "shouting." Among the most frequently documented religious practices in the lowcountry and in African American religious experience broadly, shouting is exemplified in a well-known description of "the frenzy" by famed black sociologist W.E.B. Du Bois.[52] Though the term has had multiple meanings in the lowcountry, shouting was most often used to describe the communal process called the ring shout. During meetings, lowcountry blacks would link arms, form a circle, and shuffle in a counterclockwise circular motion to the beat of a shout song—a rhythm or tune, usually religious, that would begin slowly and progress into a fast-paced rhythm. Shouting was not the same as dancing. "The lines between shouting and dancing were strictly held. Shouting could be indulged only while singing a spiritual. . . . [I]t was universally agreed that shouting was dignified, that it was a worship of the Lord, that certain motions were not fitting."[53]

Historically, shouting most often occurred during weeknights and after church services on Sundays in the plantation praise house or large cabin. "[T]he true 'shout' takes place on Sundays or on 'praise'-nights through the week, and either in the praise-house or in some cabin in which a regular religious meeting has been held. Very likely more than half the population of the plantation is gathered together. Let it be the evening, and a light-wood fire burns red before the door of the house and on the hearth."[54] At these meetings, which traditionally lasted from late night until the early morning hours, lowcountry residents could freely draw from their African and African-based traditions to express their spiritual connection to a divine presence in the midst of communal participation and ritual performance.[55] The outcome of the praise meetings and shouting was that of spirit possession. Margaret Creel suggested, "The Gullah ring shout . . . involved an altered state of consciousness and had the attributes of 'possession.' It represented either an unusual behavior inspired and controlled by an outside agent, in this case the Holy Spirit, or the outside agent displaced the individual's personality and acted in its stead."[56] As John Bennett noted, "seizures and autohypnotized [sic] cataleptic trances are common. . . . [D]uring these trances the entranced are supposed to converse with the spirit, to see visions, and to have revelations made to them by supernatural powers, sometimes they see God himself, and Mary, the mother of Jesus."[57]

Charlotte Forten noted the frequency of the "shouts" during her time on St. Helena Island, and her descriptions contested the notion that dominated the first-generation literature that women were somehow better equipped for or more sensitive to the more emotive shouting practices. She recognized that these shouts gave the community an opportunity to gather but also were a source of spiritual inspiration within the community. "The people on the place have grand 'shouts.' They are most inspiring. Went to one Thursday night. There is an old blind man, Maurice, who has a truly wonderful voice, so strong and clear. It rings out like a trumpet. One song—'Gabriel blow the Trumpet'—was the grandest thing I have yet heard. And with what fire and enthusiasm the old blind man led off. He seemed inspired." The following Sunday, Forten attended "the grandest shout" she had yet seen at the praise house. "Several of the soldiers who had come home on a visit joined in the shout with great spirit. The whole thing was quite inspiring."[58] At one point, she and Lizzie (her local companion) found themselves "in a dark corner of the Praise House" where they "amused" themselves by "practicing a little." She further posited, "It is wonderful that perfect time the people keep with hands, feet, and indeed with every part of the body. I enjoy these 'shouts' very much."[59]

Laura Towne offered some of the earliest descriptions of the ring shout in the lowcountry. In 1862 she described the following events: "To-night I have been to a 'shout,' which seems to me certainly the remains of some old idol worship. The negroes sing a kind of chorus—three standing apart to lead and clap—and then all the others go shuffling round in a circle following one another with not much regularity, turning round occasionally and bending the knees, and stamping so that the whole floor swings. I never saw anything so savage. They call it a religious ceremony, but it seems more like regular frolic to me."[60] The next night, she attended another "shout," held at Rina's house, which she described as a "savage, heathenish dance." She offered additional details about the performative aspect of the ring shout, noting that in addition to three men who "stood and sang, clapping and gesticulating," essentially keeping up the rhythm to the song, there were other men and women present in the form of a circle. They "shuffled along on their heels following one another in a circle and occasionally bending the knees in a kind of curtsey. They began slowly, a few going around and more gradually joining in, the song getting faster and faster till at last only the most marked part of the refrain is sung and the shuffling, stamping, and clapping gets furious."[61] These descriptions by Towne and Forten suggest that shouting was a lowcountry communal event that took place regularly.[62]

Women's role as shouters is historically significant. Although men and women led shouting practices in the lowcountry, it was well documented that women were particularly adept at facilitating shouts. Arguably these descriptions reflect numerous negative references to black women as being "emotional" in the earliest generations of Gullah/Geechee scholarship. Yet it is important to note women's positions as shouters because of the significance and frequency of shouting in Gullah/Geechee communities, and because it further affirms women's responsibilities as spiritual leaders and culture keepers. In a discussion of the meaning and frequency of shouting in lowcountry churches, Robert Gordon provided the following description of a worship service:

> On the several occasions when I have seen this happen in recent times, a single old auntie was responsible. Overcome by religious ecstasy and hysterical with emotion, she arose almost defiantly and led off, shuffling and swaying down the aisle. One by one others joined, till perhaps a third of the congregation were "shouting." Around and around they went, up one aisle and down the other, while the deacons and elders stood apart, their faces expressing mingled emotions of mild disapproval tempered with envy, their knees bending and their bodies swaying in time with the shouters.[63]

The physical exertion of shouting struck all who observed the practice. Often the community would gather and clear the meeting space by pushing benches and chairs to the wall. Everyone would then stand in the middle of the floor, form a circle, and wait for the singers to "line out" or "strike up" a song, to which those in the circle would move, first by walking and then by shuffling. During this shuffle, "The foot is hardly taken from the floor, and the progression is mainly due to a jerking, hitching motion, which agitates the entire shouter, and soon brings out streams of perspiration."[64] John Bennett personally witnessed the ring shout, which he called a "strange round Jericho shuffle," at an unspecified location near Charleston. "The whole body falls into motions, as the music takes hold possession of the dancers, every muscle moves in time, racking. The dancers move faster and faster, the ring seems to whirl, without warning the leader suddenly faces about and without pauses reverses the circuit/revolving. Now and then those exhausted drop out; others take their place. For hours the dance goes on until all are utterly exhausted."[65] In addition to her astonishment at "how long they kept up and how soon after a rest they were ready to begin again," the physicality of the movements was noteworthy to Laura Towne because,

"The floors shook so that it seemed dangerous. It swayed regularly to the time of the song."[66]

The interconnectedness of shouting, singing, and dancing is an additional feature of the shouting tradition in the lowcountry. It was not uncommon to hear those inside the circle singing the chorus of the song. Most often, a separate group of singers led the songs during the shouting. This was likely because of the physical exertion that shouting required. As William Allen depicted, the singing was especially prominent because it was the music—along with the physical movements of the ring shout—that led to heightened, ecstatic experience.

> [A]t regular intervals one hears the elder "deaconing" a hymn-book hymn, which is sung two lines at a time, and whose wailing cadences, borne on the night air, are indescribably melancholy. . . . But more frequently a band, composed of some of the best singers and of tired shouters, stand at the side of the room to "base" the others, singing the body of the song and clapping their hands together or on their knees. Song and dance are alike extremely energetic, and often, when the shout lasts into the middle of the night, the monotonous thud, thud of the feet prevents sleep within half a mile of the praise-house.[67]

John Bennett also recognized the importance of the singing during the shout. "The singers pitched the air, a good singer begun by the best singers and kept up the crows inside the ring, leaders, clappers and dancers all joining."[68]

The music style that accompanied shouting was complex. Charlotte Forten was a seasoned pianist yet was unable to notate or play the tune or rhythm of the music. "[O]f the tune and manner of singing it is impossible to give any idea." In addition to her difficulties in translating the shout tunes, she also found understanding the words to the songs challenging. When some of the young blacks visited her home, she noted that in addition to singing some of the "old favorites" like "Down in the Lonesome Valley," "Roll, Jordan, Roll," and "No Man Can Hender [sic] Me," the children also sang "several shouting tunes" that she had never heard before. The singing was led by "a large black boy, from Mr. R[uggle]'s place" named Prince, who "was full of the shouting spirit, and c'ld [sic] not possibly keep still. It was amusing to see his gymnastic performances. They were quite in the Ethiopian Methodists' style." Forten found it impossible to understand the words of these shouting songs, which she characterized as being "very wild and strange."[69] Hence, she was only able to write the words in such a way as to offer some suggestion of the song's tune.

This inability to describe or characterize the meaning and function of shouting caused many to conclude that the shout was African in origin. Abigail Christensen postulated that the shouts "were no doubt survivals of African dances used in fetish or idol worship."[70] John Bennett considered the religious dance among Sea Islanders as "the last reminder of the religious dance of the devotees . . . the remaining vestige of the old serpent frenzy."[71] William Allen suggested, "It is not unlikely that this remarkable religious ceremony is a relic of some native African dance, as the Romaika is of the classical Pyrrhic."[72] Although Gullah scholar William Pollitzer has suggested (incorrectly) that religion played a minimal role in the life of the Gullah, he nonetheless recognized "the call-and-response fashion of the preaching," the rhythmically compelling music, and the singing and dancing traditions associated with the ring shout as "the most striking features" of Gullah religion.[73] Contemporary scholars have further theorized that the foot shuffling, the musical patterns, and the altered state of consciousness that occurred during the ring shout connect it directly to specific ethnic groups in west and central Africa. In the seminal text *Slave Culture: Nationalist Theory and the Foundations of Black America*, Sterling Stuckey notes the importance of the circle and its ancestral function throughout the African diaspora, arguing that shuffling in a ring during ceremonies to honor ancestors is "an integral part of religion and culture."[74] Similarly, Margaret Creel argues that the ring shout was "West African in origin" and an important characteristic of the initiation process "into the Praise House."[75]

Whatever the origin, it is most important to note that shouting among lowcountry blacks has been and continues to be an important expression of religious experience. Today, there are many different forms of shouting. According to Gordon, "One might shout acceptably while standing in one place, the feet either shuffling, or rocking backward and forward, tapping alternately with heel and toe, knees bending, the body swaying, and the hands clapping. Or the singer could alternately advance and retreat."[76] Shouting thus refers to the dance also known as the ring shout; the screams, yells, and cries that indicate the manifestation of the Spirit; the physical, rhythmic movement of the body that can overtake an individual when the Spirit "hits" or enters; and the types of songs that accompany the dances and vocalizations. What is most important about all of these forms is that they are predicated on the idea of spiritual possession and ecstatic experience, they are facilitated by distinct musical practices, and they continue to be practiced by the women in this study.

"Caught Up in de Spirit"

These musical practices—including their theology, rhythmic appropriation, significance, structure, and function—are at the heart of shouting in contemporary lowcountry culture. The incorporation of the drums and Hammond organ, along with the lowcountry clap, repetition, call-and-response, and the progressive increase of tempo, invoke the Spirit and lead to shouting; "Sendin' Up My Timbah" is a great example of this. The same features of shouting as outlined by Robert Simpson regarding slave shouting practices—the involvement of everyone present in one of three roles (lead singers, basers, and shouters); the opportunity for individual expression; and the flexibility and fluidity between the singers, basers, and dancers—are still present.[77] The very repetition and tempo of the song create an environment where the air is charged with an energy that erupts into what Du Bois called "the frenzy." In this way, the rhythmic appropriation parallels the ring shout. Today, there are several communities actively continuing this tradition, the Macintosh County Shouters in coastal Georgia being one example. While their efforts are certainly laudable and important, the broader numbers of community folks who continue or are familiar with the practice are small considering the historical prominence and frequency of the ring shout. Here I am referring explicitly to the traditional, circular shuffle style that once dominated the religious expression. I am not implying that it no longer exists at all, but that the ring shout does not occur with the same frequency; it is not being taught to younger generations in a widespread way; and those who practice the ring shout often do so in an effort to preserve the practice intentionally, much like the Macintosh County Shouters in Georgia. Yet even while there are contemporary African American worship settings where aspects of the ring shout are being continued and revived, my observations of contemporary worship practices of select churches in lowcountry areas, and my own experiences growing up in a rural area of the South Carolina lowcountry lead me to conclude that the practice has considerably and significantly diminished to the point of virtual nonexistence. At the same time, while shouting in the form of the ring shout has largely been discontinued, shouting continues to be an active part of lowcountry religious practice. The goals of the ring shout—communal celebration, invocation of the Spirit and/or ancestors, spirit possession, and catharsis—are duplicated in the contemporary singing of songs and the shouting practices that accompany them. The difference is that while ecstatic experience may not occur every time, it is—along with the expression of faith and belief—the hope and goal of the music. This is particularly the case since the Spirit is invoked and therefore cannot be forced. As Beatrice described, "Whenever we sing, we hope that in all of these things God will show up."

Shouting is a ritual that can only occur in a religious context, and its frequency and style vary. In Ruth's church, St. James Presbyterian, she has described that they "used to have a lot of shouting and dancing and getting happy and those large meeting shouts and everything. Then we moved away from that. Now, praise the Lord, we're back to allowing the Holy Spirit to take control." Yenenga confirms the increased spiritedness at the church: "You know Presbyterian churches used ta be like very well, um, prim prim, stiff, you know high fallutin'. But it's not like that now. You can come to our church and you'll think you in Pentecostal church on Sunday morning. . . . It's very high-spirited! . . . Lit up with Holy Spirit! Lit up girl, high praise!" It is this sense of spirit, or spirit possession, that is crucial to the religious experiences of each of the women. Also known as "the huckabuck," "da holy dance," "gettin' hit," "feelin' da Holy Ghost," and being "caught up in de Spirit," shouting is for each of them the culmination of their personal relationship with God.[78]

In *Women in the Church of God in Christ: Making a Sanctified World*, Anthea Butler notes how spirit possession is a community-wide practice that is not exclusive to women; rather, possession and being "under the power" demonstrate the ways that "Holy Ghost power was not limited to leaders" but was broadly available and accessible to everyone who participated.[79] At the same time, Butler reasons that a special importance is ascribed to manifestations of spirit possession among women, especially those who are viewed as spiritual leaders and exemplars within the church. While none of the women in this study are members of the denomination Butler focuses on in her text, her emphasis on the importance of shouting among women who participate in spirit-filled expressions, and women who are also spiritual leaders, is relevant here. Just as Church of God in Christ (COGIC) women embrace ecstatic practices to outwardly express the internal, "sanctified," or holy existence they live day to day, Lucille, Roberta, Lucinda, Yenenga, Beatrice, Ruth, and Faye see and experience shouting as a normal and natural expression of their existence as devout Christian women—even as their encounters of the Spirit may manifest in different ways. Faye described her own shouting practice in the following way: "I have never been one of those people to dance, you know? But I'll raise my hand and rock and cry. I'll even cry out sometimes." Her account also affirms the frequency of shouting, which most often occurs in the context of community worship on Sundays and during weekly meetings. As Yenenga described, "Two, three times a week, you go to the meetin' house, sing and shout; that's where you remember all 'dem songs." Being "caught up," however, is very much an individual experience that can occur outside of church. "When you get caught up when you by yourself," Lucille explained, "that's how you know God is really with you, you know?" Whether inside or outside of formal religious meetings, the Spirit makes itself known in different ways for these women. Yet, it is the very fact that the Spirit "shows up" that is crucial to all of their experiences.

Although shouting in the "traditional" shuffle style of the ring shout has all but disappeared,[80] Lucinda, Yenenga, Lucille, Faye, Ruth, Beatrice, and Roberta have each witnessed the ring shout and could recall specific moments when it was done. None of them, however, admitted to being able to do the ring shout or acknowledged their own participation in it. Yet I have seen a variation of the ring shout on numerous occasions during worship services and choir anniversaries. During a Sunday worship service at Wesley UMC in 2005, I witnessed Lucinda doing a "holy dance" where she jumped up and down and moved her legs in a motion similar to jogging in place. Several women circled around her while she was "caught up." They joined hands in the circle and did not shuffle, instead moving in such a way to accommodate Lucinda's movement. They remained encircled until the Spirit left Lucinda and she "calmed down." When asked why this was done, Lucinda explained, "It's to protect me. When de Spirit hits, I ain't in control and ain't no tellin' what de Spirit's gonna do. So they have to come 'round and make sure I don't hurt nobody." Faye agreed with Lucinda and added, "when you're really in the Spirit, you can't get hurt, it's the people around you that you're lookin' out for."

Allowing the Spirit to take control is imperative to their religious experiences. When I asked why the Spirit "taking control" is so important, Ruth replied, "That's why some people say worship service is a little long, you know. But when you allow the Holy Spirit to take control time doesn't matter, you know." This association with the Spirit and timelessness, replicated in the music's atemporal qualities, demonstrate both the continuation of the practices and appropriation of the meanings of being "caught up in de Spirit." This modern appropriation reflects the creativity of lowcountry blacks, demonstrates the active transmission of pluralistic religiocultural practices, and confirms the continued significance of shouting as a form and practice that is very meaningful to those who participate and observe.

Ruth's comment about the diminished use of shouting, dancing, and getting happy also begs exploration because of what it reveals about the transformation of shouting practices over time. Although Ruth attributes the resurgence of shouting at her church to increased efforts by her minister and worship leaders to "allow the Spirit to take control," she was unable to account for why the more emotively expressive encounters with the Holy Ghost lessened over time before being revived. History suggests that the transition between more and less expressive worship that Ruth observed in the lowcountry paralleled broader shifts in African American worship styles across the country during the early and mid-twentieth century. Migratory patterns and the resulting changing communities, as well as increased access to popular sacred music styles such as gospel, meant that black communities had to negotiate and renegotiate understandings of their faith. In addition, many churches had to modify their worship practices to accommodate the changes in population and audience demand.[81]

Further conversation with Ruth revealed a direct correlation between when shouting and seeking stopped. Like the practice of seeking one's religion, shouting, dancing, and other "ecstatic" encounters diminished with the onset of confirmation classes and the establishment of other polity-driven formalized practices. Ironically, the reduced occurrence and diminished acceptance of more "traditional" practices, which were generally associated with the practices of the enslaved, historically coincided with increased pursuits for middle-class ideals within black communities. These ideals, which included increased education, improved economic and political conditions, and strategic efforts to debunk racist myths about black intellectual, artistic, and moral inferiority, were the direct result of respectability movements within African American culture between 1890 and 1930, which had lasting effects well into the twentieth century. Evelyn Brooks Higginbotham's *Righteous Discontent* describes the implications of notions of respectability on black religious expression in the South—namely that within the Baptist church, black women used their notions of self-help to construct a "female talented tenth" with the intent of "broadening the public arm of the church and making it the most powerful institution of racial self-help in the African American community."[82] Even as these women contested topics such as segregation, voting rights, and lynching; used notions of racial progress to promote education among African Americans; and contested the invisibility of women in the biblical text and black church broadly, the effect of their shift toward respectability meant that black ecstatic religious expression was treated as an outmoded and overly simplistic practice that should be displaced. Ruth's description of the change in worship style at St. James is indicative of this shift.

This desire for more mainstream acceptance also had a direct impact on the practice of religion within black communities, as ministers were encouraged to pursue formal education in the form of seminary training. Yenenga attributed the shift in worship style to a more diminished sense of emotive expression within St. James, which Ruth references as being a direct result of the increased education of local ministers. According to Yenenga,

> As the older ministers you know, died, the new, well I wouldn't say new, the younger ministers that come from theology schools uh, change some things and that would continue. . . . Some of the things we um say we used to go to church and be there until three o'clock, all day. You get a young minister come in from theology, now church is out one o'clock. You know what I'm saying? . . . Yeah, so change do come when you know, the younger ministers come along from school or you know all depends on their background.

It is not difficult to imagine that, like the ring shout and seeking one's religion, shouting became associated with negative stigmas regarding black religious morality. Given the role of music in these practices, that traditions like the ring shout, seeking, and shouting transitioned from being predominant to discontinued suggests, as historian Jerma Jackson affirms, that even as important as music practices are within these communities, they too succumbed to the pressures of increased secularism and education.[83]

Yet, the longstanding traditions in the lowcountry that emphasize the importance of connection to the Spirit and ancestors, as demonstrated in the practice of talking to the dead, have always left a space where communities could contest popular notions of respectability. Even as formal practices of ecstatic religious expressions like the ring shout diminished, the use of music to invoke the spirit has ensured that even when certain communities or changes in institutionalized practices seemed to thwart ecstatic expression, the necessity and importance of maintaining customs ensured these connections remained. Because many lowcountry worship styles and practices resemble the spirit-filled expressions of the COGIC church, Butler's presentation of the role of spiritual expression again becomes relevant. Butler notes that ecstatic practices such as shouting and dancing, "were linked to the worship styles of the slaves, which many of the members in the early twentieth century could still remember. Unlike their black Baptist cohorts, who shunned ecstatic practices in the hope of attaining respectability, COGIC members embraced the ecstatic workshop of the convocation services that have witness to the outpouring of the Spirit. . . . The emotionally charged environment of the convocation allowed members who had forgotten the fervor of services in their urban environments to get back in touch with the sacred and to touch the not-so-distant past of slavery."[84] Like the folks in the COGIC conventions who desired to connect with their past and to maintain that connection by way of sustained religious expression, the members of lowcountry churches have been connected to their history and their ancestors. The importance of sustaining these connections, which is demonstrated by the significance Faye, Lucinda, Beatrice, Lucille, Ruth, and Roberta place on the act of remembering, reveals that the practice of remembering bore greater significance than the performance of respectability.

The Memory of Music

The unique rhythmic patterns, overlapping harmonies, creative appropriation of religious themes, and lively spirit of lowcountry music are striking. The music is the center of religious experience for these women as individuals, but also for them as members of larger religious communities. As sung in the lowcountry, religious music offers access to a form of African American sacred music where the ideological and spiritual elements of a contemporary black community are deep and the influences of the living dead abound. These features reflect individually and communally held ideas of expression and faith. The language, intonations, and theological structure of the songs clapped, drummed, and sung in churches throughout the lowcountry have created a musical style that characterizes Sunday worship experiences. This style has extended, however, beyond the realm of traditional worship and the walls of the church into the daily activities and rituals of women. It is women who are the predominant members of churches and church choirs and, as such, they are the primary progenitors of this distinctive musical culture.

Music provides these women with a connection to those who have gone before them, gives them the opportunity to pass on the rich musical traditions, and allows them to actively practice their faith. Music in fact serves as a primary way for these lowcountry women to "tulk to de dead." As Sam Floyd suggests, music facilitates beliefs and actions that members of a culture know without knowing how they know it, that simply feel right when encountered.[85] This knowledge is at the heart of what Roberta expresses when she says, "there is something special about this music, it touches me real deep," and when Lucinda states, "I don't know where it [the lowcountry clap] come from, but I know where it come from with me." Music is not just sung, it is embodied, and it is believed in—a belief that is physically performed and transmitted to the memories of the community. In addition to the unique rhythmic practices, it is this sense of cultural memory that sustains this music and the faith of these women. The most distinctive feature of lowcountry music is therefore the deep meaning it holds for the people who sing it and what that significance communicates about their histories, present realities, and future hopes.

The music surrounding this culture is vocal and functional. It expresses the experiences of the people, their belief in God, and their undaunted spirituality, as well as their ability to communicate with those who have gone before them. Music has a liturgical and ceremonial role for these women. It is formally performed within church services and practiced during religious events, as well as during personal rituals such as prayer. It also has an everyday quality that directly mediates their daily lives. Music becomes a means of helping them accomplish work, errands, and miscellaneous tasks, and it facilitates their personal, daily expressions of faith, such as prayer. These women rely on the sacred nature of the music to help them deal with the mundane practices and challenges they face on a day-to-day basis. During a lull in choir rehearsal when Faye, Roberta, and Lucinda were together, I asked them if there was something about gospel music that inspired them. Faye commented, "It doesn't matter to me whether it's old-timey or contemporary, it all work for me and it all help me get through everyday," which the other women echoed in agreement. Faye's emphasis on how the music helps her to "get through" reflects its sustaining function in her life as a woman of faith. It is important to understand these women's individual and collective relationships to the music because they demonstrate the sustained and continuous merging between the church and their lives beyond the world of the church. The collective memory of this music is long lasting because music is as significant to religious belief, practice, and tradition as participation in church activities and belief in God. Most significant, the daily use of music has become one of the most important ways for these women to pass on religious traditions, including talking to the dead, to their families and communities. In the accompanying audio, the male vocalist that can be heard on the songs "My Hope Is Built," "When God Calls

Me," and "A Charge to Keep I Have" is Lucinda's son, David Jr. He learned how to perform those songs and to incorporate the polyrhythmic form of the lowcountry clap (he can literally be heard rapping the rhythm with his knuckles on the podium or choir stand) from his mother, and he too sees his ability to sing and move audiences as a means of accessing God, as well as his deceased father. In Lucinda's example, we see how a cultural tradition can be translated across generations.

Among these women, music thus operates as a performative feature of lived memory. The mechanisms through which music is remembered—storytelling, call-and-response, basketry, and services devoted to the rec-ollection of past musical styles—reflect how music is a part of the shared memories of these seven women. The rhythmic practices of contemporary music in their churches, which draw from the past while incorporating present experiences, also demonstrate how the community at large remem-bers and (re)appropriates lowcountry music traditions in the present. At the same time, the women's experiences of the music reflect their individual connections to music practices in the lowcountry, for each draws personal meaning from it. As Lucille, Ruth, Faye, Lucinda, Yenenga, Beatrice, and Roberta actively participate in their respective churches, music simultane-ously strengthens their individual faith and connects them to the living dead among them, but it also connects them to a larger community of faith. Addi-tionally, the bodily expression of the music—best exemplified in the active shouting and dancing traditions, the women's openness to the movement of the Spirit, and Lucinda's song-delivery style—demonstrates the various ways in which lowcountry music is performed. Hence, we see that the music produced in lowcountry culture is sung, danced, and shouted, but most important, it is lived as it is remembered.

CHAPTER 5

Lived Memory

> I was interviewed by this woman from Nigeria. She just wanted to do the
> comparison, to tell the children back home in Nigeria how we cherish
> them so much and they were getting so Americanized, you know,
> forgetting their roots, whereas we were here remembering.
> —YENENGA WHEELER

In the story "Intro," Yenenga offers the following description of
Gullah/Geechee origins: "Ahn you know what happened? Long time
years ago dey brought my ancestors over here. They say, 'well, where
dat Gullah come from?' I say, well 'e bring 'em from the shores
of Sierra Leone and dey come yeh down here in the lowcountry.
Honey . . . most of de slave trade been in Charles Town. Well dat's
what I was taught and e' fuh true too. So my ancestors was deposit
out on the farms and the plantation."[1] Yenenga's recounting of the
past reveals that the Gullah/Geechee have a specifically West African
heritage. By emphasizing the connections between Sierra Leone
and South Carolina, Yenenga accepts that the Gullah/Geechee are
descendents of slaves transported during the transatlantic trade,
and that they have direct African lineages. What is striking about
Yenenga's tale is not the story itself, for she does not reveal anything
new about Gullah/Geechee beginnings. Rather, it is the *function* of
the story as a means of connecting the present with the past that
is remarkable. In recounting a story she was taught, she indicates
the sense of responsibility she feels to pass that story on as truth to
others. This is important because it demonstrates the significance
of storytelling as a means of talking to the dead for Yenenga spe-

cifically, but also because it broadly speaks to how remembering is as much about telling a story that is accepted as truth as it is about allowing that story to merge the past, present, and future.

In the lowcountry, remembering is a crucial way of teaching and preserving traditions, and recalling the people who created customs is one way of keeping them alive.[2] Memory—synonymous with remembering—represents how knowledge is transmitted, confirms how rituals are shared, and demonstrates how narratives are transmitted through a community's experiences. While they may be written, these narratives are also discursive. Memory thus refers to what has been written as well as to what has been passed on through rituals, practices, symbols, and other unwritten aspects of culture. It also encompasses the features of the past that are very much a part of the present. Understanding the aspects of memory as they are ritualized, (re)appropriated, and performed is significant because it provides a means of understanding the social, cultural, and religious perspectives of a given community.

It is through the lens of religion that the purpose of talking to the dead as a discursive practice is revealed. For the women in the study, remembering is a spiritual practice. Jesus Christ's admonishment to believers, "this do in remembrance of me,"[3] bears witness to their faith and devotion to church life. Remembering also has communal implications as individual narratives are recounted alongside and intertwined with those of the community. Memories of times spent with deceased friends and loved ones carry as much significance as abandoned traditions and key historical events. Remembering has sacred significance to these women and is perceived as a gift from God. According to Roberta, "You have to always remember, 'cause we live in a world that wants us to forget, and God doesn't want us to forget." Forgetting one's history is therefore interpreted as a sin that can only be avoided by active remembering. Remembering is therefore a way of teaching, preserving, and celebrating lowcountry culture while honoring the ancestors. It is a spiritual practice that takes faith as a starting point and, when employed, is a means of overcoming the sin of forgetfulness.

For Ruth, Lucille, Beatrice, Roberta, Faye, Lucinda, and Yenenga, there is a direct relationship between remembering and talking to the dead, for to remember is to actively recall and establish connections with the past, which includes the deceased. This means they seek out connections to the dead in a variety of ways: through music, religio-cultural practices like sweetgrass basketry and storytelling, the incorporation of folk religious customs, and prayers and dreams. Remembering as a form of talking to the dead allows the women to recall moments of their past, like seeking, that connect them to the deceased, and to use those moments to inform how they choose to live out their present. Talking to the dead is a form of lived memory since it is one of the many ways that the importance of remembering is continued in Gullah/Geechee culture.

As important as remembering is in the lowcountry, however, it is a form of talking to the dead that is beginning to change. This is in part due to how perceptions of Gullah/Geechee culture from the outside world are transmitted within communities that are increasingly facing the challenges of cultural commodification. This shift is also the result of how remembering is being deemphasized among lowcountry women, who too have to wrestle with the implications of being part of a culture that is celebrated for its rich history and cultural distinctiveness, while it is simultaneously marketed in a tourist-driven economy. Notable changes in the practice among the women of this study leave me cautiously optimistic about remembering as a means of talking to the dead among Gullah/Geechee women.

Africa as Historical Reality and Lived Memory

Remembering is the most apparent way that connections to Africa are readily evoked in the lowcountry. Residents continuously celebrate their African ancestry and remembering becomes a means of honoring their rich history as a people who survived the bonds of enslavement. As emphasized in scholarship, cultural retentions are inconsequential to how these women interpret their African connections. This is exemplified at the Emancipation Service held at Wesley UMC, where Faye, Lucinda, and Roberta recall their past as freed blacks while celebrating their history as African descendents alongside members of their community. Another illustration is the creation of the Gullah Festival, a three-day event held each May to celebrate the history and culture of blacks, and whose primary goal is to educate everyone about the contributions of blacks to lowcountry culture.[4] Each of these practices demonstrates the continued importance of talking to the dead by way of remembering.

Understanding how Africa is remembered by the women in this study and the impact of these connections on lowcountry culture today demands recognizing, as historian of religion Charles Long has suggested, what Africa means to African Americans within a contemporary context. In "Perspectives for a Study of Afro-American Religion in the United States," Long argued that three components must be explored in order to better understand the distinctive qualities of black religion: "1) Africa as a historical reality and religious image; 2) the involuntary presence of the black community in America; and 3) the experience and symbol of God in the religious experience of blacks." Although Long's characterizations are evident in Gullah/Geechee culture, the first perspective is salient to this discussion. According to Long, that the existence of black communities in North America was a result of the transatlantic slave trade affirms the lasting impact of Africa upon black Americans. He concluded, "So even if they had no conscious memory of Africa, the image of Africa played an enormous part in the religion of blacks."[5] Jason Young affirms that Africa became a symbol that was deliberately remembered by those in the New World, and that through memory, it symbolically informed the ways that blacks created culture. "African culture did not ride Atlantic waterways as vestigial survivals or retentions but as the product of cultural memory, mediation, and creation."[6] It is clear that although African Americans were not always able to recall or identify the languages, specific cultural practices, and other authenticating details of their African ancestry (especially since they were involuntarily brought to North America and treated in ways that threatened their ability to recall these practices and traditions), the image of the land came to have a sacred meaning that was transmitted into their religious practices.[7]

It is this characterization of Africa as historical reality and sacred symbol that is key to understanding the significance of remembering Africa and its connections to talking to the dead in lowcountry culture. To the seven women of this study, Africa is the place from which their ancestors originated, and it has sacred significance because of that. To remember the importance of Africa as a historical reality is to therefore call upon the memories of deceased ancestors. Roberta, Lucinda, Lucille, and Faye cannot specifically identify their African ancestry and have little interest in doing so beyond indicating that they are "from Africa." For example, when asked about her awareness of her African heritage, Faye replied, "I don't know where in Africa I'm from, I just know I'm from Africa." Yet these women readily accept that they are African descendants, and they celebrate that history, which they have been taught predominately through oral traditions. Hence, what is most important to them is not identifying any specific geographic ancestry or any specific practices as African, but that their heritage is *African* and that it is a *shared heritage*. Lowcountry identification with Africa as a continent and symbol of home is therefore a feature of collective memory. To remember Africa in this way has sacred significance, allows these women to call upon the memories and ancestors of their symbolic home, and to use that nostalgic identification to fight the sin of forgetfulness.

These women embrace a clear sense of connection to Africa, which is evident in their recognition and acceptance of a shared African heritage. However, the extent to which each woman has embraced and actively remembers Africa varies, which speaks to some of the changes that are occurring in Gullah/Geechee culture. Of the seven women, Lucille feels only a minimal sense of connection to Africa beyond its being a symbol of her ancestry. When asked about her sense of personal identification with Africa, Lucille animatedly replied, "Oh no, no, no, I am *African American*, not African! I don't want to take anything away from that, especially since everybody here is all into Africa now, but I know I'm African American. I don't know anything about Africa and all of that. I live here, in America."[8] Lucille's reference that everyone is "all into Africa now" suggests that positive identification with Africa has become increasingly popular among lowcountry residents—a feature I have also observed over the years. Lucille does not appear to harbor anti-African sentiments, nor does she seem in any way opposed to others maintaining a strong relationship with their African heritage. Yet she expresses a desire to distance herself from any connection with Africa beyond being an African descendent in a very literal sense. Lucille's efforts to disassociate may have been the result of the negative associations reflected in the common use of the terms Gullah and Geechee, which for many residents are historically equated with being "primitive." Although Lucille recalled learning that she was from Africa at a very early age, she feels only a minimal bond to Africa because she grew up in the lowcountry and because her family "did not focus at all on our African heritage." Lucille's perspective best represents the point of view held by many of the younger populations of Gullah/Geechee descendants, who appear less interested in making any ties with an explicitly African heritage and are minimally engaged in actively calling on the memory of Africa to talk to the dead.

Beyond recognition of an African ancestry, Roberta, Faye, and Lucinda do not make any efforts to understand the details of their presumed relation to Africa. When asked whether they considered themselves African or African American, or when invited to identify whether or not specific practices were or could be African, they could not speak conclusively on the matter and appeared disinterested in the idea that there were identifiable connections. One exception was Faye, who described how Black History Month was an important time for her to explicitly celebrate her African ancestry. Every Sunday in February, Faye would don an "African style" dress or blouse, and she sponsored a "Black History Celebration" program at Wesley UMC. She utilized the program to commemorate the African American community's rich African heritage. She commented, "I feel like February is my chance to contribute to that history, but that's about all I do." Despite their seeming ambivalence, however, Faye, Roberta, and Lucinda appear to represent a generation of women who are not willing to completely disassociate themselves from their African heritage, but who only call upon the memory of Africa as a means of talking to the dead intermittently.

For Ruth, the ease with which she accepts a connection with Africa originated from her own understanding of her ancestry but also through her membership at St. James Presbyterian. As a mission-based church that emphasizes "introducing the unchurched to salvation in Jesus Christ," St. James also provides "comprehensive educational programs" to church members and the extended community. At the core of these programs, which are centered upon "Christian and cultural education ministry," is teaching lowcountry residents about their African heritage, encouraging members to celebrate that heritage, and invoking the memory of Africa as a sacred space. St. James devotes approximately 5 percent of its million-dollar budget to promote programs that increase knowledge about lowcountry-African connections. It also provides students from Nigeria and Ghana with financial support to attend college in South Carolina, and to subsidize biannual mission trips to South Africa. Within St. James, there is an intentional incorporation of African material culture, including art and dress. On any given Sunday, one will witness women, men, and children in traditional church attire of suits, ties, hats, and dresses and informal attire including khakis, summer dresses, and sandals. One can find as many members (including the ministerial staff) dressed in traditional African and African-themed garments such as Kente-patterned ties, hats, stoles, full wrapper dresses, and the like.[9] The acceptance of African culture and dress through programs, missions, or sponsorship in no way quantifies the perceived "Africanness" of the church, but it directly affects the ways parishioners and visitors understand the importance of Africa within the life of the church. This recognition by the leaders of St. James has permeated Ruth's personal life, and has affirmed the sense of openness she has toward remembering Africa as a sacred place, which she does with some regularity.

Intentionally calling upon the image of Africa has particular significance for Yenenga, whose earliest memories of Africa as an important geographic space began at an early age when her parents and grandparents told her stories about their history as enslaved people "brought over from Africa."

Interestingly, it was Yenenga's art of storytelling that truly ignited what has become a substantive relationship with the memory of Africa. In the late 1990s, Yenenga began receiving more requests for her storytelling. As a result, she took the initiative to "educate herself" about Gullah/Geechee history so that she could sharpen her craft. While she has given full credit to the stories passed on to her from her parents and grandparents, she made it clear that she "had to go about doin' things the right way." For Yenenga, the "right way" meant going to the local library to supplement her knowledge about her African ancestry, the structure of local plantations throughout James Island and Charleston, the history of black and white relations, and other aspects of her culture that she personally observed. It also confirmed what family members taught her. Yenenga's research efforts were fueled by her desire to gather greater details, and it was during her process of discovery that she "really came to better understand our history in the lowcountry."

Of all the women, Yenenga most readily calls upon the memory of Africa, so much so that she has incorporated a strong association with an African identity into her life. While Yenenga acknowledges that the influence of her parents and grandparents, as well as her natural gift, helped her to become a storyteller, it was her participation on a twenty-one-day mission trip in 1992 that ignited her professional commitment to storytelling. When she visited South Africa, she "didn't feel anyway strange" and indicated that she experienced a profound sense of being "home." While there, she was given a Zulu name that she then incorporated into her professional and personal life.[10] Once she returned from South Africa, a fellow church member called on her to replace someone at Charleston's MOJA Arts Festival. This sequence of events confirmed both her God-given purpose of communicating stories and the strong connection she felt to Africa while she visited. Thus, in addition to linking her to her personal family history, Yenenga recognizes that storytelling is for her a connection to her African roots. As she frequently reminded me, "storytelling is a part of Africa." She utilizes the term "griot" to refer to her role as a "living archive" in the lowcountry and embraces the role of storytellers commonplace in the Islamic regions of the Sudan, Senegal, and Guinea.[11] Yenenga's service to St. James Presbyterian gave her the opportunity to travel to South Africa and facilitated her profession as a local storyteller.

The recognition of Africa as a home and sacred space to which she feels intimately connected has single-handedly changed Yenenga's life. She continues to communicate with the people she met in Africa "'til this day."

She has an adopted daughter from Nigeria, and desires to return to Africa not as a part of the church's itinerary, but on her own to visit her adopted daughter's family and the friends she met during her first trip.[12] Her connection to an African heritage is very strong and, in its own way, embodies the ways that culture becomes tied to market forces, or cultural commodification. When asked whether she considers herself African, she replied, "Yes, I'm very, very much connected to Africa you know, and the ancestral thing. I just feel like a part, *very much* a part. And so nowadays after you know I got really connected with my heritage, all white paintings came down." That her relationship to Africa is so deeply tied to her connection in "the ancestral thing" indicates how her memories of Africa continue to speak to her. It also echoes Lucille's critique, "everyone's all into Africa now," or that acceptance of African cultural elements is now increasingly fashionable in the lowcountry.

Yenenga's incorporation of African culture and positive identification with Africa is evident in her personal relationships and her use of an African name. It is also prevalent in her home and style of dress. She frequently wears dashikis and wrappers that bear images of Africa and color patterns of various African nation-state flags.[13] She stopped having her hair professionally straightened and began to wear her hair in a dreadlock style because "they wear natural hairstyles in Africa." During my initial visit to her home in 2003, I was struck by the amount of African-themed artwork. Before I could inquire about the art she commented, "Of course you can see that my house is very Afrocentric."[14] The walls of every room were decorated with African-themed pictures. Near the entrance to the main hallway, there were tables that held various contemporary artworks, all of which contained black or African characters. Around the front and sides of the tables were various items—sweetgrass baskets, bowls, vases, and a water basin a friend purchased for her while visiting Accra, Ghana. Also placed around and upon the tables was a large collection of musical instruments, including two medium-sized Djembe drums, a large Ngoma and a Goumbe, an ornate clay Udu drum, two rain sticks, a small marimba, and a bamboo flute.[15] The tables in her sitting area held various sculptures and dolls, many of which have on wrapper-style dresses. One particularly noticeable doll, which stood about nine inches tall, was made of beads. It had a long red cape with black accents on the collar and white dots speckled throughout. The face was beaded red with a white nose and white eyes, and had a gold three-tiered neck ring resembling the dress of the Maasai tribe of Kenya. The bottom of the doll had a line of blue beads, then a mix of green that looked like steps on its "dress." Yenenga is very proud of her art and music collection and the ways that one can easily see her ties to Africa. Though seemingly romanticized, Yenenga's valuation reveals how Africa serves as a historical reality that has directly impacted her lived identity. For Yenenga, being connected to Africa is not just about her ability to use a craft she has inherited to talk to the dead. It is also about her living out that relationship daily.

Beatrice's ties to Africa are similar to Yenenga's insofar as they have been influenced by her craft. When her grandmother taught her how to create baskets she also explained to Beatrice that their craft was one that originated in Africa and had been passed down in their family for generations. The memory of Africa as a sacred geographic space has therefore always been a part of how she uses her craft to talk to the dead. To celebrate that connection, Beatrice has included the following description in the pamphlet that is always on her table of baskets:

> Sweetgrass basketmaking has been a part of the Mount Pleasant community for more than 300 years. Brought to the area by slaves, who came from West Africa, basketmaking is a traditional art form, which has been passed on from generation to generation. Today, it is one of the oldest art forms of African origin in the United States. Mount Pleasant South Carolina enjoys the distinction of being the only place where this particular type of basketry is practiced. Here the descendents of slaves from West Africa continue the tradition.

Ms. Bea's pamphlet also provides a description of the relationship between the art of basketry and the plantation system. In this way, Beatrice acknowledges links between crafts in the lowcountry and West Africa, while celebrating efforts to ensure the continuation of sweetgrass basketry. "With the decline of the plantation system, black families acquired land and started a new way of life. Because they felt that this basket making tradition was an important part of their cultural heritage, and that future generations would be able to retain an identity with Africa through the baskets, they kept the tradition alive."[16]

This idea of keeping the tradition alive again reflects the confluence of past and present for these women, and how that merging occurs through remembering and talking to the dead. Beatrice and Yenenga utilized research to supplement the histories they had always been told, and their occupations have made them more knowledgeable of African influences on their crafts. The information they acquired from their explorations was, however, not exactly new to them. They had always been aware of their ancestry because of what they had been told by the people around them. Yenenga and Beatrice had been living with the memory of African connections for as long as they had practiced their crafts, and especially as they used their crafts to talk to the dead.

Certainly, each woman's personal experience has shaped her knowledge of Africa, the way she remembers Africa and allows that remembering to communicate with her ancestors, and the ways she chooses to integrate (or not) remembering Africa in her personal life. Lucinda, Roberta, and Faye see the importance of remembering Africa with some regularity and, at the very least, commemorate Africa and recall the significance of Africa in their lives annually during the Emancipation Service. For Yenenga, Beatrice, and Ruth, their frequent invocation of the memory of Africa has resulted in the acceptance and incorporation of some African or Afrocentric practices, beliefs, and material items. Lucille, however, embraces the memory of Africa only in a very basic sense, and allows that connection to remind her of her relationships with her ancestors. These variations among the women reveal subtle differences in how the memory of Africa continues to live in contemporary Gullah/Geechee communities. These distinctions are most important, however, because of their implications for the continuation of talking to the dead.

Whether by articulating religious and cultural practices and having African antecedents or through efforts to identify African geographic origins, scholarship has always described Africa as a significant cultural marker for lowcountry blacks. Rather than focusing on cultural continuities, I have argued that remembering Africa as a sacred historical space is a spiritual practice and means of talking to the dead. Yet similarities in attitudes toward remembering Africa by Lucille, Faye, Roberta, and Lucinda suggest that the practice may not be as important as it once was, or at the very least, that lowcountry residents do not see invoking the memory of Africa as necessary for talking to the dead. That there is a clear desire to move away from Africa's sacred significance for Lucille, and in some ways for Roberta, Faye, and Lucinda—who only actively remember Africa in select ways—suggests that the importance of remembering Africa is diminishing. At the same time, Yenenga's role as a community storyteller, Beatrice's craft as a basket maker, and the ways St. James Presbyterian invokes the importance of remembering Africa for Ruth have helped them place ongoing importance on remembering Africa. The disparities between these women are significant because of what they suggest about the consequence of having cultural markers that emphasize the importance of remembering

Africa as a means of talking to the dead, and the significance of calling on the memory of Africa with some frequency or regularity. If something that was once such an integral component of talking to the dead is no longer as significant, then it becomes increasingly important to find new ways to remember Africa.

I do not believe that the variations in the importance the women place on remembering Africa means that talking to the dead is no longer being actively practiced. Rather, many of the women seem to be comfortable with remembering in other forms such as through the recollection of their seeking experiences, through the ancestral connections they make through music and singing traditions, and through the dreams they have where they encounter the dead. In these forms, remembering as a means of talking to the dead is alive and well in the lowcountry. Despite the ways this study has moved me beyond efforts to identify Africanisms in lowcountry culture, I cannot deny that the pervasive belief in talking to the dead, as exemplified in the lives of these seven women, is at the very least influenced by the African worldviews that have remained implicit in lowcountry culture. This does not mean that I identify talking to the dead as an "African" practice. I have discovered, unlike the preponderance of scholars of lowcountry culture, that the Africanness or non-Africanness of their practices is not what is of greatest importance to these women. With little exception, the women are uninterested in whether or not their belief in the living dead is African. What is most significant is their belief in God and the spirit world, and their intimate connections to it. To them, talking to the dead is about the *value* and *meaning* it brings to their lives as Christian women who are unwilling to put the intimate relationships they maintained with the living aside after their loved ones die. Talking to the dead by way of remembering serves a powerful purpose, for it allows them to hold on to their past while living in a present that is rapidly changing. These women use talking to the dead to navigate how their unique culture is facing an increasing threat of commodification.

The Commodification of Gullah/Geechee Culture

The lowcountry is advertised as a historic community that embraces a deep and rich history. Charleston's motto, for example, is "The City Where History Lives." The bulk of Charleston's multimillion dollar economy derives from the tourism industry rather than local taxes or development projects. This includes the twenty-day Piccolo Spoleto Festival of the Arts, which runs annually from Memorial Day Weekend through mid-June and draws more than one hundred thousand tourists and local visitors. It also includes a plethora of celebrated venues, such as the City Market and local museums, and a host of events designed to provide the tourists with a taste of the low-country's valuable history.[17] The celebration of history has also influenced the attitudes of lowcountry blacks toward Africa. As Lucille's previous comment "everybody here is all into Africa now" suggests, lowcountry residents have taken a greater interest in establishing African connections. While a general interest in celebrating and understanding one's cultural heritage is certainly a motivating factor, the profitability of embracing an "authentic" African identity has also contributed to these efforts.

Throughout the lowcountry, tourist boards, local organizations, and residents alike have recognized that celebrating the contributions of Africans and African Americans are highly marketable and profitable enterprises. As a result, more tours, museums, and festivals devoted exclusively to commemorating the relationship between Africans, African Americans, and lowcountry history have been created.[18] Among the most popular events are the Annual Hilton Head Gullah Celebration, which has occurred throughout the month of February for the past fifteen years, and as previously noted, the Gullah Festival in Beaufort, which has been held annually during Memorial Day Weekend since 1986, and now distinguishes itself from other celebrations by referring to itself as the *Original* Gullah Festival.[19] In September 2010, I received an unsolicited flyer from Stress Free Travel in Philadelphia, promoting "A Historic Gullah/Geechee Vacation." For nearly eight hundred dollars per person, participants could take "four trips for the price of one" to explore Gullah/Geechee culture, which included excursions to Beaufort and St. Helena Island, Charleston, and Myrtle Beach as well as an outing in Savannah, Georgia. The cost of the trip, which ran from May 25 to May 30, 2011, also included roundtrip travel by way of a private motor coach, hotel accommodations throughout the locales, at least one meal per day (usually breakfast or lunch), and admission to the Original Gullah Festival. Also part of the package were private tours on St. Helena Island, a visit to St. Helena's praise house, participation in a waterfront Sunday worship service, and trips to non-Gullah/Geechee locales such as the House of Blues in Myrtle Beach and Paula Deen's restaurant in Savannah.[20]

In the Beaufort area, Penn Center hosts a plethora of year-round events to promote Gullah culture. This includes its Heritage Days Celebration, which utilizes art exhibits and performances to "showcase the unique cultural heritage of the Gullah people of the Sea Islands." Penn Center has also developed a Gullah Studies Summer Institute. This two-week workshop offers courses, seminars, and lectures to educate academicians, local residents, and tourists alike about the history of the center, its relationship to the Civil Rights Movement, and other features of Gullah culture including the Gullah dialect, local cooking practices, textile designs, and folk customs. For $2,400, anyone interested in learning more about the culture can participate in the institute. The fees cover tuition and room and board.

In Charleston, the MOJA Arts Festival, a ten-day affair that celebrates African American and Caribbean art, also runs annually from September to October. Similarly, year-round exhibitions at the Gibbes Museum of Art, the Old Slave Mart Museum, Gallery Chuma, and the Avery Research Center for African-American History and Culture have flourished into landmark events and key tourist locales. The Gullah Tours, created by lowcountry native Alphonso Brown and operating from downtown Charleston, is increasingly becoming a sought-after tour for visitors.[21] For two hours and a twelve- to eighteen-dollar fare, tourists can ride an air-conditioned bus and see sites such as the Underground Railroad, sweetgrass basket makers (including Ms. Bea, whose stand is visible from the bus), the Old Slave Mart, and the presumed home of Denmark Vesey. For $375 a tour can be arranged with a private chartered bus, which allows visitors to actually get off the bus and actually "step-on" the grounds of the tour stops. Gullah storytelling is also available upon request. According to the advertisement for the Gullah Tours, these "true stories focus on the Gullah language, culture, and music. They are entertaining in nature, with bits of humor, yet remain sincere and accurate in their history and portrayal of the Gullah people."[22] All of these events, tours, and exhibitions are open to the public, but they also involve various fees or requests for donations. Hence, while efforts to celebrate and preserve the culture are important, the emphasis on fundraising for all of these activities encourages one to question whether or not Gullah/Geechee culture is for sale. It also leaves one wondering whether lowcountry inhabitants believe that marketing and selling Gullah/Geechee culture is the only way to ensure its continuation.

In 1987 Patricia Jones-Jackson published *When Roots Die*, one of the earliest assessments of increased commercialism in the lowcountry. The tourist industry has had a tremendous impact upon the ways that Gullah/Geechee culture has become commodified. Many African American residents—including the women in this study—have noticed increasing numbers of tourists, journalists, and writers entering the lowcountry. These visitors often express explicit interest in seeing and talking with the "African" people of the lowcountry. African American residents of the lowcountry are by and large presented as being proud of their African heritage. Indeed, there is a sense of pride for many lowcountry black residents, which is in some regards related to their histories as African descendants. As Lucille's narrative and clear disassociation from an African identity suggests, however, incorporating this history in a prideful manner is not always the case. The sense of pride many feel, as lowcountry resident William Saunders has suggested, may simply reflect a general sense of self-respect unrelated to an African past. "People from the universities have been writing about these islands, about African heritage, and all that. I would say that as far as the islanders were concerned, I don't think that there was much pride in heritage of the past, but that they were proud, period. I don't think that they used to connect themselves with Africa, you know, 'Roots' type stuff, but they were and are just real people who show their heritage."[23]

Whatever the source, visitors—especially white visitors—expect to see "authentic" Gullah culture and will readily pay the prices for tours, exhibitions, and sites to achieve their goal of getting a glimpse of the people who have historically been characterized and are now marketed as "the most direct repository of living African culture to be found anywhere in North America."[24] Whites, however, are not the only consumers, even if they make up the majority of the lowcountry's tourist economy. Black visitors who frequent Alphonso Brown's "Gullah Tours" also consume Gullah/Geechee culture, and in so doing, are actually paying to see and remember the lowcountry *as its own* figurative home or sacred space that connects blacks throughout the diaspora. Hence, the objectives of the people producing and reproducing the culture (whether they are black or white) are increasingly becoming focused on lifting up the culture's more marketable features. This brings the relationship between the celebration, revitalization, and preservation of Gullah/Geechee culture and commodification into question.[25] The lines are fine and becoming finer as increased efforts to advertise lowcountry culture as a "living African culture" have meant that organizations are going to greater lengths to substantiate certain features of lowcountry African American life. These features—including the Gullah dialect, lowcountry food practices, and the lowcountry clap—become marketed and sold as "real" examples of a distinctively "African" heritage at the expense of other equally important customs. The implications are tremendous and suggest that if the practice of talking to the dead is not viewed by those creating and sustaining lowcountry market economies as an important aspect of Gullah/Geechee life, it too may succumb to market forces and become less significant. Or, worse, if deemed viable to market to consumer populations, the practice of talking to the dead may end up being for sale.

This is an especially salient issue for Yenenga and Beatrice, whose economic livelihoods depend predominantly on tourism and who wrestle with the implications of cultural commodification on a day-to-day basis. Ms. Bea advertises the opportunity to purchase a sweetgrass basket as a chance to purchase a part of authentic African culture. On the front of her business's pamphlet the following phrase can be found:

SWEETGRASS BASKETS: A PROUD TRADITION, A VALUABLE INVEST-
MENT

Ms. Bea recognizes that while she is offering people a part of her heritage, she must also ensure that she makes enough money to support her family and sustain her trade—a trade that is ever-changing due to the ecological shifts that make acquiring sweetgrass increasingly difficult. By marketing sweetgrass baskets both as a tradition and an investment, she justifies her price list. The larger baskets, which can be utilized as laundry baskets, magazine holders, or as a decorative piece in one's home, begin at $500. Tourists witness the intricate weaving process required to make the baskets and observe Beatrice creating the baskets by hand. They also admire the beauty of baskets. For many, however, the prices are exorbitant. While sitting with Ms. Bea at her stand, I witnessed countless visitors express utter astonishment at their cost. Beatrice, however, does not believe that she sells her baskets at a high enough price to compensate for the length of time they take to produce. Even the smallest basket, which is capable of holding a few small pieces of jewelry, a set of keys, or coins, can take anywhere from four to six hours to complete.[26] The prices of the baskets are also driven by market factors. Downtown Charleston is home to many basket makers, most of whom position themselves in or near the City Market. As a result, Beatrice has to reduce her prices to compete with other basket makers and to ensure that she makes a sale. I have not incorporated pictures of Ms. Bea's products to protect her identity, but also because she made it clear that she did not want to have any pictures of her or her baskets included in this book. Beatrice never felt comfortable providing a picture because "too many people just want to take pictures of us now." When I later inquired about her apparent discomfort, she informed me that she has had experiences where visitors would take pictures without her permission, and it would show up in a local newspaper. She tries to manage the increasing commodification of her work and image.

Yenenga also markets her stories as a glimpse of the past and a means of preserving the rich traditions of Gullah/Geechee culture. Storytelling is, however, how Yenenga makes her living. As a result, Yenenga has at times found herself in a personal and professional quandary. Although she frequently performs at African American churches, predominately black schools, and the various festivals devoted to celebrating African American culture, Yenenga's largest and most financially lucrative audiences are predominately white. At the beginning of her story "Intro," Yenenga makes a statement that one could easily miss. She says, "'Cause listen yeh now, let me tell ounnah somethin', Buckra like for hear dem story, an when Ah done tulk 'em, Buckra got my check!"[27] In this quip lies the heart of the cost of cultural commodification. Yenenga tells stories because she is a gifted storyteller, because she loves to do it, and because it is a cherished part of her heritage. Yet she is clear that storytelling is her livelihood and the primary way she makes money—a feat that is most readily achieved by telling the stories to white people. Yenenga at times feels torn by this discrepancy. She describes, "I love speaking to our people, you know, but they don't pay as much, they just don't pay as much. White folks seem to be more willing to pay to learn about us than we are." Although Yenenga has never shared how much she financially profits from being a Gullah storyteller, she has noted that she has done "very well in the business."

In the lowcountry, cultural commodification goes hand in hand with commercial development. Beatrice has experienced the negative, rapid effects of commercialization and commodification because it has jeopardized her trade. Today, sweetgrass basket makers are challenged by one particularly dramatic change—the limited supply of sweetgrass. As the development of resorts has increased, the natural marshland habitat is being rapidly destroyed. Similarly, construction of private, gated communities that prohibit access from "outsiders" makes it difficult for Beatrice and other sweetgrass basket makers to physically acquire sweetgrass. In short, "natural habitats of sweetgrass need to be preserved, protected, or relocated if this industry is to continue. The basketmaking community will need help from local governments to continue to sell baskets."[28] Thus while the rising tourist industry in the lowcountry positively affects Beatrice in that it potentially increases her income, it makes sweetgrass more difficult to acquire.

Although blacks continue to outnumber whites within many lowcountry communities, the historic "black majority" is swiftly diminishing. According to June Thomas, the dramatic changes of African American communities, which included shifts from being predominately agricultural to comprising uneducated and minimally skilled laborers, were "brought about by the new era of corporate tourism, complete with large-scale resort and hotel ventures." Hilton Head, which is located approximately forty minutes southwest of Lucille's home in Beaufort, fits this description: "On Hilton Head Island, once entirely populated by Gullah blacks, resort development has burgeoned since the early 1960s, and all the resort hotels, villas, restaurants, and golf courses have relied on black employees for all of their ten or fifteen years of existence. While blacks on the other islands have not yet been entirely pulled into the tourist sector, but have likely instead worked in hospitals, military bases, and households of Charleston or Beaufort, resort development is spreading and has already become a major source of employment for black sea islanders."[29] Unlike the 1980s, when Thomas initially provided this description, resort development and influx of white residents are no longer limited to Hilton Head. Changes in the racial, economic, and geographic landscape of the lowcountry are occurring at an alarming rate. The building of bridges to connect smaller barrier islands to larger islands and inland locales have resulted in greater access for African American residents to better education and job opportunities. Yet rapid development has led to the commercialization of entire islands and communities.[30] "Highways, golf courses and hotels have replaced traditional graveyards and farms. Many Gullah people were forced to sell their land and move away, unable to afford the rising taxes that came with resort and suburban development. . . . Another factor in the migration out of the lowcountry [is] a tradition called 'heirs property.' . . . [O]ften, family members who have left the lowcountry are willing to sell valuable land to the highest bidder, while heirs still on the land desperately want to hold on to property that has been in the family for generations."[31]

On James Island, increasing numbers of whites have dramatically transformed the communities. When asked about transitions in land ownership and residency on James Island, Yenenga animatedly replied,

Well gyal I tell you Buckra dem done move in so fast, and the word Buckra that mean white man. Buckra dem done move in here so fast until I really don't know you'll have to look that one up you know, a little betta now 'cause they just, they move in and kinda move us out a little bit you know. . . . Yeah so, I remember when all these places useda been dut road, main highway ain't been nuttin but dut road but every ting now paved! You know, so they're really movin' in, a lot of them you see, you know they takin' over the waterfront property. . . . I remember when

I used to sell meat, cut meat and sell meats and ice cream and all those things, but you see, Buckra done bring all the supamarkets now. Everybody get in they car now and you know, shoot out to the supamarkets.[32]

Since James Island, like Moncks Corner and Mt. Pleasant, is so close to Charleston, newer residents purchase waterfront and inland properties due to the moderate cost of living. As James Island and other inland areas of the lowcountry continue to move toward development and suburbanization, the effects of the change are sure to be felt by local black inhabitants, who are rapidly losing their ownership of land and who, because of minimal education and labor skills, are increasingly at the low end of competitive job placement. Yenenga worries that like the ancestors, who picked cotton and grew rice, blacks of the island will continue to "make Buckra rich" by selling and losing their inherited properties.[33]

Yenenga has felt the effects of development in the lowcountry personally, a process she calls "legalized thievery." She owns an undeveloped three-acre plot of land on James Island that has been in her family for generations. In 2005, the property taxes amounted to $700. Only a year later, the tax had increased to an unbelievable $7,000. Fortunately, Yenenga was able to raise the money and paid the taxes on time. She is even making efforts to contest the tax increase. Most stories comparable to Yenenga's do not, however, end on such a positive note, and the lands and homes that have remained in African American families for generations are rapidly being bought out, sold, or overtaxed. Beatrice is also concerned about the impact of modern development efforts for property reasons. She angrily quipped, "They takin' all de property and openin' up de highways!" After expressing her discontent with the situation in the lowcountry she immediately commented, "We livin' in a time—a perishin' time, we have to pray, that's why you have to know how to pray, and how to put in a storeroom, cause sometimes you ain't gon be able to do it, you gotta be prayed up." It is her faith in God that sustains her in the midst of the dramatic shifts in land ownership, the increased property taxes, the influx of white residents, and the changing urban landscape that has reduced her access to the resources needed to sustain her trade. While Beatrice's faith expresses a sense of hopelessness in the possibility of change, it reflects an acceptance of an unchangeable situation that can best be met by maintaining belief in God's power to sustain those who have faith. The costs of these commercial changes are not solely economic but have had substantial religio-cultural effects. As Jones-Jackson noted, these "forces are motivating a break in cultural traditions, an upheaval of social patterns, and a general disruption of the old norms, all of which are now in some danger of becoming lost."[34]

The Protection of Gullah/Geechee Culture

The notion that Gullah/Geechee culture is becoming "lost" is a concept that has long been a part of lowcountry history. Whether recounted as generational transitions as in Julie Dash's filmic narrative *Daughters of the Dust* or as Jones-Jackson prophetically captured in her monograph title *When Roots Die*, the notion that these communities are "under threat" has been in place for almost as long as people have been trying to identify Africanisms within Gullah/Geechee culture. The impact of increasing visibility and accessibility of these communities—their dwellings, cultural practices, food, dialect, and even property—has resulted in their growing popularity and has drawn more individuals and businesses from outside of the lowcountry. As Beatrice's and Yenenga's experiences confirm, their very livelihood is being threatened by changes in the economic, social, and cultural landscapes. While tourism has led to the increased celebration, profitability, and commodification of Gullah/Geechee culture, those transitions do not come without great personal cost. It is clear that the continuation of the features of Gullah/Geechee culture that makes them unique hangs in the balance. J. Lorand Matory paints a picture of the delicate equilibrium between the loss and continuation of Gullah/Geechee culture:

> I will consider the uncertain evidence that the recent dispersion and out-migration of some Gullah/Geechees threatens the endurance of their creole language. However, I will also consider evidence that out-migration and subsequent return, along with tourism, have precipitated an unprecedented degree of cultural self-awareness, canonization of tradition, and pride, as well as profit, in Gullah/Geechee speech, foodways, handicrafts, and history. "Gullah/Geechee culture" as such is a product of interaction and return, and, far from dying out, "Gullah/Geechee culture" has become a potent weapon in the struggle to maintain landownership and access to resources.[35]

Matory's comment is provocative because of his acknowledgment of the exchange that happens when a community experiences a type of cultural resurgence as a result of tourism—and its specific effect on the Gullah/Geechee dialect. Remiss in his statement, however, is another aspect of the cost of the "canonization of tradition." If, in fact, outmigration, the return of lowcountry residents to their family "home," and tourism are viewed as potent weapons, what then are we to make of the spiritual costs that individuals like Beatrice and Yenenga, whose financial lives depend on the tourist industry, pay in their efforts to maintain access to resources? These women have a conflicted sense of their skills and their financial payoff. Yenenga brought this up in one of our conversations.

> Yenenga: . . . You gonna tell these people what kinda car I drive? Why? Dat's my business!
>
> LeRhonda: There's no judgment from me in that Yenenga, I promise. It's just that you drive a Jaguar—in many circles that is considered to be a luxury car. It gives a sense of your economic status.
>
> Y: I just dunno why dey need ta know all dat! What dey gonna think?
>
> L: They're gonna think that you've made good money in your life— enough money to buy a Jaguar. They may even think you make good money tellin' your Gullah stories. And there ain't nothin' wrong with making money doing what you're good at.
>
> Y: Well, it fuh true. But dat don't stop if from hurtin' my soul.
>
> L: What do you mean?
>
> Y: I see what I do as a gift, but it's a gift dey pay me for. And sometimes, that really just hurts my soul 'cause I shouldn't haveta do it for pay. People should be wantin' to learn this stuff, and now I gotta charge 'em what I can afford to keep eatin'. It's just a shame.[36]

This exchange does not diminish the importance of factors such as increased cultural self-awareness and cultural pride. Yet it is clear that positions that celebrate the cultural memory and commemoration of Gullah/ Geechee heritage exist alongside the creation of personal, ethical quandaries about just how much or which parts of the culture should be embraced and how that popularization can lead to commodification.

We will not be able to determine the long-term ramifications of such ethical dilemmas—often excluded from conversations about the preservation and celebration of cultural heritages—for some time. There is, however, another aspect of the celebration of Gullah/Geechee heritage in the midst of its endangerment: the recognition of these communities' need for protection and the financial and logistical support to ensure it. The Gullah/ Geechee communities of South Carolina's lowcountry have recently been recognized by Congress as one of over forty "National Heritage Areas"— places where a variety of resources (historic, natural, cultural, and scenic) are viewed as making important human and geographic contributions to the nation. After a lengthy study by the National Park Service, the Gullah/Geechee coast was named, "one of the 11 Most Endangered Historic Sites in America because they fear encroachment on these communities will result in the extinction of the culture, its language and customs."[37] National Heritage Areas are deemed "representative of the American experience through the physical features that remain and the traditions that have evolved in them. These regions are acknowledged by Congress for their capacity to tell important stories about our nation. Continued use of National Heritage Areas by people whose traditions helped to shape the landscape enhances their significance."[38] In South Carolina, Beaufort, Charleston, Colleton, Georgetown, Horry, Jasper, and parts of Berkeley and Dorchester counties are now protected under the enactment of the Gullah/Geechee Cultural Heritage Act, which was passed by the 109th Congress on October 9, 2006, as part of the larger National Heritage Areas Act. Led by the efforts of South Carolina Congressman James E. Clyburn, a native of Sumter, the Gullah/Geechee Cultural Heritage Act was one of ten newly recognized "heritage areas" deemed both important and "endangered" enough for the federal government to protect.

> The Gullah/Geechee Cultural Heritage Act has three specific purposes: (1) recognize the important contributions made to American culture and history by African Americans known as the Gullah/Geechee who settled in the coastal counties of South Carolina, Georgia, North Carolina, and Florida; (2) assist State and local governments and public and private entities in South Carolina, Georgia, North Carolina, and Florida in interpreting the story of the Gullah/Geechee and preserving Gullah/Geechee folklore, arts, crafts, and music; and (3) assist in identifying and preserving sites, historical data, artifacts, and objects associated with the Gullah/Geechee for the benefit and education of the public.[39]

The Gullah/Geechee Cultural Heritage Act ensures that the areas covered receive $1 million in annual funding over ten years. Since its enactment, a fifteen-member commission has been established, with Charleston as its home base, and its job is to help federal, state, and local authorities implement a management plan for the Heritage Corridor (map 5.1). In South Carolina, the counties included cover the areas in which all seven of the women reside.

How the efforts of the Gullah/Geechee Cultural Heritage Act will directly help women like Yenenga and Beatrice remains to be seen, especially since they are unaware of this act and do not know the specific details of what the

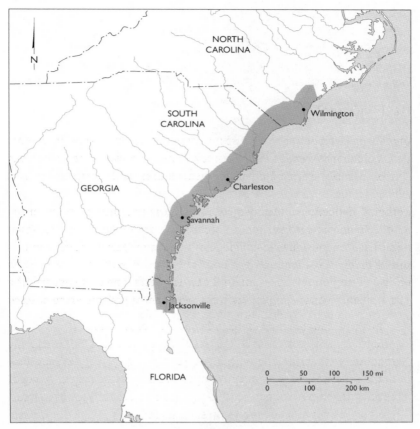

Map 5.1. Gullah/Geechee Heritage Act Corridor.

act should do at the grassroots level. Beatrice and Yenenga continue to practice their traditions of storytelling and basketmaking on an individual basis
and are unaffiliated with any formal organization beyond their churches.
As such, it is unclear how they can even make the members of the commis-
sion aware of their existence. To date, they have not received implicitly or explicitly identifiable benefits from the act, and although they both appear to
be plausible beneficiaries, they have yet to see any specific effects from the
act itself individually or within their respective communities of Mt. Pleasant
and James Island.

In a press release about the Gullah/Geechee Cultural Heritage Act, Congressman Clyburn publicly identified personal motivations for supporting the act, stating: "I felt the need to act on the Park service's recommen-
dations quickly so we can begin their implementation before the Gullah/

Geechee culture becomes more endangered. . . . [T]he Gullah/Geechee culture is the last vestige of the fusion of African and European languages and traditions brought to these coastal areas. I cannot sit idly by and watch an entire culture disappear that represents my heritage and the heritage of those that look like me."[40] Despite the efforts of the Gullah/Geechee Cultural Heritage Act, the positive effects of increased tourism, amplified cultural pride, and broader recognition of the importance of Gullah/Geechee culture, conversations about the potential erasure of Gullah/Geechee culture persist. This is in part due to the fact that many blacks of the lowcountry—including two of the women in this study—continue to be denied the economic resources necessary to ensure the continuity of their cultural practices. For Beatrice, the sweetgrass she needs to continue her own stand is not any easier to access. In fact, although she is "retired," she still on occasion "goes to clean house" for financial support. Yenenga is retired also, but struggles with accommodating the needs of the community and meeting her own fiscal responsibilities. That these seventy-year-old women continue to wrestle in these rote economic terms sheds greater light on a statement made by lowcountry resident and scholar Marquetta Goodwine: "Should the Gullah/Geechee culture vanish from this earth, it may be due not to their desire to forsake their traditions, but rather to the failure to empower socioeconomic and political institutions to ensure their collective survival."[41]

Gullah/Geechee Women and the Survival of Religion

Remembering is a way of celebrating the dialect, religio-cultural rituals, and other features that make the coastal and low-lying areas of South Carolina distinct. This is the case even when traditions such as the ring shout, seeking, and the act of invoking Africa are no longer practiced in exactly the same ways, for remembering them is as important as performing the practices themselves. Celebrating these customs is embodied in the daily use of the Gullah dialect as well as shouting during worship services. Invoking the Spirit during singing and worship honors the unique history of an African American microcosm where music facilitates a special connection with the Spirit of God and those who have gone before. Remembering is also a means of confirming the history of a diasporic people who have survived innumerable social and economic hardships and have relied on their belief to demonstrate how a community of people has "come this far by faith." Just as the old songs are remembered and sung, they invoke a communal past of oppression.

Within twenty years, the seeking tradition, which was so pivotal in the religious formation of the women in this study, was no longer being practiced. This is especially significant because seekin' was critical to the life of the church and to talking to the dead, for as Ruth indicates, "it *always* determined which church you would obtain membership with." Each woman identified seekin' as the process that introduced her to an intimate relationship with the God of Christianity and facilitated talking to the dead. For all the women, their continuous involvement in the church is directly linked to their participation in the process of seeking. Ruth was quite fond of the seeking process because "it brought you to that point where you realized that it's only you and God. It made you shut everything else out and you had to deal with that one on one relationship with God." The primary reason the seeking tradition ceased was because of changes in church membership practices. As Ruth pointed out, seeking could take "weeks and weeks." Ministers today are encouraged to increase membership to gain denominational financial support. They therefore no longer feel as if they have "weeks and weeks" to introduce potential members to the church before they can become members. This is especially true for churches that have larger memberships. Hence, to expedite the church membership process and make joining the church more accessible for all age groups, candidates for church membership are invited to join a church during the Invitation to Discipleship. This format of joining a church, which is also called "extending the right hand of fellowship," is common practice in a great number of Protestant American churches throughout the South. The person desiring membership will be invited by the minister to stand, walk to the front of the church, and give their right hand to the minister, indicating their desire to join. The expedition of the process of church membership has helped to increase the numbers of people who join churches. Ruth notes, "We no longer have to have these long, drawn out seekin' meetings. The people can just join and it's as easy as that. That helps me as a church leader 'cause now I can just call them up or meet with them one on one when it's convenient for everybody."

Changes in church membership practices also reflect generational differences in attitudes, and the women of this study—who represent the older generations of African American residents of the lowcountry—have particular attitudes about how "joining church" should occur. The exception among the seven women was Ruth, who has a moderate perspective on the changes of the church membership procedures. Although she greatly valued her seekin' process, she truly does not mind that becoming a church member entails a much shorter process, particularly since it makes her numerous duties as a member of St. James's ministerial staff easier to negotiate. The remaining women believe that "extending your right hand" to become a member has taken away the seriousness of church membership. According to Lucinda, "Now anyone can just go up and be a member, and it wasn't like that before, it wasn't so quick!" Similarly, Roberta commented, "oh yeah, we had to take our time at the mourner's bench! We had to lay before God and really get to know Him." Beatrice has taken these changes personally. "We 'aint give no preacher no hand and yo heart and things—ain't been no passin' ya hand and givin' ya heart. Back then, with them old people, man you can't tell them bout no hand en heart, you gotta seek! We ain't come up dat fast way, people call us that old timey way, people say that, but I'm glad. 'Cause there's a lot goin' wrong. In those days it take a village to raise a chile . . . right now a chile raisin 'e self—if you go to a parent and tell them somethin' about they child, they might slap you! Nobody raise nobody now, everybody raise dem self!" The older women's reflection on the seeking process is at times nostalgic, a reminder of the way things used to be. They also reflect, however, the dramatic changes in the way that becoming a member of a church is now perceived among younger generations. Younger church members do not seem interested in devoting a great deal of time to local churches, nor do they appear interested in going through an intricate process to become a member. The disparity between the attitudes of younger and older lowcountry residents is exemplified in a conversation I had with Christina, Yenenga's twenty-two-year-old grandniece:

LeRhonda: Do you consider yourself to be religious?
Christina: Yeah.
L: In what way?
C: Um, I consider myself to be Baptist. My mom used to tell me that everyone had to seek out their own religion. Um they would have to, there was some kind of ceremony that I don't, I don't remember the ceremony, but everyone had to go through a period of seeking out to be a Methodist, a Presbyterian, a Baptist. And my mom was a Baptist and I joined the Baptist church on the island. . . . Everyone, the older ones had to seek out their religion, and that was a whole ceremony that I, I don't know too much about, it's pretty disconnected from me.
L: You didn't have to do that?
C: No.
L: You don't think you would have wanted to?

C: (*snickers*) No, that was just their way of doing things, we don't do it like that no more![42]

While conducting field research, I was seldom able to convince people younger than thirty years of age to talk to me for any extended period about their experiences. This was the case whether before, during, or after church meetings and services, or at events outside of church. Although there were numerous young and middle-aged adults attending churches, they did not tend to linger after services, nor did they frequent religious events beyond Sunday worship. This left me with a sense that younger people harbored a sense of indifference toward local churches, for reasons that are virtually impossible to isolate.

The features that made seeking such a distinctive practice in the low-country—the result of church membership and the act of talking to the dead—have become lost between the generations. This process of change is the result of a complex system of variables. The contemporary disconnect from the seekin' tradition is directly affected by younger folks' lack of interest in the traditional practices and their interpretations that the traditions are out of style. This disconnect is also a result of the fact that older people do not openly speak about their experiences of joining the church. While spending time with the women, my inquiries about seekin' were consistently met with surprise and in some cases, suspicion. As a result, I began to initiate discussions of seekin' by revealing how I read about seeking in the work of Gullah/Geechee scholars. Once I became more familiar with the women and asked them why they did not talk about seekin' anymore, they each indicated that they felt that people were no longer interested or had forgotten about the tradition. Lucille admitted that her thirty-year-old daughter does not know that she seeked her religion because "they just don't do that anymore and they [the younger people] just don't care." There is also considerable difference in the attitudes among younger and older generations toward each other. Younger generations view elders as being old fashioned, strict, and conservative, and no longer view senior members of the communities as wise leaders or spiritual elders. Older generations—including the seven women in this study—embrace the attitude that the younger folks are indifferent and lazy. According to Yenenga, "these kids miss a lot, they ain't spiritually nothing." Even Ruth, the youngest woman in this study, has noticed a shift in how things once were and how they are now. "You learned everything in school, in the home, and in the church because it was all connected, family. So that was just the important thing that's missing today because those teachers in the schools worked with us, and the elders worked with us in the church . . . [for] the young adults, it's a different world because they don't have that. They have children, they have jobs, they have new cars . . . , they have to get down to the family issues, and so they don't spend as much time in the church as we did." Ruth attributed these discrepancies to the fact that churches are no longer appealing to youth and that they do not make conscious efforts to "meet them where they are." She noted that the church is not in their lives, which has had a dramatic effect. Disparities between age groups are not unique to cultural analyses. What is distinct in this case are the ways that differences in attitudes between generations have resulted in the drastic modification and elimination of cultural traditions.

The discontinuation of the seeking tradition has also been directly affected by the professionalization of religious leaders in the community, which has almost single-handedly transformed the face of religion in the lowcountry.[43] Ministerial professionalization—which is its own form of commodification—is important to consider as it has directly impacted a key way that the women of this study began talking to the dead. Similarly, the rapid spread of prosperity gospel throughout lowcountry churches has led to a dramatic emphasis on economic gain rather than spiritual growth. The women spoke vividly about the discontinuation of the seeking process due to changes in leadership and in educational levels within their church. Yenenga shared, "gyal . . . ain't like how y'all go to church now. Y'all jus up now an give ya hand an have a few classes. . . . The younger ministers that come from theology schools and uh, change some things." With the onset of new leadership, especially educated ministers, the process of seeking, which had once been such an integral part of church membership, was abandoned. The week after Ruth was welcomed into the church by the elders, the new pastor (who had baptized her and the others in the group after they seeked) told Ruth and the other new members, "Next week, I'd like to see y'all in confirmation class!" Ruth therefore experienced the seeking process and the first round of confirmation classes at St. James. "We had both because they weren't teaching that in the seminaries, you know they weren't teaching the seeking process. . . . And through the classes we learned about the Presbyterian Church because that was one of the things they were teaching in the seminary, he had to teach the polity, you know you had to teach about the church and . . . taught the books of the Bible. And he gave us a written test, you know, the test wasn't a dream, he gave a *written* test, you know!"

These transitions within the community have impacted the ways that women talk to the dead across generations. The most significant change is that talking to the dead has become less prominent as a mode of spiritual access among younger generations within lowcountry communities, a shift that can be attributed to several causes. First, as younger generations (including my own) are increasingly encouraged to succumb to the allure of capitalism and leave the lowcountry as soon as they can, they often depart as young, college-aged adults. This means that they frequently miss the opportunities to learn about the importance and longstanding tradition of the practice, a tradition that for each of the women in this project began as children, but became solidified in young adulthood. A second cause, which is the least prominent and typical of generational shifts, is that as the younger generations are encouraged to expand their horizons beyond their local, residential roots, many become disinterested in the custom, while others interpret talking to the dead as an outdated mode that becomes associated with their parents' and grandparents' "old way" of doing things. Third, the elimination of religious customs that facilitate talking to the dead, such as seeking, has led to a diminished emphasis on the value of the tradition.

My age and personal experiences curiously place me within this generational shift. As a child of the mid-1970s, I am roughly the age of the women's daughters (Lucille, Beatrice, and Ruth) and granddaughters (Lucinda, Faye, Yenenga, and Roberta). With the exception of Yenenga, who was not at all shocked, the women in this study were pleasantly surprised at my awareness of and openness to talking to the dead. As a lowcountry native, the ability to talk to the dead was something that my family acknowledged within me at a very young age and took seriously the older I became. This suggests that although none of the women in this project admitted it, a fourth cause for the generational shift may also be that older community members no longer speak openly about the practice because of the sense that younger members will either shun it or have a limited ability to access the experience.

Despite these changes, two of the women are leading efforts to restore or remind others of the traditions that have been lost and are at risk of being lost through dialogue, instruction, storytelling, and reenactment. Thus while seeking is virtually extinct, practices are being created to implant the tradition in the collective memories of their respective communities and to ensure that it is remembered. Yenenga has utilized storytelling to detail the seekin' process. She frequently narrates how "in the old days" people would "go out in de woods" during intense periods of prayer. Yenenga and Ruth acknowledge that features of the process continue to emerge in the religious lives of lowcountry residents, especially the use of dreams and visions to determine one's actions, roles, and purpose in life. Ruth accepted the call to preach by recounting the dream she experienced while seekin'. It has been a constant reminder that she often speaks about in her preaching engagements and work with the church. "Throughout history a lot of people received their call through dreams and, (she pauses) and thinking about dreams you stopped and you stayed all these years 'cause you remembered that dreams have power and they stay with you. And I know it was because and I truly believe it was because of that seeking . . . that part of my faith journey what help to stabilize me."[44]

Similar to Ruth's and Yenenga's personal efforts, some community groups are working to preserve the aspects of lowcountry culture directly affected by commercialization and commodification. To date, the most prominent of these local organizations is the Gullah/Geechee Sea Island Coalition (GGSIC). The GGSIC was formed in 1996 by St. Helena Island native Marquetta Goodwine, "[t]o promote and participate in the preservation of Gullah/Geechee history heritage, culture and language, to work toward the maintenance and (re)acquisition of Sea Island land/property, and to celebrate Gullah/Geechee culture through artistic and educational means by way of electronic (newsletter) and through 'grassroots scholarship,' or the inclusion of 'native voices' in representations of Gullah/Geechee culture."[45] Two additional goals of the GGSIC are to establish the Gullah/Geechee people as a distinct, self-operating nation with its own systems of governance and to save lowcountry communities from encroachment. As the organization's director, Goodwine travels throughout the lowcountry, the greater United States, and abroad to promote lowcountry culture. The organization also identifies her as "Chieftess of the Gullah/Geechee Nation" and utilizes the moniker "Queen Qwet." In this capacity she is "the selected and elected official head-of-state, liaison, and spokesperson for Gullah/Geechee people."[46] The efforts of Goodwine and the GGSIC have been far-reaching. In 2002, the GGSIC founded the International University of the Gullah/Geechee Nation, an institution offering courses that show direct linkages to Gullah/Geechee history, heritage, and cultural practices. The work of Goodwine and the GGSIC are reminiscent of Black Nationalist movements of the 1960s and 1970s because of their emphasis on nationhood, economic independence, and the establishment of strong ties to an African heritage. Yet their efforts to preserve and promote Gullah/Geechee culture—and to do it in ways that ensure its continuity without compromising the integrity of the practices or the practitioners—remain one of their many inimitable contributions.

That religion in the lowcountry, like many of the other cultural aspects of lowcountry life, is at risk is an understatement. Jones-Jackson asserts, "Even more striking than the economic consequences of development on the indigenous population of the Sea Islands has been its cultural impact. Modernization has caused severe social dislocations."[47] The practice of talking to the dead, while ongoing, is also increasingly becoming more "muted" because, as is the case with seeking, the women who have this fluid relationship with the deceased do not openly talk about their practice. In this way, it is now up to organizations such as the GGSIC, scholar-activists like Goodwine, and the women of this study who are still alive—Lucinda, Ruth, Lucille, Roberta, Beatrice, and Yenenga—to ensure the continuity and survival of these traditions. As Goodwine noted in her address at Wesley UMC's Emancipation Service in 2007, "times are changing, and we can sit here and pretend like they're not, or we can act with the power that God has given us."[48]

The survival of Gullah/Geechee religion and culture is contingent on these communities—and arguably the women in them—remembering and celebrating their histories. It also depends on having the resources they need to continue. The threats of commodification, commercialization, urbanization, and modernization become transparent when one compares the relationship between the practices that are now a significant part of low-country religion to those that once were. These changes have had a great impact on Gullah/Geechee cultural traditions, including religion, which was not specifically included as an endangered aspect of lowcountry culture in the Gullah/Geechee Cultural Heritage Act.

The Future of Talking to the Dead

This project began by raising the question, How do Gullah/Geechee women negotiate traditional practices associated with their cultural identity in the midst of significant historical and generational change? The extended answer to this question has unfolded over the progression of this work. Gullah/Geechee women have navigated histories that exclude them—histories that only minimally address their significant roles in Gullah/Geechee culture and simplify their complex narratives and experiences. These women have negotiated being part of a Christian tradition that sought to obliterate their folk customs, exclude them from leadership positions, and treat them as members of inferior standing within their churches. Gullah/Geechee women, represented by these seven women from different locales and of different denominations, rose against these challenges and carved their own spaces within their churches, which became recognized as viable, alternative places for women to learn and lead by example. These women structured their own religious, social, and cultural networks; created their own spaces; and articulated their religion and spirituality in the terms that best suited their experiences and social locations. At the communal level, they have relied upon each other and defined their identities as black southern women in ways that have felt most comfortable to their personal associations. They have seeked, they have sung, they have shouted, they have prayed, and they have remembered.

At the individual level, all seven of these women have struggled to balance their historical pasts with their presents and to traverse their personal challenges in such a way that they could survive with their faith and whole selves intact. Until her death, Faye saw her leadership roles in the church as a means of demonstrating that women could also be responsible, effective, and influential figures within their communities. Roberta's continued participation in the activities of her church ensures her connection with members of her church community and the community at large, and allows her a literal mobility that prevents a lifelong injury from immobilizing her. Ruth's activity at St. James and her calling to preach and care for the elderly guide her ongoing service to the church—a work she sees herself doing until she dies. Beatrice uses her hands to craft sweetgrass baskets to tell the story of a grandmother who was instrumental to her development and to continue a tradition of artistry that has crossed many waters. Lucinda's gift of healing others, coupled with her singing ability, transforms her reputation as a rootworker into that of a community participant who moves and connects with people in remarkably distinct ways. Yenenga uses her voice to reach masses of people who may not be aware of the historical and ongoing significance of Gullah/Geechee culture and the lasting imprint of the Gullah/Geechee upon American history.

The condensed answer to this question about how Gullah/Geechee women negotiate change is that despite the challenges and shifts that have accompanied modernity, they have continued to believe in the God that brought them "this far by faith" and to trust in the ancestral communities who in their unique communication provided them with guidance, knowledge, and peace. What has remained consistent and continues to be the hope for the preservation of lowcountry religion is the unyielding faith of women like Roberta, Lucinda, Faye, Lucille, Yenenga, Ruth, and Beatrice. As Yenenga has expressed in her short story "Intro," faith is "how we made it through. Because you know what? Times was tough. But then we couldn't dwell on them tough times like dat. We had to make a way, sometimes outta no way." Although the future of the transmission of Gullah/Geechee religious practices—including seeking, the intricate religious song traditions, the distinctively syncretic style of Gullah/Geechee religion, and talking to the dead—is yet to be determined, it remains certain that lowcountry women will play pivotal roles. As the culture keepers in the South Carolina lowcountry, Gullah/Geechee women continue to hold the keys to its survival and will directly shape the future of lowcountry religion.

Between the Living and the Dead

On March 11, 2007, I gathered with Roberta Legare, Lucinda Pinckney, and approximately 150 others to celebrate Faye Terry's homegoing service. As is custom, most of the attendees, including her six active and six honorary pallbearers, wore black or dark-colored suits. Two of Faye's eight great-grandchildren wore white—her favorite color—in her memory. Her alabaster casket lacked the gloss and luxury that typify modern funerary boxes, yet was simple and classy in its understatement. Its presence clearly pronounced the finality of Faye's life on this earth.

Faye's service was the programmatic embodiment of her life. Even in death she was surrounded by friends, family, and community members who loved and respected her dearly, and who sorrowfully reflected on the significance of her loss to their lives. She was heralded for her role as a nearly lifelong member of Wesley UMC, her ongoing faithfulness to the church, and her faith and unwavering commitment to God. There was no doubt among the participants that if there is any such thing as a heaven, Faye would be there, and she would be there waiting for the rest of us. During the funeral, selected speakers and the officiating minister spoke openly about her sense of humor, her generosity, and her at-times biting candor. As Sarah, the woman who offered remarks to the family on behalf of the community, stated, "no one could tell you like it is like Faye could." Music filled the program more than traditional aspects such as scripture readings and the eulogy. It included her three favorite hymns—"Amazing Grace," "Blessed Assurance," and the ever-moving "How Great Thou Art," which the audience sang with fervor.

It is custom at Wesley UMC that the choir of which the deceased was a member sings at the funeral. That slightly overcast day, the senior choir members were regally adorned in their white robes. Roberta and Lucinda sat in the choir stand on either side of Faye's robe, which lay empty in the space where she would stand—and at the end of her life, sit—during the choir's first Sunday performances. The choir sang two songs in tribute to Faye: "I've Got Victory," which Faye typically soloed, and most aptly, "Sendin' Up My Timbah," which was rendered after the scriptures were read. I had no idea in 2005 and 2006 when I recorded the songs that accompany this book that they would be a part of Faye's memorial.

When Lucinda stood to begin the solo, emotion erupted in the church, which until that moment had been solemn and silent. There were several seconds of loud weeping, crying out, and clapping that rang out from various locations in the church. It took some time for Lucinda to gain her composure, and as she did, she moved so that she was standing behind, yet literally over Faye's open casket, which was positioned in front of the altar. Lucinda then delivered the first line, "I dreamed that I dreamed, of my heavenly home," with clarity. As the choir hummed their accompaniment, something remarkably transcendent occurred, as we were all utterly transfixed by her lean figure standing over Faye's body. While Lucinda described through song her daily efforts to "send up her timber," and as the choir and organist accompanied her, the entire energy of the funeral shifted from mournful to joyous. The tempo of the song transitioned from a slow dirge to a more rapidly paced rhythm accentuated by the lowcountry clap's staccato, and people began to stand, clap, and sing—even to shout. At that moment I experienced Lucinda's soul-stirring and heartfelt rendition of the solo anew. When I looked at her performing the song I felt the urgency with which she called out—to God, to her deceased mother, and to Faye. When I looked at Roberta in the choir stand, who had been holding onto Faye's robe, she had moved from inside the choir stand to just beyond it and her lips were forming words that were not in the song—she was not only mourning the loss of her closest and dearest friend. She was praying for her, and as I later found out, praying to her.

I remember being struck by how Lucinda's posture suggested that she was making the effort to do what Faye had done—to pray every day—and hoped that she too would be rewarded at the end of her life with the peace that was cast over Faye's lifeless face. Given my conversations with Lucinda, I could not also help but wonder if, in that moment, she too was talking to Faye. This question remains unanswered, as during later discussions with

Lucinda, she could not recall the entire experience of singing the song. To her "it was like she was out of her body" then, though she could remember all the remaining details of the service.

Faye's death on March 8, 2007, was shocking to her family, friends, and community. Though she had been ill, no one expected her to deteriorate so rapidly, and no one thought she would die. I last spoke with her during a visit on March 6, 2007, which was also the last time I saw her alive. She had had two minor strokes seven months prior and had noticeably deteriorated, but not severely. Though she had no problems speaking, she no longer moved as swiftly or as fluidly as when I had last seen her four months earlier; she had lost some weight and could not walk unassisted. During our final conversation Faye was in bed "getting her rest" after lunch. At the time she complained of some stomach pain but said she was looking forward to a full recovery. I reluctantly left her, and I did not stay long because she had expressed a desire to get more rest. Yet my husband reminded me that when I spoke to him shortly after leaving Faye, I declared I did not think I would see her alive again.

The time I spent with Faye, Lucinda, Lucille, Ruth, Roberta, Beatrice, and Yenenga, in their homes, on their jobs, in their churches, and in their communities, has proven to be among the most rewarding experiences of my life. I continue to speak with and visit the remaining six women, though it never seems often enough. I cannot help but notice that all of them have aged, which I am sure they can also say about me. My interactions with these women have led me to deduce that coexistence of the worlds of the living and deceased among lowcountry inhabitants cannot be denied. Despite dramatic changes brought on by commercialization and commodification, belief in connections between the living and the dead is as real as it is ongoing. Shortly after meeting each of these women, their strong faith in God and belief in a fluid relationship between the living and the dead became obvious to me. Memorabilia of their deceased loved ones were placed near their church hymnals, next to pictures of Jesus Christ, and beside their Bibles. Like breathing, the relationships these women maintain with the deceased are assumed, implicit rather than explicit. The exchange between the living and the dead is so fluid, so understood within these communities, that the women were often surprised when I inquired about their connections with the deceased and the ways those connections were evident in their practices of prayer and singing.

Talking to the dead is a connection that these women take for granted, and it is this presumed relationship between the living and the dead that also pauses me. I fear that the implicit nature of talking to the dead and the ways that people do not openly speak of the connections between the living and the dead may place the practice at risk, for it will eventually become so assumed that it is no longer visible. Hence, if people do not speak openly and without provocation about the practice, or if one is not intimately familiar with lowcountry culture, there is a chance that the practice will continue undetected. This would be a significant loss because talking to the dead and the various ways that it manifests—through music, singing, shouting, dreams, prayer, and cultural practices—reflects the subversive ingenuity of lowcountry inhabitants to appropriate their experiences in such a way that allows them to thrive as spiritually functioning human beings.

Because of the drastic changes occurring in the lowcountry from increased urbanization, I am not sure how the fluid and open acceptance of coexistence between the living and the dead will continue. Nature once facilitated the sinuous exchange between the living and the dead in lowcountry life. It was once a place covered predominately by oak, pine, and palmetto trees. In addition to serving as reminders of their survival through violent hurricanes and tropical storms, lowcountry residents have historically considered these trees, and the wooded areas that harbor them, sacred spaces. The aged, weighted limbs and dangling moss of oak trees remind Yenenga of "the arms of God" reaching to comfort her. They also remind her of her seeking experience, where she "first really came to know God." As these areas rapidly diminish with the influx of people unfamiliar with the worldviews of lowcountry culture, I cannot help but wonder how the decrease in natural green spaces will affect the attitudes of lowcountry inhabitants toward relationships between the living and the dead. Additionally, like seeking and the ring shout, the distinctive songs and musical practices (including the lowcountry clap) that have sustained connections to the dead are rapidly diminishing. For example, Lucinda still sings "Sendin' Up My Timbah," and by example has taught her son David to embrace traditional lowcountry music practices. David, however, has since left Wesley UMC to pastor a church of his own—one that is not always open to incorporating the "old way of singing" into its worship service.

This emphasis on moving away from the past is the most alarming and threatening to the practice of talking to the dead. Modernity, commodification, and commercialization will affect the lowcountry economically, socially, culturally, and religiously in ways that have yet to be revealed. These factors notwithstanding, since history is marked by the constant evolution of customs, traditions, and narratives, I remain hopeful about the continuation of the distinctive religio-cultural practices of the lowcountry—including talking to the dead. Just as the Gullah/Geechee have maintained their culture over centuries of change, one can likely rely on their ability to maintain their identity. It is the faith and example of these seven women, best embodied in their ability to "tulk to de dead all de time," that will likely sustain and perpetuate the practices that make lowcountry religion so unique.

Though several years have passed, I have certainly not forgotten Faye. I am reminded about her significance and presence when I talk to Roberta and Lucinda, as well as when I review my field notes and recorded interviews. To hear her voice is always a reminder to me that while there was so much that I learned, there was so much that I had yet to discover about her. It leaves me with tremendous disappointment about the limitations of what we can learn about others in such a short time and also in such a constrained way through research. I know that there is a way in which Faye had remained with me because she was the first of "my women" to pass away. Though it certainly was not intentional, my wedding anniversary is one day before the anniversary of her death. Faye certainly continues to speak to me through the pages of this book. To tell her story and the stories of the six other women featured in this text is, in fact, to talk to them all. Yet I have been disappointed that my own seeming ability to talk to the dead has not resulted in any direct encounter with Faye since her death. It is almost as if I have been holding my breath waiting for her, and I have expected to see her in my dreams to no avail. I ask Roberta and Lucinda, and they have been surprisingly coy about whether or not they have actually talked with her, though they readily admit that they "feel her" often. I find myself still listening and waiting to see if she will talk to me. If and when that moment should ever come, I will listen . . .

Companion Audio Materials

The inclusion of recorded materials with this book serves several purposes. First, it is reminiscent of the earliest recordings of Gullah/Geechee folkways, where linguists (in particular) helped create an archive of Gullah/Geechee culture. I envision this material as making its own contribution to the continuation of those archives. Second, I believe that it is one thing as an ethnographer to give descriptive language to someone's metaphysical experience of encountering the Holy Spirit and talking to the dead, and another to allow someone to literally hear the transformation take place.

Third, these materials demonstrate the distinct musical practices that, like many other aspects of lowcountry culture, are now threatened by the shifts of modernity. Many of these songs are no longer (or rarely) recorded and are sung with less frequency as older members of the communities pass away and younger generations do not continue the traditions. The same holds true for Yenenga Wheeler's stories. Yenenga has never had an apprentice and does not know of anyone else who is a storyteller. She graciously granted me permission to use her stories from a recording that she made in February 2006—materials she often sells on her own. Some of the recordings of the songs I have included here are from archives of Wesley UMC rather than my own recordings because they are of much better quality than those I acquired during fieldwork. I have only included songs that I heard while I was in the field. Occasionally, however, when I could not find secure recordings as sung by the women, I included the best recording I could locate. For example, Lucinda's son David is the leader on the track "A Charge to Keep I Have." Hence, it is included here as an example of the style, content, and structure of religious music in the lowcountry and demonstrative of how Lucinda has passed on her vocal style and ability to her son.

Last, I have compiled these materials because they provide multiple, yet different examples of how the women from this study (most of whose voices are included) draw strength from their work in the church as soloists and choir members, their love for sacred music, and their belief in God. These materials are therefore critical to this work for they document the significance of these practices, demonstrate the importance of music and storytelling traditions, and exemplify (in audio form) the strong belief in God and the deep faith that sustains the women included in this project.

Access to the featured audio is provided at www.dukeupress.edu/Talking-to-the-Dead.

Audio Materials

1. "Couldn't Hear Nobody Pray"—WUMC Senior Choir, led by Roberta Legare. Recorded June 3, 2001.
2. "Way By and By"—WUMC Senior Choir, led by Lucinda Pinckney. Recorded July 4, 1999.
3. "It Is Well"—WUMC Combined Choir. Recorded circa 1997–1998.
4. "When God Calls Me"—WUMC, led by David Pinckney. Recorded February 7, 1999.
5. "A Charge to Keep I Have"—WUMC, led by David Pinckney. Recorded August 1, 1999.
6. "My Hope Is Built"—WUMC, led by David Pinckney. Recorded May 2, 1999.
7. "My Hope Is Built II"—Sung by Lucille Gaillard and LeRhonda Manigault. Recorded July 13, 2006.
8. "Meeting Songs Medley"—Sung by Yenenga Wheeler and LeRhonda Manigault. Recorderd July 15, 2006.
9. "Call to Christ"—Sung by Lucille Gaillard. Recorded July 15, 2006.
10. "Sendin' Up My Timbah"—WUMC Senior Choir, led by Lucinda Pinckney. Recorded June 6, 1999.

Interview Format and Demographics

Most of the interview data in this project derived from the time I spent with these women between March 2003 and March 2007, which consisted of the spring breaks in 2003, 2004, 2006, the summers of the same years, and nearly the entire year from June 2004 to June 2005. I also followed up with them during a residency in South Carolina in the first three months of 2007, which coincided with Faye Terry's death. All direct quotes provided are verbatim.

The women in this project were "formally" interviewed twice—once in 2003 and once in 2007, which meant, at the very least, I digitally or audio recorded two sets of interviews. I frequently turned on the recorder during observations of church services, musical performances, and informal conversations, but the background noise and the sacred moments of these spaces often meant that recording had to be discontinued. Institutional review board standards notwithstanding, it made sense to conduct an "entrance" and "exit" interview with the women. In each interview, I asked the women the same questions to note discrepancies over time, and those framing questions are included here. In almost every case, I found incongruities to be minimal and discovered that the detail given in response to the questions posed was greater in the latter interview, presumably because the women felt more comfortable with me the second time.

All ethnographers know that many revelatory moments occur during formal interviews, but the most revealing aspects of people's lives generally emerge between those formal spaces. As such, the details that I documented in this work do not always coincide with interviews I formally recorded and transcribed but are best found in my field notes and jottings. Because of the history of exploitation in these communities, I have not included any pictures of the women or their surroundings, though I have some in my possession. The crisis of exploitation and commodification of these communities also made obtaining signed consent forms and utilizing audio recorders difficult, and consent was most often obtained verbally. The only exception was Beatrice, whom I sat with most often at her sweetgrass basket stand in downtown Charleston. The outside location of the stand, the surroundings of a busy intersection, and the frequent visits by tourists or other parties interested in purchasing baskets made audio recording our time together impossible. Visits to Beatrice's home proved no less difficult. Her home was the central locale for playing and eating among her children, grandchildren, and great-grandchildren. Needless to say, the environment was not at all conducive to audio recording. Thus, when it was impossible to record, block quotes were handwritten, as I asked her to slow down and repeat herself so that I could accurately transcribe her statements.

INTERVIEW SCHEDULE

Ethnographers know that while one has a script, variation from that script is commonplace. Included here are the broad questions posed to each woman during initial and final interviews. These questions were not asked in any specific order but as they naturally emerged in the conversation, a process I call *ethnographic unfolding*. As a result, although information such as age was not a formal interview question, the details were revealed over time. Interviews, both formal and informal, were always at least one hour in length. Note that in the section entitled "engagement with written source materials," I would inquire about specific ideas, themes, and terms from the generations of written materials on lowcountry culture.

Historical Origins and Background
1) How long have you and/or your family lived in the lowcountry?
2) Can you describe the island/area generally and then specifically with reference to the area where you/your family reside?

Religion and Religious Affiliation
3) What does it mean to you to be "religious"?
4) Do you consider yourself religious? In what way?
5) How important is religion to you?
6) Are you active in a church or religious group(s)? Which one(s)?
7) How did you become a member or participant in the church or group?
8) Do you know what seeking is? Did you seek your religion? Can you describe the process?
9) Are there any religious moments or events you have experienced that you would like to share?

Religious Ceremonies, Practices, and Rituals
10) Can you describe religious activities that you participate in on a regular basis?
11) Are there practices that you do outside of the church/organization that you consider religious?
12) Are there activities that are done in your community around births, deaths, and marriages? Can you describe them?

13) Can you recall any significant events from your life that you would consider religious?

Gullah/Geechee Women in Religion

14) Are you affiliated with a church or religious group? In what way?
15) Is your church/group predominantly female, male, or equal in membership?
16) Are there women who are leaders in your church or group?
17) As a woman, do you feel that you have equal rights in your church or religious affiliation?
18) What is your role in your church/religious community?
19) Why do you participate? (or not?)
20) Do you believe that Gullah/Geechee women are treated with respect, honor, equality? Why or why not?
21) Is there anything else that you would like to tell me about your life as a woman in the lowcountry?

Engagement with Written Source Materials

22) Are you familiar with the following concept, idea, etc.? How did you become familiar with that?
23) I read in [insert source] that [insert subject] meant [insert description from written materials]. Were you aware of that? Have you ever heard of that? If so, how/when and in what context(s)? Do you agree with it? Why or why not? Can you tell me anything about it?
24) Have you ever read [specifically named source(s)]?

Self-Identification

25) Do you consider yourself African, a descendent of Africa, or African American? How do you make these distinctions?
26) Do you consider yourself Gullah? Geechee? Are you comfortable with either/any term? Why or why not?

A NOTE ABOUT DEMOGRAPHICS

In chapter 1, I cite demographic data about median incomes and city and county populations. Although their numbers are steadily increasing, I have excluded data for people identified as Hispanic and Asian in keeping with how the women of this study perceive race dynamics in their communities as an ongoing exchange between blacks and whites, and because these populations comprise less than 4 percent of the populations in each of the areas. South Carolina's average of residents below the poverty line is 17.1 percent. Demographic and statistical information is compiled from released data of the 2010 census. See the 2010 census data for complete details, http://www.census.gov/.

TABLE APPB.1 Lowcountry Demographic Data

Town or City	County	Total Population	White Population	Black Population	Median Household Income	Below Poverty Line
Beaufort	Beaufort	49,000	69%	25%	$36,000	13%
Cross	Berkeley	less than 1,000	35%	60%	$33,000	17%
James Island	Charleston	34,000	45%	43%	$48,000	18%
Moncks Corner	Berkeley	8,000	57%	37%	$37,000	17%
Mt. Pleasant	Charleston	68,000	90%	7.25%	$61,000	5%

NOTES

PROLOGUE

1. The enslaved were sold at the Custom House on East Bay Street and the Old Slave Mart on Chalmers Street, both less than two blocks away from the City Market. Historical data indicate that slaves were never sold in the City Market. I suspect my visit there produced a startling experience because of the proximity of the trade.
2. The historical timeline as published by the City of Charleston documents the first sale and trade of an enslaved woman named Lucinda in the Old Slave Mart in 1856, a date too late to encompass the mass marketing, sale, and trade of the millions of enslaved bodies that passed through the Charleston port before being dispersed to other colonies.

INTRODUCTION: GULLAH/GEECHEE WOMEN

1. Dash, *Daughters of the Dust*.
2. Chireau, *Black Magic*, 2.
3. These names are pseudonyms.
4. McKoy, "The Limbo Contest."
5. I am indebted to one of my anonymous reviewers, who framed the scope of my project in these terms.
6. "The lowcountry" is a term used in South Carolina to refer to the lower third of South Carolina (including the Sea Islands), which is distinguished from the piedmont and upstate regions because of the presence of Atlantic-bound rivers.
7. Here I employ Margaret Creel's use of "culture" to signify communal systems of meaning that directly inform beliefs, thoughts, feelings, histories, and behavior. Culture is dynamic and is passed on from generation to generation through creative, encompassing, and adaptive modes of communication. Creel, *A Peculiar People*, 1.

8. The term "Geechee" (also spelled Geechie) has been used to distinguish the inhabitants of Georgia from those of the coastal areas of South Carolina ("Gullah"). I use Geechee synonymously with Gullah to refer to one who is from the South Carolina Sea Islands and surrounding areas, and to differentiate the people of the Sea Islands from the vernacular. The women included in this study support my distinction, though they use the terms interchangeably. It should also be noted that Geechee has been associated with negative characterizations of lowcountry residents and utilized pejoratively to label them as "primitive," "backward," "slow," and "country." It was not uncommon in the 1980s for children to taunt someone by calling him "Geechee." In this project, all uses of Gullah or Geechee presuppose positive characterizations.

9. The Windward Coast, also known as the Rice Coast, refers to coastal West African areas encompassing Senegal to the north and Sierra Leone and Liberia as its southernmost points. See Young, *Rituals of Resistance*; Creel, *A Peculiar People*; Wood, *Black Majority*; Littlefield, *Rice and Slaves*; Carney, *Black Rice*; Curtin, *The Atlantic Slave Trade*; and Eltis et al., *The Trans-Atlantic Slave Trade* for additional details.

10. Considered a Creole language, the Gullah dialect is a variant of English that consists of condensed sentences and varied displacement of verbs, pronouns, and adjectives. Hence, to many English-speaking people, Gullah may sound "backward." Gullah has been spoken for hundreds of years, from its black Atlantic origins to its residency and development in the Unites States during slavery. To lowcountry blacks, the Gullah dialect was a survival mechanism as it was key to shared communication.

11. Scholarship has typically attributed Gullah cultural distinctiveness to its geographic isolation. Contemporary examinations of Gullah/Geechee culture—including this one—contest notions of "absolute" or "complete" isolation within these communities, instead celebrating the dynamism inherent in the amalgamation of diverse populations. Waterway travel, interstate and intrastate trading systems, and other forms of translocal communication resulted in, and necessitated, dynamic cultural exchange. It would be as erroneous to presume that the Gullah were in no way influenced by cultures outside of their own as it would be to assume they had no influence upon the cultures they encountered. To ignore the fact that Gullah/Geechee culture simultaneously functions as both product and producer is simply outmoded. See Matory's timely essay "The Illusion of Isolation." Matory also contends—and I agree—that rather than a seeming loss in isolation, loss of land and access to maritime resources are more influential factors in the changes occurring in contemporary Gullah/Geechee culture.

12. For an overview of the transition of Gullah/Geechee customs, see Jones-Jackson, *When Roots Die*.

13. Here "discourse" refers to the broad body of knowledge relevant to any subject

or field of interest, and to the imaginative, ideological, intellectual, cultural, religious, and/or literary modes of production represented by individuals and communities.

14. Braude, "Women's History Is American Religious History"; Brown, "What Has Happened Here"; Higginbotham, *Righteous Discontent*; Gilkes, *If It Wasn't for the Women*.

15. A number of monographs within the past decade have specifically focused on the dynamics of religion among black women: Ross, *Witnessing and Testifying*; Frederick, *Between Sundays*; Butler, *Women in the Church of God in Christ*; and Weisenfeld and Newman, *This Far by Faith*.

16. Herskovits, *The Myth of the Negro Past*. The search for Africanisms in American culture originated as a response to the limited critical scholarship about African and African American communities in North America. Before this movement, scholars monolithically grouped the experiences, histories, and narratives of blacks into one of two general categories. The first category was people who had no past except a history of primitive, African savagery from which they had been delivered by contact with (Christian) Europeans. The second group wholly and uncritically accepted the cultural, racial, and religious identities ascribed to blacks through their contact with Europeans (this includes Phillips, *American Negro Slavery*; Elkins, *Slavery*; and Stampp, *The Peculiar Institution*). In an effort to refute these narrow claims and simultaneously speak to the diversity and depth of African American experiences, scholars of all disciplines began to argue that blacks in North America had distinctively African identities and histories that were relevant to the development of American culture. They also contended that these continuities could validate the resilient dynamism and self-efficacy of blacks in America. Finally, they affirmed the identification of Africanisms as a viable means of investigating African American communities.

17. Herskovits admitted that studying Africanisms in North America would prove difficult because differentials in the degree of contact and accommodation between European and African traditions determined the persistence of survivals. This is an argument supported by Herskovits's most avid challenger, E. Franklin Frazier. Like Herskovits, Frazier recognized African continuities in the West Indies, Latin America, and the Caribbean—and even in the South Carolina lowcountry. Yet in *The Negro Church in America* Frazier refuted Herskovits's claim that one can look to religion in North America to locate Africanisms (the lowcountry being the only exception) and suggested that black religion is exclusively American. According to Frazier, Christianity replaced African traditional systems of familial and social cohesion. In addition, the processes of capture, transport, enslavement, and trade reduced (if not altogether negated) the possibility of the retention and transmission of African culture in North America. To Frazier, African American culture began without any African antecedents, and African culture only survived inasmuch as it adapted to the planta-

tion economy. Scholars who have argued against the idea of Africanisms since Frazier have employed this idea.

18. Scholars have classified the discussion of African retentions as a "debate" between proponents of two extremes: those who believe religious practices in black American communities exhibit clear connections to African traditional religious practices versus those who do not. I contend that this dichotomy fails to adequately address or consider the complexities in classifying practices, beliefs, and symbols that often remain unnoticed by human observation and are inadequately expressed by human speech. This discussion of cultural retentions has since given way to conversations about religious syncretism. See Leopold and Jensen, *Syncretism in Religion*, and Scott, "That Event, This Memory."

19. Charles A. Raymond's three-part series is among the first published works to devote specific attention to the Gullah of South Carolina. See Raymond, "The Religious Life of the Negro Slave." Between 1863 and 1908, there were several additional published works that focused exclusively on the Gullah, including Forten, "Life on the Sea Islands"; Benjamin, "The Sea Islands"; Rowe, "The Negroes of the Sea Islands"; Christensen Jr., "The Negroes of Beaufort County, South Carolina"; and Bennett, "Gullah." Laura M. Towne (1825–1901) presented the earliest documentations of lowcountry religious life in *Letters and Diary of Laura M. Towne*. Towne's diary was not published until 1969, but I include it in this listing of early sources. In addition, Abigail Christensen published a book of lowcountry folk stories entitled *Afro-American Folk Lore*. These works are part of the first generation of scholarship on Gullah/Geechee culture.

20. Turner explicitly connected the origins of the Gullah to areas of Senegal, Gambia, Sierra Leone, the Gold Coast, Togo, Liberia, Angola, and Nigeria. Turner argued that while the Gullah language was a creolized form of English, it contained numerous survivals from the languages of specific ethnic groups (Twi, Dahomey, Mandingo, Yoruba, Ibo, Fula, and other northern groups of Nigeria). Turner was also the first to treat the lack of knowledge about African languages and cultures as an academic "handicap," and he openly challenged scholars to take the African heritage of the Gullah/Geechee peoples seriously and to do so methodologically. For an overview of Turner's influence in Gullah research, see Wade-Lewis, *Lorenzo Dow Turner*. For greater detail on Turner's limitations and the ways that his analysis of the Gullah dialect has been challenged by other linguists, refer to articles by Montgomery and Sengova in Montgomery's, *The Crucible of Carolina*. Refer also to volume 10 (1980) of the *Journal of Black Studies* entitled "Sea Island Culture," pages 379–496.

21. I draw from Paget Henry's expanded use of the term "text," which notes the power of *language* as a form of communication (see *Caliban's Reason*). This includes written sources as well as modes of communication that are demonstrated in performative acts, myths, language, speech, sound, rhythm, and

music, which can become living texts. I contend that his expansion of the notion of "text" is especially useful for communities like the Gullah/Geechee, where there are scant written materials by blacks to investigate black religious life. This expansive use of the term "text" offers a creative lens through which to view the discursive religious practices in the lives of lowcountry women.

22. This more widely accepted idea of connecting lowcountry blacks to an African heritage was not new, for as early as 1908 Charleston resident John Bennett— an attorney, writer, poet, and artist who devoted extensive time between 1900 and 1940 exploring Gullah history and culture—had already noted the correlation between the Gullah dialect, religion, and their African heritage. Bennett, *John Bennett Papers*, 1176.00.

23. Lawton, "The Religious Life of South Carolina Coastal and Sea Island Negroes"; Crum, *Gullah*; Guthrie, *"Catching Sense"*; Jones-Jackson, *When Roots Die*; Creel, *A Peculiar People*; and Wolfe, *The Abundant Life Prevails.*

24. The first generation of scholarship predominantly described the Gullah as "deeply religious" and did little to account for how the Gullah/Geechee appropriated the complex religious worldviews they brought with them. Within the earliest documentations of lowcountry religion, the integration of folk or non-Christian customs was treated as an aberrant form of religious practice, and it was argued that missionary efforts to introduce the Gullah to Christianity "bettered" them because it eradicated their "primitive" traditional African and African-derived practices such as conjure, voodoo, and hoodoo. These texts suggested that "innate, deep religiosity" and "emotionalism," rather than a complex religious worldview, made the Gullah especially suited for Christianity. In *The Burden of Black Religion*, Curtis J. Evans argues that this feature of literature about blacks (which he calls "romantic racialism") was a subset of racial essentialism.

25. The literature I reference here exclusively includes nonfiction, published articles and books, and unpublished archival materials. The reader will observe a noticeable gap between the first and second generations of scholarship. The resurgence of Gullah/Geechee scholarship that denotes the second generation directly coincides with the historical quest for Africanisms that dominated African American scholarship in the 1970s.

26. For a helpful analysis of domination and silencing of Gullah women through religious influence, see Creel, "Community Regulation and Cultural Specialization in Gullah Folk Religion," 47–49.

27. Hosley examines the ongoing implications of historical memory in *Routes of Remembrance*. Through an in-depth exploration of the African, diasporic, and European narratives, Hosley analyzes the "politics of memory" of the Cape Coast and Elmina in coastal West Africa and how they have influenced contemporary understandings of Ghana's role and place in the transatlantic slave trade.

28. See Long, *Significations*.
29. See especially Hosley, *Routes of Remembrance*; Gilroy, *The Black Atlantic*; Matory, *Black Atlantic Religion*; and Young, *Rituals of Resistance*.
30. Using language as a vehicle for communicating past and present experiences in the narratives of African American women is well documented in Etter-Lewis, "Black Women's Life Stories."
31. That all of the women are Christian is coincidental. That none of these women is from Edisto or St. Helena Island, however, is intentional of my efforts to provide a more expansive overview of religious practices in the lowcountry. Nearly all studies of the Gullah have focused on communities from those two areas.
32. Refer to the appendix for details about interview procedures.
33. See the epilogue.
34. Geertz, *The Interpretation of Cultures*.
35. Here I must acknowledge Samuel Lawton's 1939 dissertation. Lawton was not the first to use interviews and observations to understand Gullah/Geechee life. He was the first, however, to incorporate the personal expressions, quotes, and prayers of those he observed to demonstrate their religious understandings. This, however, did not mean that Lawton's ethnographic approach was not without limitation because his descriptions suggest that he hid his intentions from the communities he studied and members actively questioned his role as a "genuine" participant.
36. In addition to being a black feminist or feminist of color, a womanist, according to Walker, is one who desires "to know more and in greater depth than what is considered 'good' for one"; is "outrageous, audacious, courageous"; "appreciates and prefers women's culture"; "loves other women, sexually and/or nonsexually"; "sometimes loves individual men sexually and/or nonsexually"; "loves music, loves dance, and loves herself *regardless*"; and as one who is "committed to survival and wholeness of entire people, male *and* female." For Walker's entire description, see *In Search of Our Mothers' Gardens*, 1. Though not exactly alike, "womanist" has thus in many ways become synonymous with "African American feminist." For an analysis of the relationship between womanism and black feminism, refer to Collins, "What's in a Name? Womanism, Black Feminism and Beyond," and Phillips, *The Womanist Reader*.
37. This study embraces a rich connection to the work of black feminist anthropologists, who have for decades employed ethnography as a viable approach to understanding black women's experiences. See McClaurin, *Black Feminist Anthropology*, and Harrison and Harrison, *African-American Pioneers in Anthropology*, for additional information on the use of ethnography to explore the lives of black women. Zora Neale Hurston's (1891–1960) imaginative use of ethnography to illuminate black women's experiences should also be acknowledged. Hurston utilized her training in anthropology with Franz Boas and Melville Herskovits to design an ethnographic style that allowed her to speak from the

pulse of the African American communities she investigated. For an excellent summary of Hurston's unique contributions, see Hernández, "Multiple Subjectivities and Strategic Positionality."

38. When Walker first proposed the term "womanist," it became widely—though not exclusively—employed by black female theologians. Among the first community of scholars to embrace Walker's term as a personal position and methodology, womanist theologians investigated the multiple and interlocking systems of oppression that were particular to black women's experiences under the guise of a theological rubric. Cannon, Black Womanist Ethics, and Grant, White Women's Christ and Black Women's Jesus, are considered the first works in womanist theological discourse. Also refer to Townes, A Troubling in My Soul; Williams, Sisters in the Wilderness; and Douglas, The Black Christ.

39. Frederick, Between Sundays, is one of only a few contemporary book-length works in black feminist anthropology that treats religion as a central means of interpreting black women's experiences. See also Thomas, "Womanist Theology, Epistemology, and a New Anthropological Paradigm."

40. As a moniker for black feminist theology, womanism became limited. First, as the earliest womanist works focused on the meaning, role, and significance of Christianity in black women's lives, womanist theological discourse maintained a predominantly Christian focus. Second, womanist scholars relied on written texts, including the Bible, fiction, and nonfiction works as primary sources of interpretation and investigation. Through this methodological paradigm, they continuously gave preeminence to written works as a normative basis for analysis of women's experiences. A number of scholars are now moving womanism beyond its Christian-based theological beginnings; see Cole and Guy-Sheftall, Gender Talk; Hucks, "Burning with a Flame in America"; Ross, Witnessing and Testifying; and Stewart, Three Eyes for the Journey. See also the critique offered in Coleman, "Must I Be Womanist," and the subsequent roundtable discussion in the Journal of Feminist Studies of Religion, 85–134.

41. Bennett was not the first to write about the Sea Islands and the people who reside there, yet his contributions to the South Atlantic Quarterly are particularly significant because he was among the first to attribute the name Gullah to the black residents of the Sea Islands in a scholarly work. He was also a pioneer among those who devoted their time and effort to studying the culture and language of the Gullah. See Bennett, "Gullah," and Bennett, John Bennett Papers.

42. Heyward's contributions are significant because she produced hundreds of poems and short stories on her life as a white southerner growing up on a rice plantation. She traveled throughout South Carolina, North Carolina, and Florida, where she held her dialect recitals for churches, women's groups, schools, local colleges, and tourists. Heyward gained a great deal of notoriety as an "unusually gifted" storyteller and specialist of the Gullah dialect, and she recounted the short stories and tales that she either overheard or was

told by blacks on her father's plantation. Documentation by the *Savannah Press* and other sources referred to her "perfect" dialect. Heyward reportedly had a true love and devotion toward lowcountry blacks. Yet her recitals were troubling for the ways she characterized lowcountry blacks as "savages"; how she emphasized black benevolence toward whites as a defining, positive feature of Gullah culture; and for her performance of the Gullah dialect and recounting of Gullah folklore as a means of entertaining white audiences. Yet, the descriptions provided in her Gullah recitals offer important insight into African American religious culture that have continuously framed how Gullah/Geechee religious life has been represented. Heyward, *Jane Heyward Papers*.

43. An additional area for exploration would be the examination of the work of South Carolinian Chalmers S. Murray. A journalist and lifelong resident of Edisto Island, Murray researched and published works on local Gullah/Geechee culture. He wrote several manuscripts about his life on Edisto and his interactions with the blacks of the community, and worked as a staff journalist at the *Charleston Evening Post*, where he published several articles on Edisto Island. Some of these titles were published in the *Charleston Evening Post* and the *News and Courier* (Charleston), and are included in his personal papers. Murray, *Chalmers S. Murray Papers*.

44. In the late 1920s, the Social Science Research Council provided $30,000 to research the culture of the Sea Islands, namely St. Helena. While the exact reason for the exclusive focus on St. Helena is unknown, it is presumed that the success and prominence of Penn School played a key role in its selection as a research site. From this funding, three texts were published the same year: Johnson, *Folk Culture on St. Helena Island*; Johnson, *A Social History of the Sea Islands*; and Woofter, *Black Yeomanry*. Each text is significant because it supported the existence of Africanisms on St. Helena, detailed the history and lives of African Americans, and described the impact of Penn School.

45. Crum's *Gullah* was a sociohistorical analysis of plantation life on Edisto and St. Helena Islands. Crum concluded that while isolation produced many of the distinctive features of Gullah culture, the influence of whites had the most profound and lasting effects on their culture. Crum's personal papers reveal that his interest in the Gullah stemmed from his biographical beginnings as a white southerner from South Carolina and his involvement in the Social Gospel Movement.

46. We cannot underestimate the significance of Lawton's contributions. In addition to being the first work to limit its investigation to religion (which in a practical sense means that all who have written about lowcountry religion have referenced Lawton's work), it was the first study of lowcountry culture that did not focus predominantly on the African American communities of St. Helena or Port Royal Islands. Lawton based his conclusions upon his residency on Port Royal Island, which included observing and participating in the lives of African

Americans on St. Helena, Port Royal, Lady's, Parris, and Coosaw Islands. Second, Lawton examined the themes that emerged from the first generation of scholarship in such extensive detail that he single-handedly transformed the way in which scholars understood lowcountry religion. His analysis of the significance of the praise house, the nature and function of the religious service, the role of religious leaders, and the physical and psychological characteristics of the seekin' experience set the standard for how these practices would be explored.

47. Heyward, Jane Heyward Papers [Gullah Notebook #4]. The items related to her Gullah dialect recitals are dated in the 1920s. Notably, Heyward's son DuBose authored Porgy (New York: George H. Doran, 1925), which George and Ira Gershwin turned into the hit musical Porgy and Bess.

48. Heyward maintained a particular format during her public recitals, which would last from twenty to eighty minutes. She began her program by showing "pictures of the old time"—photographs of lowcountry blacks, local plantations, and the slaves with whom she grew up. After that, she performed the Gullah dialect, and read poems and short stories describing her personal interactions with enslaved blacks, and subsequently published a book that synthesized her public lectures.

49. Evans, The Burden of Black Religion.

50. The terms "racist" and "paternalist" have been employed in a variety of contexts. I use the term "racist" to refer to the belief and/or ideology that Africans, Negroes, blacks, and/or African Americans are culturally, biologically, and/or intellectually inferior to another race (especially whites) because they are African, black, Negro, and/or African American. Paternalism is generally defined as the use of power and authority to dominate a person or group for the benefit of those in power. This domination is usually said to be in the "best interest" of the subordinate. I use this term to include the ways that white planters/missionaries utilized their power to dominate Africans and African Americans, specifically as it led to the system of racial subordination in North America during the eras of enslavement, Reconstruction, and Jim Crow, and up to the Civil Rights Movement. I also use the term "paternalist" to account for the subversive and subtle ways that the goals, objectives, and methods of this ideology have continued to dominate scholarly work about or geared toward Africans and African Americans. For a helpful discussion of the long-term effects of white paternalism on blacks in America, see Genovese, Roll Jordan Roll, 6 passim.

51. Despite the pioneering efforts of Turner, Johnson, and others, nonfiction works and investigations of Gullah/Geechee communities ceased from 1950 to 1974. It is unclear why this historical lapse occurred. One can, however, speculate that increased social and political activity in the South surrounding the widespread lynching of African Americans in the 1950s, the landmark case

Brown v. Board of Education (1954), and the Civil Rights Movement in the 1960s received the attention of scholars during this time. This absence of scholarship is perhaps most significant because it opened up opportunities (and time) for subsequent scholars to examine, interrogate, challenge, and reinterpret the findings of the earlier sources, and to present findings of lowcountry African American communities with broadened perspectives.

52. The resurgence of Gullah/Geechee scholarship in 1974 began with Peter Wood's seminal text, *Black Majority*, in which he presented numerical and statistical data that explicitly documented the ten-to-one, black-to-white ratio in the lowcountry and the social, political, and historical implications for that numerical disparity. Wood's *Black Majority* was followed by subsequent contributions of Mary Twining and Patricia Jones-Jackson, both of whom attended to elements of folk-culture in the lowcountry and documented the originality and creativity of oral traditions and the impact of increased commercialization on the islands. After Twining and Jones-Jackson, numerous dissertations, articles, and texts explored Gullah/Geechee culture with renewed fervor. These works analyzed the effects of the rise of urbanization within Sea Island communities and produced studies on language, religion, social history, and cultural practices. They explicitly argued for the positive recognition of the unique aspects of lowcountry culture and connections between lowcountry inhabitants and Africa.

53. It is worth mentioning that Pollitzer suggests that the extended family played more of an important social and economic role than religion among lowcountry blacks. He thus concludes that it is the Gullah's Africanness that has historically united them rather than their shared experiences during enslavement, their navigation of an American identity, or their religion.

54. Raboteau, *Slave Religion*, 4–5.

55. Nikki Lynn Rogers' dissertation, "The Affinity of South Carolina's 'Gullah' African Americans" (2000), uses biological research to identify specific African ethnicity among the Gullah. The three texts that engage the ongoing conversation about cultural survivals include Hargrove, "Reinventing the Plantation"; Moore, "Gullah/Geechee Cultural Survival"; and Cross, *Gullah Culture in America*. Two dissertations have continued the discourse on linguistics and literature in the lowcountry: Hirsch, "A Lie for True," and Hamilton, "Gullah Gullah City." See also Anderson, "Gullah Christianity," and Lanier, "Home Going," which explore the significance of religion in the lowcountry.

56. For more information on constructivism and collaboration as a distinct form of ethnography, see Lassiter, *The Chicago Guide to Collaborative Ethnography*, 5.

57. Collins, *Fighting Words*, xx.

58. Tweed, "Between the Living and the Dead."

59. My engagement with memory studies includes the foundational work on the subject of collective memory by Maurice Halbwachs (*On Collective Memory*) and

subsequent writers; the study of social memory and how memory becomes embodied and remembered via bodily movements, rituals, and practices by Paul Connerton (*How Societies Remember* and *The Spirit of Mourning*); and the analysis of cultural memory by Jan Assman (*Religion and Cultural Memory*). These texts are important for the ways they articulate the impact of memory upon living societies and transitioning cultures. See also Kleinman and Kleinman, "How Bodies Remember."

60. An additional subset of scholarship in memory studies involves the employment of memory in ethnography and oral history. These sources, which include Lewis, "To Turn As on a Pivot"; Fields, "What One Cannot Remember Mistakenly"; and K'Meyer and Crothers, "If I See Some of This in Writing I'm Going to Shoot You," have proved especially useful in my analysis of how African diaspora communities negotiate memory.

61. Chireau, *Black Magic*, 3.

62. McKoy, "The Limbo Contest," 209–10.

63. There are a number of sources that have influenced my definitions of religion and religious experience. They include Taylor, *Critical Terms for Religious Studies* (see the essays by Sharf and Smith); Eliade, *The Sacred and the Profane*; and James, *The Varieties of Religious Experience*. See also Otto, *The Idea of the Holy*, and Proudfoot, *Religious Experience*.

64. www.dukeupress.edu/Talking-to-the-Dead.

65. Weisenfeld and Newman, *This Far by Faith*, 1.

66. Gordon and Gordon, *Not Only the Master's Tools*, ix–xi.

CHAPTER 1: CULTURE KEEPERS

1. See appendix A.

2. When cited, all statements by the women included in this study are direct quotes.

3. Faye died in March 2007. See the epilogue.

4. Of additional note is the former community of Scanlonville, a nearby 614-acre locale, and its neighboring entertainment pavilion, Riverside, an all-black neighborhood. In 1975, the entire area was purchased by the City of Charleston and reconfigured into exclusive gated communities.

5. For a description of the rich history of sweetgrass basketry in the lowcountry, see Coakley, *Sweetgrass Baskets and the Gullah Tradition*. For additional exploration of the use of basketry as a means of Gullah/Geechee connections to Africans, Native Americans, and the formerly living, see Rosengarten, "Spirits of Our Ancestors" and *Row upon Row*.

6. Although the numerous contributions black women have made to American culture through service industries should be celebrated, womanist and black feminist scholars have bemoaned black women's relegation to positions of servitude. Through critical explorations of black women's class status, their

access to economic and educational resources, and the ways their access to these resources are also in part determined by their gender and race, we learn that black women continue to struggle with multiple and layered forces of oppression.

7. Davis, *Women, Race & Class*, 99.

8. Collins, *Black Feminist Thought*, 74.

9. Buckra is a colloquial term used throughout the lowcountry and Anglophone Caribbean to refer to Caucasians.

10. There has been an increase in scholarship that embraces womanist and black feminist perspectives to account for black women's subjectivities as poor and working-class women. See McElya, *Clinging to Mammy*; Hunter, *To 'Joy My Freedom*; Clark-Lewis, *Living In, Living Out*; Tucker, *Telling Memories among Southern Women*; Hondagneu-Sotelo, *Doméstica*; and general texts on domestic workers and perceptions of women's labor, such as Katzman, *Seven Days a Week*; Jones, *Labor of Love, Labor of Sorrow*; and Morgan, *Laboring Women*. Yet more work is needed on the long-term effects of these traditions within the American South specifically, and on the lingering implications upon white attitudes toward black women nationally.

11. See especially McElya, *Clinging to Mammy*, and Wallace-Sanders, *Mammy*.

12. For texts that take up the issue of women's employment within the context of religion, see Higginbotham, *Righteous Discontent*; Wiggins, *Righteous Content*; Gilkes, *If It Wasn't for the Women*; Butler, *Women in the Church of God in Christ*; Ross, *Witnessing and Testifying*; and Collier-Thomas, *Jesus, Jobs, and Justice*.

13. Combined total.

14. See also Pinn, *The Black Church in the Post-Civil Rights Era*. Current interrogations about the relevance of "the black church" as a category is best captured by the initial ruminations and subsequent debate surrounding Eddie Glaude Jr., "The Black Church Is Dead," *The Huffington Post*, February 24, 2010. Accessed June 6, 2010. http://www.huffingtonpost.com/eddie-glaude-jr-phd/the-black-church -is-dead_b_473815.html.

15. Church rosters are often misleading as they provide data for membership numbers, but beyond adding new members, are seldom updated with enough frequency to accurately provide an account of membership trends. I therefore utilize the church's average Sunday attendance to give a sense of the size and participation in church life.

16. Wesley UMC, Poplar Hill, and Greater Goodwill AME were each founded between 1866 and 1890.

17. Since their inception, Presbyterian (U.S.A.) churches have historically been adamant about having educated ministers lead their congregations. For additional details as well as a broader history of the Presbyterian Church and its black members, see Parker, *The Rise and Decline of the Program of Education*, and Wilmore, *Black and Presbyterian*.

18. For additional information about the prominence of popular and prosperity gospel ministries in the lives of African American churchgoers, refer to Walton, *Watch This! The Ethics and Aesthetics of Black Televangelism* (New York: New York University Press, 2009). For examination of the role of evangelical ministries on black women, see Frederick-McGlathery, "But It's *Bible*."

19. Field note description.

20. Rowe, "The Negroes of the Sea Islands," 710.

21. Christensen, "The Negroes of Beaufort County, South Carolina," 484.

22. Johnson, *A Social History of the Sea Islands*, and Crum, *Gullah*. Notably, both studies peripherally engaged the analysis of religion.

23. Lawton, "The Religious Life of South Carolina Coastal and Sea Island Negroes," 80, 70.

24. *Journals of Charlotte Forten Grimké*, Sunday, November 23, 1862; Sunday, November 30, 1862.

25. *Diary of Laura M. Towne*, October 26, 1862; March 25, 1863, passim.

26. *Diary of Laura M. Towne*, July 20, [1862] Sunday; October 26, 1879. The exact frequency or process surrounding the designation of "baptizing Sunday" was unspecified.

27. Raboteau, *Slave Religion*, 225.

28. *Journals of Charlotte Forten Grimké*, Sunday, November 23, 1862; *Diary of Laura M. Towne*, May 4, 1862, passim; Raymond, "Religious Life of the Negro Slave," part 2, 676 passim.

29. Forten, "Life on the Sea Islands," part 2, 672. Emphasis is mine.

30. *Journals of Charlotte Forten Grimké*, Sunday, January 25, 1863. Forten also references this baptism in "Life on the Sea Islands," part 2, 670.

31. *Diary of Laura M. Towne*, Frogmore, January 28, 1877. Note how Towne describes six generations of women living together.

32. This tradition of having funerals on weekends continued long after Emancipation. The present structure of the five-day workweek and the shifting attitudes and practices toward funerals held by lowcountry blacks continues to influence the frequency of funerals. For more information on burial practices in the lowcountry, see Pollitzer, *The Gullah People and Their African Heritage*, and Creel, "Gullah Attitudes toward Life and Death." For a broader description of African American attitudes toward funeral practices, refer to Holloway, *Passed On*, and McIlwain, *Death in Black and White*. For an exposition of American attitudes toward death and contemporary funerary practices, see Laderman, *Rest in Peace*.

33. Raymond, "Religious Life of the Negro Slave," part 2, 678.

34. Shouting was a prevalent tradition among lowcountry black communities. This description of a "shout" is intentionally brief as I detail the history and significance of the tradition in chapter four.

35. *Diary of Laura M. Towne*. Rina was a St. Helena resident and Towne's friend.

36. Guthrie, *Catching Sense*, 34. One standing praise house remains on St. Helena today.

37. There are numerous works that examine the roles of black preachers and deacons within the slave community, including Raboteau, *Slave Religion*; Blassingame, *Slave Community*; Stuckey, *Slave Culture*; and Levine, *Black Culture and Black Consciousness*, to name a few. The intent here is not to reiterate the general ideas about the black preachers and deacons on the plantation, but to present nineteenth- and twentieth-century descriptions of their roles in the lowcountry.

38. Jackson, "Religious Instruction," 108.

39. Lawton, "The Religious Lives of South Carolina Coastal and Sea Island Negroes," 36.

40. Raymond, "Religious Life of the Negro Slave," part 2, 676.

41. Crum, *Gullah*, 90.

42. For more information about the significance of the call in the black ministerial tradition, see Myers, *God's Yes Was Louder than My No: Rethinking the African American Call to Ministry* (Trenton, NJ: Africa World Press, 1994), and Bryant, "Journeys along Damascus Road."

43. Raymond, "Religious Life of the Negro Slave," part 2, 677.

44. Raymond, "Religious Life of the Negro Slave," part 1, 479.

45. Refer especially to chapter 5, "Religious Life in the Slave Community," in Raboteau, *Slave Religion*; Stuckey, *Slave Culture*; Gomez, *Exchanging Our Country Marks*; and Wilmore, *Black Religion and Black Radicalism*.

46. Lawton, "The Religious Lives of South Carolina Coastal and Sea Island Negroes," 70, 75.

47. Guthrie, *Catching Sense*, 96.

48. Creel, *A Peculiar People*, 2, 243, 246–48, 280. See also pages 243–47.

49. Wolfe, *The Abundant Life Prevails*, 95–96.

50. This discussion of women is limited to six pages within the text: 80, 95–98, 117.

51. I engage the significance of Gullah/Geechee women's roles within these practices in chapter 4.

52. The varied challenges that women in leadership face have been well documented. See Hull, Scott, and Smith, *But Some of Us Are Brave*; Davis, *Women, Race & Class*; Jones, *Labor of Love, Labor of Sorrow*. For sources that document the specificities of black women's experiences, and specifically black southern women's experiences within Protestant Christianity, see Higginbotham, *Righteous Discontent*; Frederick, *Between Sundays*; Wiggins, *Righteous Content*; and Gilkes, *If It Wasn't for the Women*.

53. St. Jamse Presbyterian Church (USA). Accessed May 2, 2013. http://stjamespc-usa.org/meet_our_pastors.

54. Grant, "Black Theology and the Black Woman," 323.

55. Weisenfeld and Newman, *This Far by Faith*, 3.
56. The phrase, "God is good all the time and all the time God is Good," is a popular call and response trope in contemporary African American churches.
57. Ross, *Witnessing and Testifying*, 12.
58. Gilkes, "Exploring the Religious Connection," 180.
59. In some churches, children are offered a separate sermon within the order of service, which is often a modification of the message delivered to the adults. These sermons can be delivered by the pastor or minister, but also by Sunday school teachers.
60. Presbyterian elders are laypersons elected by a local congregation who hold governing authority within that local church and are ordained for administering service to the life of the church. Along with ordained ministers who deliver the Word and Sacrament, they are responsible for the ecumenical life of the church and retain ordination beyond their elected terms. For information on their roles, see *The Book of Church Order of the Presbyterian Church in America*.
61. According to Gilkes, women who serve in roles as religious professionals often employ a hybridized skill set of efficiency combined with empathy in ways that men do not. This helps them to mediate systems and structures within the male-dominated arena of church leadership that often thwart their inclusion. See Gilkes, "Exploring the Religious Connection," 192–94.
62. For a history of the United Methodist Church, and the United Methodist Women, see Norwood, *The Story of American Methodism*; *The Book of Discipline of the United Methodist Church*; Heitzenrater, *Wesley and the People Called Methodists*; and Born, *By My Spirit*.
63. For more discussion of women as the predominant members and leaders of African American churches, see Andrews, *Sisters of the Spirit*; Dodson, "Nineteenth-Century AME Preaching Women"; Higginbotham, *Righteous Discontent* and "The Black Church."
64. Ruth's narrative confirms Patricia Guthrie's assessment that women who served in the capacity of committee persons, deaconesses, etc., were also religious exemplars for younger women.
65. Mrs. Ona Belle Sanders [not a pseudonym] was a prominent missionary and teacher at St. James from 1923 to 1961. Reverend Marion A. Sanders, her husband, served as the church's pastor from 1923 to 1963.
66. Because of its connection to the practice of talking to the dead, I address the significance of the seeking tradition in greater detail in chapter 3.
67. Lucille was the only woman to reference the role of female "evangelists" in her own religious development. When asked why they were called evangelists rather than ministers or pastors, she was uncertain. It is my estimation that they were called evangelists because they could not formally be ordained but were still recognized within the community as religious leaders.
68. Gilkes methodically documents black churchwomen's self-perceptions of their

role and positions within religious institutions and organizations in her text *If It Wasn't for the Women*.

69. The autobiographies of Lee, Elaw, and Foote are reprinted in Andrews, *Sisters of the Spirit*. A later account of the difficulties women have faced in the AME Church is in Angell, "The Controversy over Women's Ministry."

70. Grant, "Black Theology and the Black Woman," 302.

71. Weisenfeld and Newman, *This Far by Faith*, 3.

72. Gilkes, "The Roles of Church and Community Mothers," 50, and *If It Wasn't for the Women*; Higginbotham, *Righteous Discontent*; and Frederick, *Between Sundays*.

73. Gilkes, "Exploring the Religious Connection," 180–81.

74. Hammonds, "Toward a Genealogy of Black Female Sexuality."

75. See chapter 5 of Guthrie, *Catching Sense*. According to Guthrie, although Gullah/Geechee women were expected to maintain roles as "keepers of the hearth" upon marriage and the division of labor among the sexes was clear, they were not perceived as subservient to men because they maintained a social life and church membership separate from their husbands.

76. Collier-Thomas, *Jesus, Jobs, and Justice*, xx.

77. Use of the term "back seat" to refer to someone who is backslidden, or fallen out of the will of God, is confirmed in the early literature on lowcountry religion. William Francis Allen noted that the phrase "on the back seat" refers to one who is "under the censure of the church authorities for bad behavior." See Allen, *Slave Songs of the United States*, xiii.

78. These perspectives directly refute the argument of William Pollitzer, who in 1999 noted, "a girl in her teens may have a baby—without marriage and without stigma." See Pollitzer, *The Gullah People and Their African Heritage*, 130–35.

79. See Guthrie, *Catching Sense*, 43–45, and Beoku-Betts, "We Got Our Way of Cooking Things," for discussion of domestic roles that lowcountry women fulfill. Beoku-Betts is also beneficial for her discussion of how women function as cultural preservers in the lowcountry.

80. Higginbotham, *Righteous Discontent*, 2.

81. This statement was housed on their former website. Accessed June 6, 2008. http://www.stjamespcusa.org/History.htm#Hist_WomenInAction.

CHAPTER 2: FOLK RELIGION

Heyward, *Jane Heyward Papers, 1892–1940*, "Gullah Notebook #4 (Program 3)," from the Collections of the South Carolina Historical Society, Charleston, transliteration by the author. *Diary of Laura M. Towne*, St. Helena Village, Sunday afternoon, November 10, 1867. Emphasis in original.

1. Higginbotham, *Righteous Discontent*, 2.

2. Jones, *The Religious Instruction of the Negroes*, 127–28.

3. Raymond, "Religious Life of the Negro Slave," part 2, 676; part 3, 816. Ray-

mond's three-part series presented a picture of religious practice among enslaved communities of coastal South Carolina.

4. Herron, "Conjuring and Conjure Doctors," 117.
5. John Bennett Papers, "Untitled Oversized Scrapbook," 132.
6. Pinckney, Blue Roots, 76.
7. John Bennett Papers, "Untitled Oversized Scrapbook," 10.
8. Benjamin, "The Sea Islands," 859.
9. John Bennett Papers, "Untitled Oversized Scrapbook," 59.
10. Benjamin, "The Sea Islands," 858–59. The "rebellion" mentioned here is likely a reference to the Vesey revolt.
11. John Bennett Papers, "Negro: Gullah Scrapbook," cover page.
12. Chireau, Black Magic, 2–3.
13. In Conjuring Culture, Smith employs the phrase to signify the ways blacks used aesthetics within religion, art, music, and politics to construct a theo-spiritual system.
14. See Smith, Conjuring Culture; chapter 5 of Raboteau, Slave Religion; and Hucks, "Burning with a Flame in America." While I am cautious about Chireau's attempt to pinpoint an "intermediary category" between religion and "other" supernatural traditions, I fully support her analysis and description of the inseparability of supernaturalism of all kinds within African American cultural patterns.
15. Chireau has brought our attention to the ways famed anthropologist Zora Neale Hurston identified a kind of hierarchy among folk practitioners and noted key distinctions between conjurers and healers (hoodoo doctors). According to Hurston, conjurers performed root-work and crafted medicinal remedies that treated relational and physical ailments, while hoodoo doctors solely worked on the healing arts. See Chireau, Black Magic, especially chapter 5; and Hurston, Mules and Men.
16. Bennett Papers, "Untitled Oversized Scrapbook," 1.
17. Herron, "Conjuring and Conjure," 118. For more detailed description of the communal role of conjurers in enslaved communities, see Rucker, "Conjure, Magic, and Power."
18. Herron, "Conjuring and Conjure," 117, 118.
19. Jane Heyward Papers (Gullah Notebook #4 [Program 3]), transliteration by LeRhonda S. Manigault-Bryant. The Gullah/Geechee ritual burial practices, and their specific connections with the deceased, have been well documented. See Bolton, "Decoration of Graves of Negroes in South Carolina"; Pinckney, Blue Roots; Creel, "Gullah Attitudes toward Life and Death" and A Peculiar People; Lanier, "Home Going"; and Young, "Burial Markers and Other Remembrances of the Dead" in Rituals of Resistance.
20. See chapters 4 and 5 of Chireau, Black Magic, which document the numerous customs used by African American folk practitioners for healing and harming

purposes; Hurston, *The Sanctified Church* and *Mules and Men*; Pinckney, *Blue Roots*, chapter 3; and Fett, *Working Cures*.

21. In this quote, the variant spellings are reproduced as originally written.

22. John Bennett Papers, "Untitled Oversized Scrapbook," 1, 4.

23. Fett, *Working Cures*.

24. Hucks, "Burning with a Flame in America," 91.

25. Creel, *A Peculiar People*, 6.

26. Chalmers S. Murray Papers, "Voodoo Gods Yet Alive on Islands," circa 1932–40.

27. Lucille's reference to "presence" is also a comment about the connection with the living dead, which I discuss in chapter 3.

28. Hucks, "Burning with a Flame in America," 90.

29. Weisenfeld and Newman, *This Far by Faith*, 7–8.

30. Raymond, "Religious Life of Negro Slave," part 2, 676, emphasis in original.

31. Raymond, "Religious Life of Negro Slave," part 3, 817.

32. Raymond, "Religious Life of Negro Slave," part 3, 819.

33. Raymond, "Religious Life of Negro Slave," part 3, 819.

34. Raymond, "Religious Life of Negro Slave," part 2, 682.

35. See Young, *Rituals of Resistance*; and Simpson, "The Shout and Shouting." I discuss lowcountry shouting practices in chapter 4.

36. Reference to Alfred, Lord Tennyson's (1809–1892) "The Brook."

37. Jane Heyward Papers, "Gullah Notebook #2."

38. John Bennett Papers, "Untitled Oversized Scrapbook," 4.

39. John Bennett Papers, "Untitled Oversized Scrapbook," 45–50.

40. See also Brown, "What Has Happened Here"; Higginbotham, "Beyond the Sounds of Silence," and "African American Women's History"; Braude, "Women's History Is American Religious History"; and Weisenfeld and Newman, *This Far by Faith*.

41. Wolfe, *The Abundant Life Prevails*, 13, 14.

42. *Diary of Laura M. Towne*, December 18, 1864; Christmas, 1864, Village, St. Helena, SC.

43. Raboteau, *Slave Religion*, 4–5; and Creel, *A Peculiar People*, 322.

44. Chireau, *Black Magic*, 41.

45. Stewart, *Three Eyes for the Journey*, describes the prevalence of the visionary in African diasporic religious traditions and highlights the significant role of the seer in divination rites among the Bakongo in the Jamaican parish of St. Thomas.

46. John Bennett Papers, "Untitled Oversized Scrapbook," 10.

47. *Diary of Laura M. Towne*, St. Helena Village, Sunday afternoon, November 10, 1867.

48. Forten, "Life on the Sea Islands," parts 1 and 2. Forten (1837–1914) lived on the Sea Islands from October 1862 to May 1864 as part of the Port Royal Experiment and maintained a diary throughout much of her life, which has since

been published as *The Journal of Charlotte L. Forten* (1953) and *The Journals of Charlotte Forten Grimké* (1988). Of the five journals that make up her diary, two reference her time in the lowcountry (Journal Three, 1858–1863, and Journal Four, 1863–1864). The five journals are published in their entirety in *The Journals of Charlotte Forten Grimké*, which, unless otherwise noted, are the main source of citation.

49. This does not mean that Forten was more sympathetic to the plight of the recently freed blacks of the Sea Islands or presented them in a more positive light than whites. Forten's descriptions of the Gullah—especially her characterizations of the Islanders as "simple" and "strange"—suggest that she "never established close social relationships with the black ex-slaves she came to know" and that she "had difficulty considering these blacks her peers because of their cultural differences, personal histories, and lack of intellectual sophistication" (*Journals of Charlotte Forten Grimké*, 44). In short, while race and gender were common denominators, the experiential worlds between Forten and the Gullah were gravely distinct.

50. For details on the history and scope of religious instruction and Christian conversion in the South and in South Carolina, see Jackson, "Religious Instruction of Negroes"; Raboteau, *Slave Religion* and "The Black Experience in American Evangelicalism"; Cornelius, *Slave Missions and the Black Church*; Smith, *In His Image, But*; and Evans, *The Burden of Black Religion*.

51. Galatians 3:28, Authorized (King James) Version. Unless otherwise noted, all biblical references cited herein are from the King James Version of the Bible.

52. For a greater examination of the impact of South Carolina's Stono Rebellion, refer to Wood, *Black Majority*, and Thornton, "African Dimensions of the Stono Rebellion." South Carolina officials referred to the Stono Rebellion as "*the Gullah war*" (emphasis in original).

53. After Turner's uprising, most of the slave states, including South Carolina, passed laws against teaching blacks to read and write and prohibited blacks from holding meetings or gathering without having a white person present. Missionaries utilized oral instruction to circumvent these statutes, which were in effect until the Civil War. "By this method the instructed was called upon to repeat verbally by rote memory certain sentences or passages given by the instructor." Jackson, "Religious Instruction of Negroes," 85.

54. Conversion efforts were not uniform among Methodist, Episcopal, Presbyterian, and Baptist churches (the four denominations that dominated lowcountry religious affiliation) by any means. Methodist attempts began as early as 1830 with the organization of the Methodist Missionary Society. Presbyterian clergy devoted time to converted blacks in Sabbath schools as early as 1836. The Episcopal Church formed its Society for the Advancement of Christianity in South Carolina and changed the constitution of its Board of Missions to include every baptized member of the church by 1834. Organized missionary efforts of low-

country Baptists, who held the largest numbers of black members, did not begin in any concentrated way until 1844.

55. Jones, *The Religious Instruction of the Negroes*, 71.

56. Jones, *The Religious Instruction of the Negroes*, 73 passim; Jackson, "Religious Instruction of Negroes," 84.

57. In 1845, ministers of South Carolina and Georgia met at a conference in Charleston to discuss the status of the conversion of blacks, data of which had been obtained from a questionnaire sent out to churches throughout the slaveholding states. According to Jackson, the questionnaire inquired about "the different plans or means of instruction, the catechism adopted, the expediency of employing Negro preachers and teachers, provisions made for the slaves worshipping with the whites, the houses of worship available for Negroes on plantations, and the influence of religious instruction on labor, discipline, and good order of the plantation." Jackson, "Religious Instruction of Negroes," 89. The proceedings of the meeting were published as *Proceedings of the Meeting in Charleston, S.C., May 13–15, 1845* (Charleston: B. Jenkins, 1845).

58. Jones, *The Religious Instruction of the Negroes*, 101–11.

59. Curtis Evans suggests that this ideology was not only the direct result of "romantic racialist conceptions" of blacks, but that these ideas informed what African Americans later came to understand as their mutual contributions to the creation of American Protestantism. For greater detail as well as an in-depth exploration of the historically varied social and cultural meanings of black emotionalism and religiosity, see Evans, *The Burden of Black Religion*.

60. This included Capers, *A Catechism for Little Children*; and Jones, *A Catechism for Colored Persons*. The literature of Jones and Capers were the most widely used. For analysis of the impact of this literature, see Matthews, "The Methodist Mission to the Slaves," and Jackson, "Religious Instruction of Negroes."

61. By 1862, with the onset of the Port Royal Experiment, religious instruction emphasized teaching the freed slaves Christianity. See the *Diary of Laura M. Towne*, Monday, April 28, 1862, and *The Journals of Charlotte Forten Grimké*, Sunday, November 16, 1862.

62. The significance of using the "Curse of Ham" narrative from Genesis 9:18–27 must be noted, as missionaries appropriated the history of Noah's relationship with his sons Shem, Ham, and Japheth to prove that God had created the institution of human bondage and that darker-skinned peoples were descendants of Ham and were thus created for the purposes of servitude. The far-reaching impact of this biblical appropriation cannot be underestimated. For greater discussion of the impact of the Curse of Ham and a broader analysis of the use of religion in the perpetuation of racial ideologies, see Peterson, *Ham and Japheth*; Smith, *In His Image, But*; Goldenberg, *The Curse of Ham*; and Harvey, "A Servant of Servants Shall He Be."

63. Jackson, "Religious Instruction of Negroes," 72.

64. Earl, *Dark Symbols, Obscure Signs*.
65. Earl's use of "ideal type" is an appropriation of sociological concepts introduced by Max Weber and explicated by Albert Schutz, which suggest that one can collect enough facts to construct an ideal or model that fits within the scheme of set characteristics. I employ the term here to capture Earl's argument about the dominant ideologies espoused by the planter class.
66. Riggins Earl, Margaret Creel, and Luther Jackson do not discuss the significance of the use of the Curse of Ham text among missionaries as a primary means of justifying the enslavement and the perpetuation of slavery in the South.
67. I contend that this ideology was most prominent *before* the mass efforts to convert and Christianize slaves in the 1830s and 1840s and that the efforts to introduce blacks to Christianity during the 1830s and 1840s marked a shift in ideology from the soulless body type to the bodiless soul type.
68. Earl, *Dark Symbols, Obscure Signs*, 11–23.
69. Earl, *Dark Symbols, Obscure Signs*, 5.
70. Peterson, *Ham and Japheth*, 70.
71. Raymond, "Religious Life of the Negro Slave," part 3, 816.
72. Analysis of slave responses to bondage is well documented, and scholarship emphasizes subversive, covert, and blatant means of resistance. See Berlin, *Generations of Captivity*; Blassingame, *The Slave Community*; Hine and Gaspar, *More than Chattel*; Harding, *There is a River*; Levine, *Black Culture and Black Consciousness*; Stuckey, *Slave Culture*; and Johnson, "On Agency."
73. Earl sifts through the religio-ethical constructs in the slave conversion narratives and characterizes the enslaved as active agents in their conversion experiences. I wholeheartedly agree with his argument that critical examinations of slave sources are foundational for ethical and theological reflection in scholarly investigations of African American experience.
74. See the electronic edition of the *Journal of the Proceedings of the Seventy-fifth Annual Council of the Protestant Episcopal Church in South Carolina*, which can be found online at http://docsouth.unc.edu/imls/episc75th/episc75th.html. The genealogical information of Jane Heyward can be found in the online description of the *DuBose Heyward* collection and the *Jane Heyward Papers*, both housed at the South Carolina Historical Society.
75. The Port Royal Experiment, which began in 1862 as a call for educators to help newly freed blacks in coastal South Carolina, has continuously been described as a "social experiment" to better the lives of the enslaved and formerly enslaved of the Beaufort and Hilton Head areas. I contend that it was a socioreligious experiment because of the program's focus on preparing blacks for their lives as full citizens by "converting them" into "happy, industrious, law-abiding, free and Christian people." In addition, that the first school for freed blacks in South Carolina (Penn Center) began in a Baptist church should not

go unnoticed. See *The Journal of Charlotte Forten*, 20; *The Journals of Charlotte Forten Grimké*; the *Diary of Laura M. Towne*; and Rose, *Rehearsal for Reconstruction*.

76. Raymond, "Religious Life of the Negro Slave," part 1, 479–80.

77. Raymond, "Religious Life of the Negro Slave," part 1, 479.

78. See Raboteau, "The Black Experience in American Evangelicalism," 100–103; and Pinn, *Varieties of African American Religious Experience*, 34–39.

79. *Journals of Charlotte Forten Grimké*, Sunday, November 23, 1862.

80. *Journals of Charlotte Forten Grimké*, introduction, 17.

81. Laura Towne noted that on St. Helena, "The colored people here are all ardent and settled Baptists, with a little sprinkling of Methodists." *Diary of Laura M. Towne*, October 28, 1877.

82. Raymond, "Religious Life of the Negro Slave," part 1, 479; part 2, 676.

83. *Diary of Laura M. Towne*, St. Helenaville, SC, February 25, 1864. St. Helenaville was where Towne and Ellen Murray, the other founder of Penn School, lived after leaving the Oaks, or Frogmore Plantation.

84. *Journals of Charlotte Forten Grimké*, November 2, 1862. Forten also references this same service in part 1 of "Life on the Sea Islands," stating: "The people came in slowly; for they have no way of knowing the hour, except by the sun," 589.

85. Raymond, "Religious Life of the Negro Slave," part 2, 677.

86. Mbiti, *African Religions and Philosophy*, 17. See also chapter 3, "The Concept of Time," 15–28.

87. Creel, *A Peculiar People*, 193–94, 273.

88. Creel, *A Peculiar People*, 274.

89. Wolfe, *The Abundant Life Prevails*, 42. This statement contradicts Wolfe's use of Margaret Creel's work and his own theory that the religious culture of low-country blacks was both African and Protestant.

90. *John Bennett Papers*, "Untitled Oversized Scrapbook," 69.

91. Raymond, "Religious Life of the Negro Slave," part 1, 479. Creel's characterization of the Gullah as a "peculiar people" is a double entendre that plays upon the negative stereotyping whites maintained about lowcountry religious practices, while revealing that Gullah religious ways were not so strange after all.

92. This description of the development of African American religion from the arrival of Africans in North America to the mass Christianization and development of exclusively African American churches began out of conversations with Dianne Stewart. During her graduate course "Theoretical Issues in the Study of Black Religion" (fall 2002) she presented a "Typology of African Diasporic Religious Formation," which is also detailed in the preface of her book *Three Eyes for the Journey*.

93. Young, *Rituals of Resistance*, 44.

CHAPTER 3: "AH TULK TO DE DEAD ALL DE TIME"

Murray, Chalmers S. Murray Papers, "Edisto Negroes Close to Spirits," from the *News and Courier*, circa 1935, from the Collections of the South Carolina Historical Society, Charleston. Historically, Gullah/Geechee connections with the deceased have been documented via their burial rites and funerary rituals. See Bolton, "Decoration of Graves of Negroes in South Carolina"; Creel, "Gullah Attitudes toward Life and Death" and *A Peculiar People*; Lanier, "Home Going"; and Young, *Rituals of Resistance*.

1. Ras Michael Brown has argued that this belief in communication with spirits in the lowcountry parallels references to belief in *simbi* spirits, West-Central African nature deities. He has also suggested that this parallel belief in spirits demonstrates the continued relevance and extension of African ancestral cultures in North America. See Brown, *African-Atlantic Cultures* and "Walk in the Feenda"; and Creel, *A Peculiar People*, chapter 10.

2. Moore, "Africanisms among Blacks of the Sea Islands," 467.

3. I address music and shouting traditions in chapter 4 and examine the act of remembering as spiritual practice in chapter 5.

4. *Oxford Dictionary of English*. 2nd rev. ed. (Oxford: Oxford University Press, 2005).

5. Burton is approximately four miles from Beaufort on Parris Island. New Hope Christian Church is a part of the Disciples of Christ denomination.

6. Spirit (capital "S") and spirit (lowercase "s") are employed throughout to distinguish between the Holy Spirit as associated with Christian theology and spirits as other metaphysical forms.

7. I describe the role of music as a means of talking to the dead in greater detail in chapter 4.

8. I also discuss the significance of her visit to South Africa in the context of her self-professed African identity in chapter 5.

9. Lowcountry folklore has been among the most well-documented aspects of Gullah/Geechee culture. See Stuckey, *Slave Culture*; Joyner, *Down by the Riverside*; Twining, "An Examination of African Cultural Retentions"; Twining and Baird, *Sea Island Roots*; and Goodwine, *The Legacy of Ibo Landing*. See also Puckett, *Folk Beliefs of the Southern Negro*; and Rhyne, *Before and After Freedom*.

10. Holloway, "Time in the African Diaspora," 200.

11. Coakley, *Sweetgrass Baskets and the Gullah Tradition*, 9.

12. Sweetgrass basketry also connects Ms. Bea to one of her daughters, who died two years ago. Ms. Bea taught her daughter how to make baskets, and often thinks of her when she is teaching her grandchildren.

13. In the lowcountry, the origins of seeking—which are reminiscent of various rites of passage ceremonies throughout the African diaspora—coincided with the mass Christianization efforts of the 1830s. In addition to the analysis provided in *A Peculiar People*, Creel has offered accounts of the seeking tradition in the essays "Community Regulation" and "Gullah Attitudes toward Life and

Death." See also Brown, *African-Atlantic Cultures*; Steiner, "Seeking Jesus"; Guthrie, *Catching Sense*; and Wolfe, *The Abundant Life Prevails*. It should also be noted that Samuel Lawton provided extensive details of the seeking tradition in his unpublished dissertation, "The Religious Life of South Carolina Coastal and Sea Island Negroes."

14. Creel, *A Peculiar People*, 286–87.
15. Raymond, "Religious Life of the Negro Slave," Part 2, 680.
16. Devoted exclusively to St. Helena Island, Guthrie's *Catching Sense* utilized the materials she collected during her dissertation research in 1975, 1976, 1979, and revisits in 1992. Guthrie did not extensively detail the intimacies of the catching sense process, though she included some descriptions of the orders of service. She also did not describe how long catching sense took or what type of religious instruction catching sense entailed other than to note that the religious belief system was based on the Scriptures. Instead, she focused on how, through the catch-sense system, members of the praise house were governed by church law and collective consensus.
17. Guthrie, *Catching Sense*, 21.
18. Guthrie, *Catching Sense*, 32, 36.
19. Guthrie, *Catching Sense*, 116–17.
20. Creel, *A Peculiar People*, 286–87.
21. Raymond, "Religious Life of the Negro Slave," Part 2, 680–81.
22. In "The Religious Life of South Carolina Coastal and Sea Island Negroes," Samuel Lawton distinguishes church membership between adult seeking and youth seeking. The women of this study were not at all familiar with this differentiation and solely identified seeking as a practice that occurred among young adults. Instead, they identified with the process of adults "rejoining" church, a practice in which adults had to once again go before the "mourner's bench," pray to God, and repent for one's errant ways.
23. Lawton, "The Religious Life of South Carolina Coastal and Sea Island Negroes," 138.
24. Lawton, "The Religious Life of South Carolina Coastal and Sea Island Negroes," 141.
25. Creel, *A Peculiar People*, 285.
26. Lawton, "The Religious Life of South Carolina Coastal and Sea Island Negroes," 138.
27. Lawton, "The Religious Life of South Carolina Coastal and Sea Island Negroes," 160.
28. Creel compared seeking to spiritual initiation ceremonies among West African ethnic groups including the Mano, Limba, Mende, Gola, and Temne. Refer to *A Peculiar People*, 285, 287.
29. Scholars have suggested that the time spent seekin' varied from two days to two months in length.

30. Some of these objects included angels, light, white women and men, people dressed in white, a Bible or hymn book, or white horses. See Lawton, "The Religious Life of South Carolina Coastal and Sea Island Negroes," 150–53.

31. According to Margaret Creel, these contacts with the deceased by way of dreams and visions produced fear in the seeker and were interpreted as negative. This claim is not supported by any of the descriptions offered by the women.

32. Emphasis in original. Although the women did not readily discuss a focus on confession, Ruth's seeking experience suggests that seeking also incorporated a confessional aspect.

33. March 16, 2003.

34. Mbiti, *African Religions and Philosophy*, 75.

35. I discuss the significance of music and song traditions and how they facilitate talking to the dead in chapter 4.

36. I discuss the implications of seeking as a discontinued tradition in chapter 5.

CHAPTER 4: "SENDIN' UP MY TIMBAH"
Crum, *Gullah*, 132, 150.

1. *Journals of Charlotte Forten Grimké*, October 28, 1862. Forten also noted the beauty of the boatmen's singing on Friday, March 13, 1863, and her surprise on Saturday, January 31, 1863, when the boatmen did not sing on their way to or from Beaufort. She commented, "*that* is most surprising. I thought *everybody* sang down here. Certainly every boat crew *ought*."

2. *Diary of Laura M. Towne*, Beaufort, SC, April 17, 1862.

3. *Journals of Charlotte Forten Grimké*, October 29, 1862.

4. *Journals of Charlotte Forten Grimké*, Christmas Day, 1862.

5. *Journals of Charlotte Forten Grimké*, Sunday, November 2, 1862.

6. *Diary of Laura M. Towne*, December 25, 1862. The song is John Greenleaf Whittier's "Oh, None in All the World Before," which is taken from his work *In War Time and Other Poems* (Boston: Ticknor and Fields, 1864).

7. Between 1905 and 1910 John Bennett sent a manuscript of 150 spirituals he, his wife, and his sister-in-law collected from their observations of blacks in the lowcountry to an undisclosed publisher. The manuscript was rejected. It is feasible that Bennett's work influenced the Works Progress Administration's collections of lowcountry folklore in the 1930s.

8. Smythe et al., *The Carolina Low-Country*, v–vi.

9. Smythe et al., *The Carolina Low-Country*, vi–vii. The society, which was made up exclusively of white Charlestonians, was not the first to notice the unique quality of music in the lowcountry. In 1867, William Francis Allen, Charles Pickard Ware, and Lucy McKim Garrison published the first collection of African American sacred music, *Slave Songs of the United States*, designated exclusively to the documentation of the "musical capacity of the negro race." The bulk of the

text (part I) was devoted to music of the southeastern slave states, "including South Carolina, Georgia and the Sea Islands." Additional works include Barton, *Old Plantation Hymns*; Parrish, *Slave Songs of the Georgia Sea Islands*; and Courlander, *Negro Folk Music, U.S.A.* These texts are among the earliest to document the rich history of what are now called Negro spirituals in the South, especially the lowcountry, and continue to be useful sources when examining the musical practices of early African American sacred music.

10. Gordon, "The Negro Spiritual," 191.

11. Costen, "Singing Praise to God in African American Worship Contexts," 394. For additional discussion of the role of music in the religious life of lowcountry blacks, see Starks, "Singing 'Bout a Good Time"; Carawan and Carawan, *Ain't You Got a Right to the Tree of Life*; and Lawton, "The Religious Life of South Carolina Coastal and Sea Island Negroes," chapter 5.

12. The music analyzed in this chapter is exclusively the songs that the women recounted and noted as significant; that were sung at services I attended; that I recorded during interviews and observations; that were discussed during interviews; and that were found in the archives of Wesley UMC, hereafter identified as WUMC Archives.

13. Faye, Lucinda, and Roberta provided additional descriptions of the Emancipation Service during interviews.

14. Refer to "When God Calls Me," on the companion audio. See also the *Songs of Zion* hymnal for a listing of traditional African American hymns and spirituals.

15. Refer to "Meeting Songs Medley," and "My Hope is Built II" on the companion audio.

16. There are a plethora of sources in musicology, ethnomusicology, and history that investigate the dynamic features of African American music, though a great deal of this literature does not specifically attend to lowcountry music, let alone its contemporary forms. Their contributions are, however, notable as they inform the theoretical formulations in this chapter. See especially Levine, *Black Culture, Black Consciousness*; Southern, *The Music of Black Americans*; Reagon, *If You Don't Go, Don't Hinder Me*; Floyd, *The Power of Black Music*; Burnim and Maultsby, *African American Music*; and Jackson, *Singing in My Soul*. In addition, Raboteau, *Slave Religion*; Smith, *Conjuring Culture*; and Matthews, *Honoring the Ancestors* offer detailed analyses of sacred music. I utilize the remaining sections of this chapter to analyze the similarities and differences in these characteristics of lowcountry music.

17. In her descriptions of the purpose of her storytelling, Yenenga frequently recited this quote from the African American spiritual, "We've Come This Far by Faith."

18. Johnson, "The Negro Spiritual: A Problem in Anthropology," 170.

19. Lawton, "The Religious Life of South Carolina Coastal and Sea Island Negroes," 110.

20. Southern, *The Music of Black Americans*, 190. For a distinction between gospel, hymns, and spirituals, see Burnim and Maultsby, *African American Music*.

21. Levine, "Slave Songs and Slave Consciousness," 66.

22. Atlanta International Records, released May 1, 1984. Copyright PA0000215479/ 1984-06-11.

23. The lowcountry clap is almost impossible to document through formal scaling, scoring, and musical notation practices, yet is readily used in most lowcountry music, including spirituals, hymns, and contemporary gospel songs. For an example of the sound, refer to any of the companion audio, especially "When God Calls Me," and "Way By and By." For additional examples of this sound, listen to Disc 3, "Blow Gabriel" (track 11), of Alan Lomax's work, *Sounds of the South*.

24. These notions of taking a song up or down do not refer to the tonal structure of the song, but to the spiritual level of the song. To take a song up means to continue to take a song higher to the point of spiritual ecstasy, where shouting and dancing often occur. Bringing a song down usually means lowering the level of the song so as to move on to the next song or move on in the order of service.

25. Reagon, *If You Don't Go, Don't Hinder Me*.

26. Lomax, Notebook, Disc 3, "Negro Church Music," from *Sounds of the South*.

27. "Pure Religion" is a derivative of the Negro spiritual "You Must Have that True Religion," which was made famous by the American folk and blues musician Huddie William Ledbetter (1888–1949), better known as Leadbelly. To date, I have been unable to acquire a recording of this song as rendered in the lowcountry, but include it here as Lucinda, Faye, and Roberta each spoke to its particular significance. Keep in mind that the verses as described at the end of this song may be altered or placed in any order depending on the leader. It should also be noted that hereafter items in parentheses refer to phrases sung by a choir, which the lead vocalist may also sing.

28. Throughout the documentation of these songs, the phrases without parentheses refer to the lead or soloist's part, while the sections in parentheses represent the choir and congregation. Where applicable, I have maintained the authenticity of pronunciation.

29. Southern, *The Music of Black Americans*, 197.

30. Recorded July 4, 1999, WUMC Archives. I utilize some of the songs from the church archives because the recordings are better quality than those offered by my digital recorder. All of the songs continue to be sung with minor variation.

31. Cleveland, *Songs of Zion*, 1.

32. "It is Well with My Soul" was recorded at the funeral of a member of Wesley UMC, circa 1997–1998. "A Charge to Keep I Have" was recorded August 1, 1999. "My Hope Is Built" was recorded May 2, 1999, WUMC Archives. "My Hope Is Built, 2" was recorded July 13, 2006, and sung by Lucille and me. According to Joyce Coakley, the rendition of "A Charge to Keep I Have" was one of the songs

frequently utilized during seeking meetings and regular worship services held throughout the week in the lowcountry. See Coakley, *Sweetgrass Baskets and the Gullah Tradition*, 89–96.

33. Levine, "Slave Songs and Slave Consciousness," 68. For additional description of hymn lining, see Dargan, "Congregational Singing Traditions in South Carolina"; and Carawan and Carawan, *Aint You Got a Right to the Tree of Life*.

34. Lomax, *Sounds of the South*, Notebook, Disc 3.

35. Hayes, "The Theology of the Black Pentecostal Praise Song," 31.

36. The theological analysis offered here is not an exhaustive explanation of Christian theology, or of the themes that exist in lowcountry sacred music.

37. Costen, "Singing Praise to God," 394.

38. William McCain, "Preface," in Cleveland, *Songs of Zion*, x. See also Maultsby, "Africanisms in African American Music"; and Costen, "Singing Praise to God."

39. I must acknowledge the work of Jon Michael Spencer in *Theomusicology* and *Re-Searching Black Music*. Spencer purports an area of study called "theomusicology," which argues that humans are inescapably religious and create arts expressing that religiosity. Although I utilized my seminary training and my roles as a minister of music and choir director to construct this chapter long before encountering Spencer's labeling, his work has offered a theoretical framework from which to understand the importance of theological analysis of African American sacred music.

40. "Operator," recorded July 19, 2006.

41. Moore, Jr., "The Spiritual: Soul of Black Religion," 80.

42. "Sit Down Servant," as observed February 26, 2006, St. James Presbyterian Church. Other verses can be inserted. On this date, the other two verses included were "you've come a long way" and "you will get home soon."

43. Some of the traditional songs that incorporated these characters and places are "Joshua Fought the Battle at Jericho" and "Ezekiel Saw the Wheel." See Cleveland, *Songs of Zion* for additional songs.

44. As recorded on April 1, 2001, WUMC Archives.

45. Among the first publications of an arrangement of "I Couldn't Hear Nobody Pray" was in Work, *American Negro Songs: 230 Folk Songs and Spirituals, Religious and Secular*, first published in 1940.

46. As recorded June 3, 2001, WUMC Archives.

47. Adjaye, "Time in Africa and Its Diaspora," 1.

48. Adjaye, "Time in Africa and Its Diaspora," 15. For the purposes of this project, the assessment of time is brief and broad, with the goal of providing a general understanding of its significance and role in music.

49. Holloway, "Time in the African Diaspora," 200. An additional connection between Gullah/Geechee music practices and African traditions is explored in the documentary *The Language You Cry In*, which traces a song sung by Sea Island inhabitants of the Georgia coast to the Mende people of Sierra Leone.

50. Written by Lloyd Woodard (Universal Music), "Sending Up My Timber" was made popular by The Ever Ready Gospel Singers and The Five Blind Boys of Mississippi in the 1960s. The version sung at Wesley UMC, which can be heard on the companion audio, is a combination of the two popularized versions in composition and structure, but distinctive in its rhythm, tempo, linguistic appropriation, and soloist improvisation.

51. The insertion of the verse distinguishes it from the versions made popular in the 1960s. While personal to Lucinda, it also reflects the connection with those who have gone on before that is a part of this culture and reflected in the metaphor talking to the dead.

52. Du Bois, *The Souls of Black Folk*, 1903. See chapter 10, "Of the Faith of Our Fathers," where Du Bois famously articulates the three prominent features of black religious experience: the preacher, the music, and the frenzy.

53. Gordon, "The Negro Spiritual," 200.

54. Allen, Ware, and Garrison, *Slave Songs of the United States*, xiii. A similar description is offered in the journals of Thomas Wentworth Higginson, colonel of the first African American army regiment during the Civil War. Higginson was well known for his suffragist and abolitionist efforts (including his support of the John Brown raid of Harper's Ferry, Virginia, in 1859) and served as commander of the First South Carolina Volunteers out of Beaufort from November 1862 to October 1864. See Higginson, "Negro Spirituals," for details.

55. Margaret Creel has suggested that the ring shout reflected both the African and African American efforts to connect the natural and supernatural, the sacred and the secular. See Creel, "Community Regulation," 73.

56. Creel, *A Peculiar People*, 299.

57. John Bennett Papers, "Untitled Oversized Scrapbook," 5–6. Bennett also remarked that these trances could be genuine or "simulated." It should also be noted that Bennett's description that the possessed sometimes see God and Mary the mother of Jesus (Christian-based) leads one to presuppose that possession by African deities—though not named by Bennett—was also probable.

58. *Journals of Charlotte Forten Grimké*, Saturday, April 25, 1863, and Sunday, April 26, 1863.

59. *Journals of Charlotte Forten Grimké*, Sunday, May 3, 1863. Elizabeth "Lizzie" Hunn was Forten's companion and the daughter of the local storekeeper on St. Helena.

60. *Diary of Laura M. Towne*, St. Helena's, Sunday, April 27, 1862.

61. *Diary of Laura M. Towne*, St. Helena's, Monday, April 28, 1862.

62. Additional documentation of "shouts" include Monday, April 8, 1862; Sunday, May 4, 1862; and June 9, 1862, in the *Diary of Laura M. Towne*, and February 22, 1862; November 30, 1862; and December 25, 1862, in the *Journals of Charlotte Forten Grimké*.

63. Gordon, "The Negro Spiritual," 192.

64. Allen, *Slave Songs of the United States*, xii–xiv.
65. *John Bennett Papers*, "Untitled Oversized Scrapbook," 5. Abigail Christensen offers a similar description of the physicality of the ring shout in her essay, "Spirituals and 'Shouts' of Southern Negroes," 155.
66. *Diary of Laura M. Towne*, Monday, April 28, 1862. Also cited in Spencer, *Protest and Praise*.
67. Allen, *Slave Songs of the United States*, xii–xiv. Also cited in Spencer, *Protest and Praise*. Allen did not personally observe this shout, but cited an unnamed article from the *Nation* dated May 30, 1867. His conclusion about the statement is most significant: "In the form described here, the 'shout' is probably confined to South Carolina and the states South of it," xiv.
68. *John Bennett Papers*, "Untitled Oversized Scrapbook," 5.
69. *Journals of Charlotte Forten Grimké*, Sunday, November 23, 1862. Mr. Ruggles (T. Edwin Ruggles) was the plantation superintendent of St. Helena Island. Forten also mentions her inability to understand the words in the entry dated Sunday, November 30, 1862.
70. Christensen, "Spirituals and 'Shouts' of Southern Negroes," 155.
71. *John Bennett Papers*, "Untitled Oversized Scrapbook," 5.
72. Allen, *Slave Songs of the United States*, xiv.
73. Pollitzer, *The Gullah People and Their African Heritage*, 8.
74. Stuckey, *Slave Culture*, 11.
75. Creel, *A Peculiar People*, 299. See also *Something to Shout About: Reflections on the Gullah Spiritual*, by Sally Plair, and "The Shout and Shouting in the Slave Religion of the United States," by Robert Simpson.
76. Gordon, "The Negro Spiritual," 200.
77. Simpson, "The Shout and Shouting in the Slave Religion of the United States," 36–37.
78. These are the terms given to spirit possession by each of the women. It is also important to note that the presence of the Spirit is always the Spirit of God (Christian) rather than an ancestor.
79. Butler, *Women in the Church of God in Christ*, 71–72.
80. Samuel Lawton noted the disappearance of this tradition as early as 1939. See "The Religious Life of South Carolina Coastal and Sea Island Negroes," 75.
81. For greater analysis of this history, see Floyd, *The Power of Black Music*; Burnim and Maultsby, *African American Music*; and Williams and Dixie, *This Far by Faith*, the textual companion to the six-part PBS documentary. For analysis of the impact of the movement for expressive worship that emerged in 1940s Chicago, which also coincided with the advent of Thomas Dorsey's "gospel music" form, see Jackson, *Singing in My Soul*, chapter 3.
82. Higginnbotham, *Righteous Discontent*, 1. For more in-depth examinations of the impact of the cult of respectability within African American communities, see also Wolcott, *Remaking Respectability*; Schechter, *Ida B. Wells-Barnett and American*

Reform, 1880–1930; White, *Dark Continent of Our Bodies: Black Feminism and the Politics of Respectability*; Harris, "Gatekeeping and Remaking"; and Kelly, *Right to Ride*.

83. Jackson, *Singing in My Soul*.

84. Butler, *Women in the Church of God in Christ*, 72.

85. Floyd, *The Power of Black Music*. See also Waugh, *Memory, Music, and Religion*.

CHAPTER 5: LIVED MEMORY

1. For discussion of how Yenenga uses storytelling as a heuristic device, see chapter 3.

2. Maurice Halbwachs (*On Collective Memory*), Paul Connerton (*How Societies Remember* and *The Spirit of Mourning*), and Karen Fields ("What One Cannot Remember Mistakenly") have argued in support of the interconnectedness of individual and collective memories.

3. Luke 22:19.

4. See http://www.gullahfestival.net for additional information.

5. Long, *Significations*, 188, 190.

6. Young, *Rituals of Resistance*, 3.

7. Long's conceptualization parallels that of V. Y. Mudimbe, whose works *The Invention of Africa* (1988) and *The Idea of Africa* (1994) argue that Africa was an idea, space, and image invented in the European mind to exoticize black peoples. As a result, Africa became implanted in the minds and memories of African diasporic communities and treated as a foreign, yet sacred holy-other home. Similar notions about the construction of Africa as a geographic space are reflected in Hartman's *Lose Your Mother* (2007) and Hosley's *Routes of Remembrance* (2008).

8. Emphasis in original.

9. Wrappers are garments for women and are worn predominately in West African cultures. The skirts are approximately two and a half feet wide, spun from various materials (often cotton or batik), can be worn at almost any length, and are secured at the waist. Blouses, which are most often coordinated in color and style, can be short or long-sleeved, are slipped over the head, and can be worn inside or outside of the wrapper.

10. Yenenga claims that her name is Zulu in origin.

11. Pollitzer, *The Gullah People and Their African Heritage*, 154.

12. Yenenga's "adoption" of her Nigerian daughter is not a legalized, but an informal way of assuming parentage.

13. Dashikis are loose-fitted pullover shirts with a V-collar. A boubou is a wide-sleeved flowing robe consisting of three pieces—a long-sleeved shirt, a pair of trousers that tie at the waist and are narrow at the ankles, and a sleeveless gown that is worn on top of the pants and shirt.

14. Afrocentrism is connected to an academic, historical, and philosophical

approach that seeks to decenter Eurocentrism. For a full description of its purpose, definition, and objectives, see Asante, *Afrocentricity*.

15. These instruments, especially the drums and the marimba, originate from various African locales. Djembes are among the most common drums and are easily located along the Ivory Coast and Ghana. The origins of the Ngoma are unclear, but it is currently played throughout regions of southern Africa. The Goumbe (also known as the Congo) drum was created in Sierra Leone, and the Udu is said to originate from the Igbo and Hausa peoples of Nigeria. See Thompson, *Flash of the Spirit*.

16. Coakley provides a similar description in *Sweetgrass Baskets and the Gullah Tradition*.

17. Among the most popular events for tourists are horse-drawn views of the city and visits to historic homes and plantations.

18. In chapter 3 of *Routes of Remembrance*, Hosley provides a striking analysis of the ramifications of diasporic tourism, which has striking parallels to the constructions of Gullah/Geechee tourism.

19. Within the past five years similar festivals have developed throughout the lowcountry in areas including James Island and downtown Charleston.

20. Flyer received at my work e-mail address on September 26, 2010.

21. For more information on each of these events and locales, refer to the following websites: http://www.penncenter.com; http://www.gibbesmuseum.org; http://www.sitesandinsightstours.com/; http://www.gallerychuma.com/; http://www.cofc.edu/avery; http://www.gullahtours.com.

22. Excerpt from the pamphlet provided when I took the tour in 2004.

23. William Saunders, "Sea Islands: Then and Now," 485. The reference to *Roots* is to Alex Haley's landmark text and film series.

24. John F. Szwed, "Africa Lies Just off Georgia," 29.

25. John Smith has argued that African American communities in the lowcountry transitioned from being largely isolated communities to communities that are readily included in national society. He noted that transition occurred in five phases: (1) colonization to freedom (1760–1861); (2) Reconstruction and isolation (1865–1930); (3) the Depression and renewed physical contact (1930–1960); (4) the coming of condominiums (1960–1975); and (5) cultural retrenchment and organization (1975–present). I find the latter two categories most useful for understanding contemporary market forces. See Smith, "Cultural Preservation of the Sea Island Gullah."

26. See Coakley, *Sweetgrass Baskets and the Gullah Tradition*.

27. A paraphrase is, "Listen here, let me tell you something. White folks love to hear these Gullah stories, but when I'm done telling them, they pay me!"

28. Dufault, Jackson, and Salvo, "Sweetgrass: History, Basketry, and Constraints to Industry Growth," 442.

29. Thomas, "The Impact of Corporate Tourism on Gullah Blacks," 1, 3–4.

30. In 1972, Kuwaitis purchased Kiawah Island in its entirety. The island was thereafter developed by Sea Pines Corporation, the same company responsible for the development of Hilton Head. The purchase incited a long and turbulent history between developers who sought to commercialize the island, and environmentalists, African Americans, and Sephardic Jews, who desired to preserve the island's ecology, culture, and economy.

31. Shelley Walcott, "Unique Gullah/Geechee Culture at Risk."

32. "Dut road" is a dirt or unpaved road.

33. See Moore, "Gullah/Geechee Cultural Survival," which examines how families are navigating landownership and cultural identity in light of increased residential and commercial development.

34. Jones-Jackson, *When Roots Die*, 19.

35. Matory, "The Illusion of Isolation," 950.

36. Emphasis in interview.

37. Clyburn, "Congressman Clyburn Introduces Gullah/Geechee Cultural Heritage Act."

38. National Park Service, U.S. Department of the Interior. Accessed June 7, 2008. http://www.nps.gov/guge/index.htm.

39. U.S. Congress, National Heritage Areas Act of 2006.

40. Clyburn, "Congressman Clyburn Introduces Gullah/Geechee Cultural Heritage Act."

41. Goodwine, *The Legacy of Ibo Landing*, preface.

42. Personal interview, 2003. I had minimal contact with Christina during the course of the research. She moved from James Island to attend college in Georgia and law school in New England and returned home only during holidays and breaks.

43. See Bryant, "Journeys along Damascus Road."

44. Emphasis in original.

45. See the coalition's website: http://gullahgeecheenation.com. Accessed October 20, 2013.

46. See also http://www.officialgullahgeechee.info. Accessed October 20, 2013.

47. Jones-Jackson, *When Roots Die*, xv.

48. January 1, 2007.

Adjaye, Joseph K. "Time in Africa and Its Diaspora: An Introduction." In *Time in the Black Experience*, edited by Joseph K. Adjaye, 1–16. Westport, CT: Greenwood Press, 1994.

Allen, William Francis, Charles Pickard Ware, and Lucy McKim Garrison. *Slave Songs of the United States*. New York: Peter Smith, 1951.

Anderson, Frank, Jr. "Gullah Christianity: An Analysis of the Ethical Dimensions of Gullah Culture and Their Implications for the Practical Theology of Contemporary African-American Churches." Ph.D. diss., Mid-America Baptist Theological Seminary, 2000.

Andrews, William L., ed. *Sisters of the Spirit: Three Black Women's Autobiographies of the Nineteenth Century*. Bloomington: Indiana University Press, 1986.

Angell, Stephen Ward. "The Controversy over Women's Ministry in the African Methodist Episcopal Church during the 1880s: The Case of Sara Anne Hughes." In *This Far by Faith: Readings in African-American Women's Religious Biography*, edited by Judith Weisenfeld and Richard Newman, 94–109. New York: Routledge, 1996.

Asante, Molefi K. *Afrocentricity: The Theory of Social Change*. Rev. and expanded ed. Chicago: African American Images, 2003.

Assman, Jan. *Religion and Cultural Memory: Ten Studies*. Translated by Rodney Livingstone. Palo Alto, CA: Stanford University Press, 2006.

Bailey, Cornelia Walker. *God, Dr. Buzzard, and the Bolito Man: A Saltwater Geechee Talks about Life on Sapelo Island, Georgia*. New York: Anchor Books, 2001.

Barton, William E. *Old Plantation Hymns: A collection of hitherto unpublished melodies of the slave and the freedman, with historical and descriptive notes*. 1899. Reprint. New York: AMS Press, 1972.

Benjamin, S. G. "The Sea Islands." *Harper's New Monthly Magazine* 57 (November 1878): 839–61.

Bennett, John (1865–1956) Papers, 1865–1956. 1176.00. From the Collections of the South Carolina Historical Society, Charleston.

Bennett, John (1865–1956) Papers, 1865–1956. 1176.00. "Gullah: A Negro Patois: Part 1." *South Atlantic Quarterly* 7, no. 4 (October 1908): 332–47.

Bennett, John (1865–1956) Papers, 1865–1956. 1176.00. "Gullah: A Negro Patois: Part 2." *South Atlantic Quarterly* 8, no. 1 (January 1909): 39–52.

Beoku-Betts, Josephine. "We Got Our Way of Cooking Things: Women, Food, and Preservation of Cultural Identity among the Gullah." *Gender and Society* 9 (October 1995): 535–55.

Berlin, Ira. *Generations of Captivity: A History of African American Slaves.* Cambridge, MA: Harvard University Press, 2003.

Blassingame, John. *The Slave Community: Plantation Life in the Antebellum South.* New York: Oxford University Press, 1973.

Bolton, H. Carrington. "Decoration of Graves of Negroes in South Carolina. *Journal of American Folklore* 4, no. 14 (July–September 1891): 214.

The Book of Church Order of the Presbyterian Church in America. Lawrenceville, GA: Office of the State Clerk of the General Assembly of the Presbyterian Church in America, 2006.

The Book of Discipline of the United Methodist Church, 2004. Nashville, TN: United Methodist Publishing House, 2004.

Born, Ethel. *By My Spirit: The Story of Methodist Protestant Women in Mission, 1879–1939.* Cincinnati: Women's Division of the General Board of Global Ministries, 1990.

Braude, Ann. "Women's History *Is* American Religious History." In *Retelling U.S. Religious History*, edited by Thomas A. Tweed, 87–107. Berkeley: University of California Press, 1990.

Brown, Elsa Barkley. "'What Has Happened Here': The Politics of Difference in Women's History and Feminist Politics." *Feminist Studies* 18 (summer 1992): 295–312.

Brown, Ras Michael. *African-Atlantic Cultures and the South Carolina Lowcountry.* Cambridge: Cambridge University Press, 2012.

Brown, Ras Michael. "'Walk in the Feenda': West-Central Africans and the Forest in the South Carolina-Georgia Lowcountry." In *Central Africans and Cultural Transformations in the American Diaspora*, edited by Linda M. Heywood, 289–317. Cambridge: Cambridge University Press, 2002.

Bryant, James A. "Journeys along Damascus Road: Black Ministers, the Call, and the Modernization of Tradition." Ph.D. diss., Brown University, 2002.

Burnim, Mellonee V., and Portia K. Maultsby, eds. *African American Music: An Introduction.* New York: Routledge, 2006.

Butler, Anthea. *Women in the Church of God in Christ: Making a Sanctified World.* Chapel Hill: University of North Carolina Press, 2007.

Campbell, Emory S. *Gullah Cultural Legacies: A Synopsis of Gullah Traditions, Custom-*

ary Beliefs, Artforms and Speech on Hilton Head Island and Vicinal Sea Islands in South Carolina and Georgia. Hilton Head, SC: Gullah Heritage Consulting Services, 2002.

Cannon, Katie G. Black Womanist Ethics. Atlanta: Scholars Press, 1988.

Capers, William. A Catechism for Little Children and for Use on the Missions to the Slaves in South Carolina. Charleston, SC: J. S. Burges, 1833.

Capers, William. A Catechism for the Use of Methodist Missions. Charleston, SC: J. S. Burges, 1833.

Carawan, Guy, and Candie Carawan. Ain't You Got a Right to the Tree of Life? The People of Johns Island, South Carolina—Their Faces, Their Words, and Their Songs. Athens: University of Georgia Press, 1989.

Carney, Judith. Black Rice: The African Origin of Rice Cultivation in the Americas. Cambridge, MA: Harvard University Press, 2002.

Chireau, Yvonne. Black Magic: Religion and the African American Conjuring Tradition. Berkeley: University of California Press, 2003.

Christensen, Abigail M. Holmes. Afro-American Folk Lore, Told round Cabin Fires on the Sea Islands of South Carolina. Boston: published by author, 1892.

Christensen, Abigail M. Holmes. "Spirituals and 'Shouts' of Southern Negroes." Journal of American Folklore 7, no. 25 (April 1894): 154–55.

Christensen, Niels, Jr. "The Negroes of Beaufort County, South Carolina." Southern Workman 32 (October 1903): 481–85.

Clark-Lewis, Elizabeth. Living In, Living Out: African American Domestics and the Great Migration. New York: Kodansha America, 1996.

Cleveland, James. Songs of Zion. Nashville, TN: Abington Press, 1981.

Clyburn, James E. "Congressman Clyburn Introduces Gullah/Geechee Cultural Heritage Act." Congressional Press Release, Sixth District, South Carolina. July 12, 2004.

Coakley, Joyce V. Sweetgrass Baskets and the Gullah Tradition. Charleston, SC: Arcadia Publishing, 2005.

Cole, Johnnetta Betsch, and Beverly Guy-Sheftall. Gender Talk: The Struggle for Freedom and Equality in African American Communities. New York: One World/Ballantine Books, 2003.

Coleman, Monica A. "Must I Be Womanist?" Journal of Feminist Studies in Religion 22, no. 1 (spring 2006): 85–134.

Collier-Thomas, Bettye. Jesus, Jobs, and Justice: African American Women and Religion. New York: Knopf, 2010.

Collins, Patricia Hill. Black Feminist Thought: Knowledge, Consciousness, and the Politics of Empowerment. New York: Routledge, 2000.

Collins, Patricia Hill. Fighting Words: Black Women and the Search for Justice. Minneapolis: University of Minnesota Press, 1998.

Collins, Patricia Hill. "What's in a Name? Womanism, Black Feminism and Beyond." Black Scholar 26, no. 1 (winter/spring 1996): 9–17.

Connerton, Paul. *How Societies Remember*. Cambridge: Cambridge University Press, 1989.

Connerton, Paul. *The Spirit of Mourning: History, Memory and the Body*. Cambridge: Cambridge University Press, 2011.

Cornelius, Janet Duitsman. *Slave Missions and the Black Church in the Antebellum South*. Columbia: University of South Carolina Press, 1999.

Costen, Melva W. "Singing Praise to God in African American Worship Contexts." In *African American Religious Studies: An Interdisciplinary Anthology*, edited by Gayraud Wilmore, 392–404. Durham, NC: Duke University Press, 1989.

Courlander, Harold. *Negro Folk Music, U.S.A.* New York: Columbia University Press, 1963.

Creel, Margaret Washington. "Community Regulation and Cultural Specialization in Gullah Folk Religion." In *African American Christianity: Essays in History*, edited by Paul E. Johnson, 47–79. Berkeley: University of California Press, 1994.

Creel, Margaret Washington. "Gullah Attitudes toward Life and Death." In *Africanisms in American Culture*, edited by Joseph E. Holloway, 69–97. Bloomington: Indiana University Press, 1990.

Creel, Margaret Washington *A Peculiar People: Slave Religion and Community-Culture among the Gullahs*. New York: New York University Press, 1988.

Cross, Wilbur. *Gullah Culture in America*. Westport, CT: Praeger Publishers, 2008.

Crum, Mason. *Gullah: Negro Life in the Carolina Sea Islands*. Durham, NC: Duke University Press. 1940.

Curtin, Philip. *The Atlantic Slave Trade: A Census*. Madison: University of Wisconsin Press, 1969.

Curtin, Philip. *The Rise and Fall of the Plantation Complex: Essays in Atlantic History*. New York: Cambridge University Press, 1998.

Dargan, William T. "Congregational Singing Traditions in South Carolina." *Black Music Research Journal* 15, no. 1 (spring 1995): 29–73.

Dash, Julie. *Daughters of the Dust*. Produced, written, and directed by Julie Dash. 113 min. New York: Kino on Video, 1991. DVD.

Dash, Julie. *Daughters of the Dust*. New York: Plume/Penguin Books, 1997.

Davis, Angela Y. *Women, Race and Class*. New York: Random House, 1983.

Dodson, Jualynne. "Nineteenth-Century A.M.E. Preaching Women: Cutting Edge of Women's Inclusion in Church Polity." In *Women in New Worlds: Historical Perspectives on the Wesleyan Tradition*, vol. 1, edited by Hilah F. Thomas and Rosemary Skinner Keller, 276–92. Nashville, TN: Abingdon Press, 1981.

Douglas, Kelly Brown. *The Black Christ*. Maryknoll, NY: Orbis Books, 1994.

Du Bois, W. E. B. *The Souls of Black Folk*. New York: Vintage Books, 1990.

Dufault, Robert J., Mary Jackson, and Stephen K. Salvo. "Sweetgrass: History, Basketry, and Constraints to Industry Growth." In *New Crops*, edited by J. Janick and J. E. Simons, 442–45. New York : Wiley, 1993.

Earl, Riggins R. *Dark Symbols, Obscure Signs: God, Self, and Community in the Slave Mind.* Knoxville: University of Tennessee Press, 2003.

Eliade, Mircea. *The Sacred and the Profane: The Nature of Religion.* New York: Harcourt Brace, 1987.

Elkins, Stanley M. *Slavery: A Problem of American Institutional and Intellectual Life.* Chicago: University of Chicago Press, 1959.

Eltis, David, Stephen D. Behrendt, David Richardson, and Herbert S. Klein. *The Trans-Atlantic Slave Trade: A Database on CD-ROM.* New York: Cambridge University Press, 1999.

Etter-Lewis, Gwendolyn. "Black Women's Life Stories: Reclaiming Self in Narrative Texts." In *Women's Words: The Feminist Practice of Oral History,* edited by Sherna Berger Gluck and Daphne Patai, 43–58. New York: Routledge, 1991.

Evans, Curtis J. *The Burden of Black Religion.* New York: Oxford University Press, 2008.

Fett, Sharla M. *Working Cures: Healing, Health, and Power on Southern Slave Plantations.* Chapel Hill: University of North Carolina Press, 2002.

Fields, Karen. "What One Cannot Remember Mistakenly." In *History and Memory in African-American Culture,* edited by Genevieve Fabre and Robert O'Meally, 150–63. New York: Oxford University Press, 1994.

Fields, Mamie Garvin. *Lemon Swamp and Other Places: A Carolina Memoir.* New York: Free Press, 1985.

Floyd, Samuel A., Jr. *The Power of Black Music: Interpreting Its History from Africa to the United States.* New York: Oxford University Press, 1995.

Forten, Charlotte (Grimké). *The Journal of Charlotte L. Forten.* Introduction and notes by Ray Allen Billington. New York: Dryden Press, 1953.

Forten, Charlotte (Grimké). *The Journals of Charlotte Forten Grimké.* Edited by Brenda Stevenson. New York: Oxford University Press, 1988.

Forten, Charlotte (Grimké). "Life on the Sea Islands: Part 1." *Atlantic Monthly* 13 (May 1864): 587–96.

Forten, Charlotte (Grimké). "Life on the Sea Islands: Part 2." *Atlantic Monthly* 13 (June 1864): 666–76.

Frazier, E. Franklin. *The Negro Church in America.* New York: Schocken Books, 1974.

Frederick, Marla F. *Between Sundays: Black Women and Everyday Struggles of Faith.* Berkeley: University of California Press, 2003.

Frederick-McGlathery, Marla. "'But It's Bible': African American Women and Television Preachers." In *Women and Religion in the African Diaspora: Knowledge, Power, and Performance,* edited by R. Marie Griffith and Barbara Dianne Savage, 266–92. Baltimore: Johns Hopkins University Press, 2006.

Geertz, Clifford. *The Interpretation of Cultures: Selected Essays.* New York: Basic Books, 1973.

Genovese, Eugene. *Roll, Jordan, Roll: The World the Slaves Made.* 2nd ed. New York: Oxford University Press, 1979.

Gilkes, Cheryl Townsend. *If It Wasn't for the Women: Black Women's Experience and Womanist Culture in Church and Community*. New York: Orbis Books, 2001.

Gilkes, Cheryl Townsend. "Exploring the Religious Connection: Black Women Community Workers, Religious Agency, and the Force of Faith." In *Women and Religion in the African Diaspora: Knowledge, Power, and Performance*, edited by R. Marie Griffith and Barbara Dianne Savage, 179–96. Baltimore: Johns Hopkins University Press, 2006.

Gilkes, Cheryl Townsend. "The Roles of Church and Community Mothers: Ambivalent American Sexism or Fragmented African Familyhood?" *Journal of Feminist Studies in Religion* 2, no. 1 (spring 1986): 41–59.

Gilroy, Paul. *The Black Atlantic: Modernity and Double Consciousness*. Cambridge, MA: Harvard University Press, 1993.

Goldenberg, David M. *The Curse of Ham: Race and Slavery in Early Judaism, Christianity, and Islam*. Princeton, NJ: Princeton University Press, 2003.

Gomez, Michael A. *Exchanging Our Country Marks: The Transformation of African Identities in the Colonial and Antebellum South*. Chapel Hill: University of North Carolina Press, 1998.

Goodwine, Marquetta L., ed. *The Legacy of Ibo Landing: Gullah Roots of African American Culture*. Atlanta: Clarity Press, 1998.

Gordon, Avery F. *Ghostly Matters: Haunting and the Sociological Imagination*. Minneapolis: University of Minnesota Press, 1996.

Gordon, Lewis R., and Jane Anna Gordon. *Not Only the Master's Tools: African-American Studies in Theory and Practice*. Boulder, CO: Paradigm Publishers, 2006.

Gordon, Robert. "The Negro Spiritual." In *The Carolina Low-Country*, edited by Augustine T. Smythe et al., 191–224. New York: Macmillan, 1931.

Grant, Jacquelyn. "Black Theology and the Black Woman." In *Words of Fire: An Anthology of African American Feminist Thought*, edited by Beverly Guy-Sheftall, 320–36. New York: New Press, 1995.

Grant, Jacquelyn. *White Women's Christ and Black Women's Jesus: Feminist Christology and Womanist Response*. Atlanta: Scholars Press, 1989.

Guthrie, Patricia. "'Catch Sense:' The Meaning of Plantation Membership on St. Helena Island, S.C." Ph.D. diss., University of Rochester, 1977.

Guthrie, Patricia. *Catching Sense: African American Communities on a South Carolina Sea Island*. Westport, CT: Bergin and Garvey, 1996.

Halbwachs, Maurice. *On Collective Memory*, translated by Lewis A. Coser. Chicago: University of Chicago Press, 1992.

Hall, David D., ed. *Lived Religion in America: Toward a History of Practice*. Princeton, NJ: Princeton University Press, 1997.

Hamilton, Kendra Yvette. "Gullah Gullah City: Race, Representation, and the Romance of History in the 20th Century Narratives of Charleston, South Carolina." Ph.D. diss., University of Virginia, 2010.

Hammonds, Evelynn M. "Toward a Genealogy of Black Female Sexuality: The

Problematic of Silence." In *Feminist Theory and the Body: A Reader*, edited by Janet Price and Margrit Shildrick, 93–104. New York: Routledge, 1999.

Harding, Vincent. *There Is a River: The Black Struggle for Freedom in America*. San Diego: Harcourt Brace, 1981.

Hargrove, Melissa Denise. "Reinventing the Plantation: Gated Communities as Spatial Segregation in the Gullah Sea Islands." Ph.D. diss., University of Tennessee, 2005.

Harris, Jane Paisley. "Gatekeeping and Remaking: The Politics of Respectability in African American Women's History and Black Feminism." *Journal of Women's History* 15, no. 1 (spring 2003): 212–20.

Harrison, Ira, and Faye V. Harrison, eds. *African-American Pioneers in Anthropology*. Urbana: University of Illinois Press, 1999.

Hartman, Saidiya. *Lose Your Mother: A Journey along the Atlantic Slave Trade Route*. New York: Farrar, Straus and Giroux, 2007.

Harvey, Paul. "'A Servant of Servants Shall He Be': The Construction of Race in American Religious Mythologies." In *Religion and the Creation of Race and Ethnicity*, edited by Craig R. Prentiss, 13–27. New York: New York University Press, 2003.

Hayes, Michael G. "The Theology of the Black Pentecostal Praise Song." *Black Sacred Music* 4, no. 2 (fall 1990): 30–34.

Heitzenrater, Richard P. *Wesley and the People Called Methodists*. Nashville, TN: Abington Press, 1995.

Henry, Paget. *Caliban's Reason: Introducing Afro-Caribbean Philosophy*. New York: Routledge, 2000.

Hernández, Graciela. "Multiple Subjectivities and Strategic Positionality: Zora Neale Hurston's Experimental Ethnographies." In *Women Writing Culture*, edited by Ruth Behar and Deborah Gordon, 148–65. Berkeley: University of California Press, 1995.

Herron, Leonora. "Conjuring and Conjure Doctors." *Southern Workman* 24, no. 7 (July 1895): 117–18.

Herskovits, Melville J. *The Myth of the Negro Past*. Boston: Beacon Press, 1958.

Heyward, Jane Screven DuBose (1864–1939) Papers, 1882–1940. 1172.03.01. From the Collections of the South Carolina Historical Society, Charleston.

Higginbotham, Evelyn Brooks. "African-American Women's History and the Metalanguage of Race." *Signs: Journal of Women in Culture and Society* 17 (1992): 251–74.

Higginbotham, Evelyn Brooks. "Beyond the Sounds of Silence: African American Women in History." *Gender and History* 1, no. 1 (March 1989): 50–67.

Higginbotham, Evelyn Brooks. "The Black Church: A Gender Perspective." In *African-American Religion: Interpretive Essays in History and Culture*, edited by Timothy E. Fulop and Albert J. Raboteau, 201–25. New York: Routledge, 1997.

Higginbotham, Evelyn Brooks. *Righteous Discontent: The Women's Movement in the*

Black Baptist Church, 1880–1920. Cambridge, MA: Harvard University Press, 1993.

Higginson, Thomas Wentworth. *Army Life in a Black Regiment*. New York: Crowell-Collier Publishing, 1962.

Higginson, Thomas Wentworth."Negro Spirituals." *Atlantic Monthly* 19, no. 116 (June 1867): 685–94.

Hine, Darlene Clark, and Barry Gaspar, eds. *More than Chattel: Black Women and Slavery in the Americas*. Bloomington: Indiana University Press, 1996.

Hirsch, Diane Sullivan. "A Lie for True: Ethnolinguistic Origins of Gullah/ GeeChee." Ph.D. diss., Union Institute and University, 2003.

Holloway, Joseph E. "Time in the African Diaspora: The Gullah Experience." In *Time in the Black Experience*, edited by Joseph K. Adjaye, 199–212. Westport, CT: Greenwood Press, 1994.

Holloway, Karla FC. *Passed On: African American Mourning Stories: A Memorial*. Durham, NC: Duke University Press, 2002.

Hondagneu-Sotelo, Pierrette. *Doméstica: Immigrant Workers Cleaning and Caring in the Shadows of Affluence*. 2nd ed. Berkeley: University of California Press, 2007.

Hosley, Bayo. *Routes of Remembrance: Refashioning the Slave Trade in Ghana*. Chicago: University of Chicago Press, 2008.

Hucks, Tracey. "Burning with a Flame in America: African American Women in African-Derived Traditions." *Journal of Feminist Studies in Religion* 17, no. 2 (fall 2001): 89–106.

Hucks, Tracey. *Yoruba Traditions and African American Religious Nationalism*. Albuquerque: University of New Mexico Press, 2012.

Hull, Gloria T., Patricia Bell Scott, and Barbara Smith, eds. *But Some of Us Are Brave: All the Women Are White, All the Blacks Are Men: Black Women's Studies*. New York: Feminist Press, 1993.

Hunter, Tera. *To 'Joy My Freedom: Southern Black Women's Lives and Labors after the Civil War*. Cambridge, MA: Harvard University Press, 1998.

Hurston, Zora Neale. *Mules and Men*. New York: Harper Perennial, 1990.

Hurston, Zora Neale. *The Sanctified Church*. New York: Marlowe and Company, 1981.

Jackson, Jerma A. *Singing in My Soul: Black Gospel Music in a Secular Age*. Chapel Hill: University of North Carolina Press, 2004.

Jackson, Luther P. "Religious Instruction of Negroes, 1830–1860, with Special Reference to South Carolina." *Journal of Negro History* 15, no. 1 (January 1930): 72–114.

James, William. *The Varieties of Religious Experience: A Study of Human Nature*. New York: Random House, 2002.

Johnson, Guy B. *Folk Culture on St. Helena Island, South Carolina*. Chapel Hill: University of North Carolina Press, 1930.

Johnson, Guy B. "The Negro Spiritual: A Problem in Anthropology." *American Anthropologist*, New Series 33, no. 2 (April–June 1931): 157–71.

Johnson, Guion Griffin. *A Social History of the Sea Islands*. Chapel Hill: University of North Carolina Press, 1930.

Johnson, Walter. "On Agency." *Journal of Social History* 37, no. 1 (fall 2003): 113–24.

Jones, Charles Colcock. *A Catechism for Colored Persons*. Savannah, GA: T. Purse, 1837.

Jones, Charles Colcock. *The Religious Instruction of the Negroes in the United States*. 1842. Reprint. Freeport, NY: Books for Libraries Press, 1971.

Jones, Jacqueline. *Labor of Love, Labor of Sorrow: Black Women, Work, and the Family from Slavery to the Present*. New York: Basic Books, 1985.

Jones-Jackson, Patricia. *When Roots Die: Endangered Traditions on the Sea Islands*. Athens: University of Georgia Press, 1987.

Journal of Black Studies 10, no. 4, "Sea Island Culture" (June 1980): 379–496.

Joyner, Charles. *Down by the Riverside: A South Carolina Slave Community*. Urbana: University of Illinois Press, 1984.

Katzman, David. *Seven Days a Week: Women and Domestic Service in Industrializing America*. Champaign: University of Illinois Press, 1981.

Kelly, Blair L. M. *Right to Ride: Streetcar Boycotts and African American Citizenship in the Age of Plessy vs. Ferguson*. Chapel Hill: University of North Carolina Press, 2010.

Kleinman, Arthur, and Joan Kleinman. "How Bodies Remember: Social Memory and Bodily Experience of Criticism, Resistance and Delegitimation Following China's Cultural Revolution." *New Literary History* 25, no. 3 (summer 1994): 707–23.

K'Meyer, Tracy E., and A. Glenn Crothers. "'If I See Some of This in Writing I'm Going to Shoot You': Reluctant Narrators, Taboo Topics, and the Ethical Dilemmas of the Oral Historian." *Oral History Review* 34, no. 1 (winter–spring 2007): 71–93.

Laderman, Gary. *Rest in Peace: A Cultural History of Death and the Funeral Home in Twentieth-Century America*. New York: Oxford University Press, 2003.

The Language You Cry In: Story of a Mende Song. Directed by Alvaro Toepke and Angel Serrano. Inko Productions, 1998. DVD.

Lanier, Michelle M. A. "Home Going: A Spirit-Centered Ethnography Exploring the Transformation Journey of Documenting Gullah/Geechee Funerals." Ph.D. diss., University of North Carolina, Chapel Hill, 2008.

Lassiter, Luke Eric. *The Chicago Guide to Collaborative Ethnography*. Chicago: University of Chicago Press, 2005.

Lawton, Samuel Miller. "The Religious Life of South Carolina Coastal and Sea Island Negroes." Ph.D. diss., George Peabody College for Teachers, 1939.

Leopold, Anita Maria, and Jeppe Sinding Jensen, eds. *Syncretism in Religion: A Reader*. New York: Routledge, 2005.

Levine, Lawrence. *Black Culture and Black Consciousness: Afro-American Folk Thought from Slavery to Freedom*. New York: Oxford University Press, 1977.

Levine, Lawrence. "Slave Songs and Slave Consciousness: An Exploration in

Neglected Sources." In *African-American Religion: Interpretive Essays in History and Culture*, edited by Timothy E. Fulop and Albert J. Raboteau, 57–87. New York: Routledge, 1997.

Lewis, Earl. "To Turn As on a Pivot: Writing African Americans into a History of Overlapping Diasporas." *American Historical Review* 100 (June 1995): 765–87.

Lincoln, C. Eric, and Lawrence H. Mamiya. *The Black Church in the African-American Experience*. Durham, NC: Duke University Press, 1990.

Littlefield, Daniel C. *Rice and Slaves: Ethnicity and the Slave Trade in Colonial South Carolina*. Baton Rouge: Louisiana State University Press, 1981.

Lomax, Alan. *Sounds of the South. A Musical Journey from the Georgia Sea Islands to the Mississippi Delta*. Sound Recording. 4 sound discs: digital; 4¾ in.+1 booklet. New York: Atlantic, 1993.

Lomax, Alan. *Southern Journey*, vol. 12, "Georgia Sea Islands." Sound Recording. 13 sound discs: digital; 4¾ in. Cambridge: Rounder Records, ℗1997–1998.

Long, Charles H. *Significations: Signs, Symbols, and Images in the Interpretation of Religion*. Aurora, CO: Davies Group, 1995.

Love, Velma E. *Divining the Self: A Study in Yoruba Myth and Human Consciousness*. University Park: Pennsylvania State University Press, 2013.

Matory, J. Lorand. *Black Atlantic Religion: Tradition, Transnationalism, and Matriarchy in the Afro-Brazilian Candomblé*. Princeton, NJ: Princeton University Press, 2005.

Matory, J. Lorand. "The Illusion of Isolation: The Gullah/Geechees and the Political Economy of African Culture in the Americas." *Comparative Studies in Society and History* 50, no. 4 (2008): 949–80.

Matthews, Donald G. "The Methodist Mission to the Slaves, 1829–1844." *Journal of American History* 51, no. 4 (March 1965): 615–31.

Matthews, Donald H. *Honoring the Ancestors: An African Cultural Interpretation of Black Religion and Literature*. New York: Oxford University Press, 1997.

Maultsby, Portia K. "Africanisms in African American Music." In *Africanisms in American Culture*, edited by Joseph E. Holloway, 185–210. Bloomington: Indiana University Press, 1991.

Mbiti, John S. *African Religions and Philosophy*. London: Heinemann, 1969.

McClaurin, Irma, ed. *Black Feminist Anthropology: Theory, Politics, Praxis, and Poetics*. New Brunswick, NJ: Rutgers University Press, 2001.

McElya, Micki. *Clinging to Mammy: The Faithful Slave in Twentieth-Century America*. Cambridge, MA: Harvard University Press, 2007.

McIlwain, Charlton D. *Death in Black and White: Death, Ritual, and Family Ecology*. Cresskill, NJ: Hampton Press, 2003.

McKoy, Sheila Smith. "The Limbo Contest: Diaspora Temporality and Its Reflection in *Praisesong for the Widow* and *Daughters of the Dust*." *Callaloo* 22, no. 1 (1999): 208–22.

Montgomery, Michael, ed. *The Crucible of Carolina: Essays in the Development of Gullah Language and Culture*. Athens: University of Georgia Press, 1994.

Moore, Janie G. "Africanisms among Blacks of the Sea Islands." *Journal of Black Studies* 10, no. 4, "Sea Island Culture" (June 1980): 467–80.

Moore, Leroy, Jr., "The Spiritual: Soul of Black Religion." *Church History* 40, no. 1 (March 1971): 79–81.

Moore, Lisa Lynelle. "Gullah/Geechee Cultural Survival: Negotiating Family, Land, and Culture on St. Helena Island, South Carolina." Ph.D. diss., California Institute of Integral Studies, 2008.

Morgan, Jennifer L. *Laboring Women: Reproduction and Gender in New World Slavery.* Philadelphia: University of Pennsylvania Press, 2004.

Mudimbe, V. Y. *The Idea of Africa.* Bloomington: Indiana University Press, 1994.

Mudimbe, V. Y. *The Invention of Africa: Gnosis, Philosophy, and the Order of Knowledge.* Bloomington: Indiana University Press, 1988.

Murray, Chalmers S., Papers, 1905–1970. 1178.00. From the Collections of the South Carolina Historical Society, Charleston.

Norwood, Frederick Abbott. *The Story of American Methodism: A History of the United Methodists and Their Relations.* Nashville, TN: Abington Press, 1974.

Otto, Rudolph. *The Idea of the Holy: An Inquiry into the Non-Rational Factor of the Idea of the Divine and Its Relation to the Rational.* Translated by John W. Harvey. London: Oxford University Press, 1958.

Parker, Inez Moore. *The Rise and Decline of the Program of Education for Black Presbyterians of the United Presbyterian Church, U.S.A., 1865–1970.* San Antonio, TX: Trinity University Press, 1977.

Parrish, Lydia. *Slave Songs of the Georgia Sea Islands.* New York: Creative Age Press, 1942.

Peterson, Thomas Virgil. *Ham and Japheth: The Mythic World of Whites in the Antebellum South.* Metuchen, NJ: Scarecrow Press, 1978.

Phillips, Layli. *The Womanist Reader.* New York: Routledge, 2007.

Phillips, Ulrich B. *American Negro Slavery.* New York: D. Appleton, 1918.

Pinckney, Roger. *Blue Roots: African-American Folk Magic of the Gullah People.* St. Paul, MN: Llewellyn Publications, 2000.

Pinn, Anthony B. *The Black Church in the Post-Civil Rights Era.* New York: Orbis Books, 2002.

Pinn, Anthony B. *Varieties of African American Religious Experience.* Minneapolis: Fortress Press, 1998.

Plair, Sally. *Something to Shout About: Reflections on the Gullah Spiritual.* Mt. Pleasant, SC: Molasses Lane Publishers, 1972.

Pollitzer, William. *The Gullah People and Their African Heritage.* Athens: University of Georgia Press, 1999.

Proudfoot, Wayne. *Religious Experience.* Berkeley: University of California Press, 1985.

Puckett, Newbell N. *Folk Beliefs of the Southern Negro.* Chapel Hill: University of North Carolina Press, 1926.

Raboteau, Albert J. "The Black Experience in American Evangelicalism." In
African-American Religion: Interpretive Essays in History and Culture, edited by
Timothy E. Fulop and Albert J. Raboteau, 89–106. New York: Routledge, 1997.

Raboteau, Albert J. Slave Religion: The "Invisible Institution" in the Antebellum South.
New York: Oxford University Press, 1978.

Raymond, Charles A. "The Religious Life of the Negro Slave, Part 1." Harpers New
Monthly Magazine 27, no. 160 (September 1863): 479–85.

Raymond, Charles A. "The Religious Life of the Negro Slave, Part 2." Harpers New
Monthly Magazine 27, no. 161 (October 1863): 676–82.

Raymond, Charles A. "The Religious Life of the Negro Slave, Part 3." Harpers New
Monthly Magazine 27, no. 162 (November 1863): 816–25.

Reagon, Bernice Johnson. If You Don't Go, Don't Hinder Me: The African-American
Sacred Song Tradition. Lincoln: University of Nebraska Press, 2001.

Rhyne, Nancy. Before and After Freedom: WPA Narratives of Lowcountry Folklore.
Charleston, SC: History Press, 2005.

Rogers, Nikki Lynn. "The Affinity of South Carolina's 'Gullah' African Americans: Biological Tests of Cultural and Historical Hypotheses." Ph.D. diss., University of Tennessee, 2000.

Rosaldo, Renato. Culture and Truth: The Remaking of Social Analysis. Boston: Beacon
Press, 1993.

Rose, Willie Lee. Rehearsal for Reconstruction: The Port Royal Experiment. New York:
Oxford University Press, 1976.

Rosengarten, Dale. Row upon Row: Sea Grass Baskets of the South Carolina Lowcountry.
Columbia: McKissick Museum, University of South Carolina, 1986.

Rosengarten, Dale. "Spirits of Our Ancestors: Basket Traditions in the Caro-
linas." In The Crucible of Carolina: Essays in the Development of Gullah Language and
Culture, edited by Michael Montgomery, 133–57. Athens: University of Georgia
Press, 1994.

Ross, Rosetta E. Witnessing and Testifying: Black Women, Religion, and Civil Rights.
Minneapolis: Fortress Press, 2003.

Rowe, George C. "The Negroes of the Sea Islands." Southern Workman 29 (December 1900): 709–15.

Rucker, Walter. "Conjure, Magic, and Power: The Influence of Afro-Atlantic Religious Practices on Slave Resistance and Rebellion." Journal of Black Studies 32,
no. 1 (September 2001): 84–103.

Saunders, William C. "Sea Islands: Then and Now." Journal of Black Studies 10,
no. 4, "Sea Island Culture" (June 1980): 481–92.

Schechter, Patricia. Ida B. Wells-Barnett and American Reform, 1880–1930. Chapel
Hill: University of North Carolina Press, 2001.

Scott, David. "That Event, This Memory: Notes on the Anthropology of African
Diasporas in the New World." Diaspora: A Journal of Transnational Studies 1, no. 3
(winter 1991): 261–84.

Simpson, Robert. "The Shout and Shouting in the Slave Religion of the United States." *Southern Quarterly* 23, no. 3 (spring 1985): 34–48.

Smith, H. Shelton. *In His Image, But . . . Racism in Southern Religion, 1780–1910*. Durham, NC: Duke University Press, 1972.

Smith, John P. "Cultural Preservation of the Sea Island Gullah: A Black Social Movement in the Post-Civil Rights Era." *Rural Sociology* 56 (1991): 284–98.

Smith, Theophus. *Conjuring Culture: Biblical Formations of Black America*. New York: Oxford University Press, 1994.

Smythe, Augustine T., et al. *The Carolina Low-Country*. New York: Macmillan, 1931.

Southern, Eileen. *The Music of Black Americans: A History*. 3rd ed. New York: W.W. Norton, 1997.

Spencer, Jon Michael. *Protest and Praise: Sacred Music of Black Religion*. Minneapolis: Fortress Press, 1990.

Spencer, Jon Michael. *Re-Searching Black Music*. Knoxville: University of Tennessee Press, 1996.

Spencer, Jon Michael. *Theomusicology*. Durham, NC: Duke University Press, 1994.

Stampp, Kenneth. *The Peculiar Institution: Slavery in the Antebellum South*. New York: Vintage, 1956.

Starks, George L., Jr. "Black Music in the Sea Islands of South Carolina—Its Cultural Context: Continuity and Change." Ph.D. diss., Wesleyan University, 1973.

Starks, George L., Jr. "Singing 'Bout a Good Time: Sea Island Religious Music." *Journal of Black Studies* 10, no. 4, "Sea Island Culture" (June 1980): 437–44.

Steiner, Roland. "'Seeking Jesus': A Religious Rite of Negroes in Georgia." *Journal of American Folklore* 14, no. 54 (July–September 1901): 172.

Stewart, Dianne M. *Three Eyes for the Journey: African Dimensions of the Jamaican Religious Experience*. New York: Oxford University Press, 2005.

Stuckey, Sterling. *Slave Culture: Nationalist Theory and the Foundations of Black America*. New York: Oxford University Press, 1987.

Szwed, John F. "Africa Lies Just off Georgia: Sea Islands Preserve Origins of Afro-American Culture. *Africa Report* (October 1970): 29–31.

Taylor, Mark C., ed. *Critical Terms for Religious Studies*. Chicago: University of Chicago Press, 1998.

Thomas, June Manning. "The Impact of Corporate Tourism on Gullah Blacks: Notes on Issues of Employment." *Phylon* 41, no. 1 (1980): 1–11.

Thomas, Linda E. "Womanist Theology, Epistemology, and a New Anthropological Paradigm. *Cross Currents* 48, no. 4 (winter 98/99): 1–7.

Thompson, Robert Farris. *Flash of the Spirit: African and Afro-American Art and Philosophy*. New York: Vintage Books, 1984.

Thornton, John K. "African Dimensions of the Stono Rebellion." *American Historical Review* 96, no. 4 (October 1991): 1101–13.

Towne, Laura M. *Letters and Diary of Laura M. Towne; written from the Sea Islands of*

South Carolina, 1862–1884, edited by Rupert Sargent Holland. New York: Negro Universities Press, 1969.

Townes, Emilie M., ed. *A Troubling in My Soul: Womanist Perspectives on Evil and Suffering*. Maryknoll, NY: Orbis Books, 1993.

Trott, Wendy Carmen. "An Afrocentric Analysis of the Transition and Transformation of African Medicine (Root Medicine) as Spiritual Practice among Gullah People of Lowcountry South Carolina." Ph.D. diss., Temple University, 2003.

Tucker, Susan. *Telling Memories among Southern Women: Domestic Workers and Their Employers in the Segregated South*. Baton Rouge: Louisiana State University Press, 2002.

Turner, Lorenzo Dow. *Africanisms in the Gullah Dialect*. Ann Arbor: University of Michigan Press, 1949.

Tweed, Thomas. "Between the Living and the Dead: Fieldwork, History and the Interpreter's Position." In *Personal Knowledge and Beyond: Reshaping the Ethnography of Religion*, edited by James Spickard et al., 63–74. New York: New York University Press, 2002.

Twining, Mary A. "An Examination of African Cultural Retentions in the Folk Culture of South Carolina and the Georgia Sea Islands." Ph.D. diss., Indiana University, 1977.

Twining, Mary A., and Keith E. Baird, eds. *Sea Island Roots: African Presence in the Carolinas and Georgia*. Trenton, NJ: African World Press, 1991.

U.S. Congress. House of Representatives. *National Heritage Areas Act of 2006*. 109th Congress, October 9, 2006. Public Law 109–338.

Wade-Lewis, Margaret. *Lorenzo Dow Turner: Father of Gullah Studies*. Columbia: University of South Carolina Press, 2007.

Walcott, Shelley. "Unique Gullah/Geechee Culture at Risk." CNN.com, February 26, 2002. Accessed July 7, 2009. http://archives.cnn.com/2002/fyi/news/02/13/gullah.

Walker, Alice. *In Search of Our Mothers' Gardens: Womanist Prose*. New York: Harcourt Brace, 1983.

Wallace-Sanders, Kimberly. *Mammy: A Century of Race, Gender, and Southern Memory*. Ann Arbor: University of Michigan Press, 2008.

Waugh, Earle H. *Memory, Music, and Religion: Morocco's Mystical Chanters*. Columbia: University of South Carolina Press, 2005.

Weisenfeld, Judith, and Richard Newman, eds. *This Far by Faith: Readings in African-American Women's Religious Biography*. New York: Routledge, 1996.

White, E. Francis. *Dark Continent of Our Bodies: Black Feminism and the Politics of Respectability*. Philadelphia: Temple University Press, 2001.

Wiggins, Daphne C. *Righteous Content: Black Women's Perspectives of Church and Faith*. New York: New York University Press, 2006.

Williams, Delores. *Sisters in the Wilderness: The Challenges of Womanist God-Talk*. Maryknoll, NY: Orbis Books, 1993.

Williams, Juan, and Quinton H. Dixie, eds. *This Far by Faith: Stories from the African American Religious Experience*. New York: HarperCollins, 2003.

Wilmore, Gayraud. *Black and Presbyterian: The Heritage and the Hope*. Rev. ed. Louisville, KY: Witherspoon Press, 2006.

Wilmore, Gayraud. *Black Religion and Black Radicalism: An Interpretation of the Religious History of African Americans*. Maryknoll, NY: Orbis Books, 2000.

Wolcott, Victoria. *Remaking Respectability: African American Women in Interwar Detroit*. Chapel Hill: University of North Carolina Press, 2001.

Wolfe, Michael C. *The Abundant Life Prevails: Religious Traditions of St. Helena Island*. Waco, TX: Baylor University Press, 2000.

Wood, Peter H. *Black Majority: Negroes in Colonial South Carolina from 1670 through the Stono Rebellion*. New York: Knopf, 1974.

Woofter, Thomas Jackson, Jr. *Black Yeomanry: Life on St. Helena Island*. New York: Henry Holt, 1930.

Work, John W. *American Negro Songs: 230 Folk Songs and Spirituals, Religious and Secular*. New York: Dover Publications, 1998.

Young, Jason R. *Rituals of Resistance: African Atlantic Religion in Kongo and the Lowcountry South in the Era of Slavery*. Baton Rouge: Louisiana State University Press, 2007.

faith traditions: body-soul dichotomy and, 90–95, 237n66; Christianity, 4; conceptions of, 8; as enactment of agency, 63–65, 86–87, 147, 169–71, 237n72; folk religions, 4, 68–81; as lived religion, 18–20, 48–55; religious practice and, 51–52; remembering as, 169–71; seeking as, 120–21, 123; use of term *faith*, 1, 50–51

feminist theory, 10–11, 86, 222n37, 223n39, 227n6, 228n10

Fett, Sharla M., 73–74, 233n23

Fields, Mamie Garvin, 112, 227n60

Five Blind Boys of Mississippi, 245n50

Floyd, Sam, 169–70

folk practices/practitioners: blue eyes, 77–78, 80–81; conjuring/conjurers, 1, 4, 7, 68–74, 89–90, 133–34, 233n15; folk religions, 76–81; healers, 233n15; herbalists, 20, 74, 78–79, 158; importance of, 20, 70–74, 80–81; medicinal traditions, 73–74, 75, 233n23; mourning, 85–86, 226n60, 247n2; physical spaces for, 73–74; religious expression and, 20; religious identity and, 20; religious practice and, 20; as resistance, 101–3; root-workers, 7, 23, 67, 68, 70–71, 74, 76, 96, 101, 202, 233n15; social power of, 71–73; supernatural power of, 68–70, 75; superstitious beliefs, 68–75, 89–90; theomusicology, 244n39; use of term, 233n15; use of term *Spirit/spirit*, 239n6; voodoo (folk religious practice), 19, 76–77, 78, 133; west-central African religious practice and, 101

Foote, Julie, 58

Forten, Charlotte (Grimké): bio of, 90, 95, 234n48, 245n59; on baptism, 229n30; on fluidity of worship time, 97, 238n84; on Gullah, 235n49, 246n69; journals of, 220n19, 234n48; on musicality of the low-country, 136–37; at Penn School, 87, 137, 236n61, 237n75; on praise house and worship services, 39–41; relationship with

Islanders, 235n49; shouts, 160, 162–63; work music, 142, 241n1

Frederick, Marla F., 5, 51, 219n15, 223n39, 230n52

funerary rituals/burial rites, 40–41, 42, 45, 205–6, 229n32, 233n19, 238n, 243n32

Gaillard, Donald, 25

Gaillard, Lucille: "Call to Christ," 212; class status, 28–30; domestic work, 28–29; evangelism, 231n67; faith traditions, 140; folk practices, 80; folk religions, 76; influence of church women on, 57; intergenerational relationships, 57; life story, 25–26, 107–8; marital status of, 25, 61; musical practices, 139, 140, 153, 170–71; "My Hope Is Built II," 212; Poplar Hill Christian Church and, 25–26, 47, 52–53, 57; religious beliefs, 102; religious leadership, 52–53; religious practice, 52–53, 102–3; sacred music, 140–41, 144; seeking process, 121, 122–23, 124, 126–27, 129; shouting, 165–66; talking to the dead, 2, 108, 109

Garrison, Lucy McKim, 241n9

Geechee. *See* Gullah/Geechee

Geertz, Clifford, 10

Gilkes, Cheryl Townsend, 52, 59, 228n12, 231n61, 231n68

Gilroy, Paul, 8

glossolalia (speaking in tongues), 35

Goodwine, Marquetta, 13, 194, 200–201

Gordon, Jane Anna, 23

Gordon, Lewis R., 23

Gordon, Robert, 161

gospel ministries, 34, 36, 37, 43, 92, 100, 198, 224n45, 229n18, 243n20

Grant, Jacquelyn, 48, 58, 223n38

Greater Goodwill AME (Greater Goodwill African American Episcopal Church), 31, 32, 33, 34–35, 57, 115, 125–26, 139–40, 228n16

griots, 65, 110, 112, 113, 178

Gullah/Geechee: Africanisms and, 5–7;

changing meanings of religious practices, 6–7; Christianity and, 90–95;
commercialization/commodifica-
tion of, 182–90, 208, 214–15, 249n30;
commodification of, 22, 208, 214–15,
249n30; contemporary changes in,
207–9, 218n11; cultural distinctiveness of, 218n11; ethnographic unfolding process, 214–15; exploitation of,
214–15, 218n11; Gullah dialect, 10,
12, 83, 85, 142, 144, 146, 190, 218n10,
220n20, 246n69; historiography, 5,
6, 11; impact of exploitation on, 214–
15; impact of transatlantic slave trade
on, 88, 100, 101, 172–75, 218n10,
221n27; limitations of scholarship
on, 6–7; as a peculiar people, 99–100,
224n91, 238n91; religious autonomy
of, 95–101; romantic racialism of, 13;
self-identification among, 8; understanding of time, 98; use of term, 2–3,
218n8, 223n41; Windward Coast and,
218n9
Gullah/Geechee Sea Island Coalition
(GGSIC), 200
Gullah/Geechee women: absence of
scholarship on, 6–7; African cultural
retentions of, 4–7; African identities
and, 88, 178, 185, 239n8; agency and,
59–63, 63–65; gender roles of, 59–63;
as griots, 65; impact of, on religious
life, 62–63, 87–90; importance of
Africanisms for, 182; importance of
faith/religious traditions to, 46–47;
as keepers of culture, 20, 21, 46–47,
63–65, 104–6, 109–16, 134–35, 139,
161, 202–3, 217n7; mourning, 85–86,
226n60, 247n2; religious practice,
4–5; scholarship on women's leadership, 44–47; self-identification
among, 8; as spiritual leaders, xiv,
7–8, 17–18, 43–44, 67–68, 105–6, 116,
122, 138, 165–66; as unintelligible,
81–87
Guthrie, Patricia, 6, 13, 45, 46–47, 117,
118, 231n64, 232n75, 240n16

Halbwachs, Maurice, 226n59, 247n2
Hall, David, 18
Hammonds, Evelyn M., 59
Hartman, Saidiya, 8, 247n7
herbalists, 20, 74, 78–79, 158
Herron, Lenora, 68–69, 71
Herskovits, Melville J., 5, 6, 14, 219nn16–
17, 222n37
Hervieu-Léger, Danièl, 18
Heyward, Dubose, 225n47
Heyward, Jane Dubose: bio of, 12–13, 95,
223n42, 237n74; dialect recitals of, 81,
83–84, 86, 225nn47–48; significance
of her work, 11–12, 86; "The Devil's
Spell," 66–67, 72–73
Heyward, Reverend Carolyn, 47–49
Heyward, Reverend Doctor Charles, 33,
35, 132
Higginbotham, Evelyn Brooks, 63, 67
Higginson, Thomas Wentworth, 245n54
Holloway, Joseph, 112, 155, 229n32
Hosley, Bayo, 8, 221n27, 247n7, 248n18
Hucks, Tracey, 75, 80–81, 223n40,
233n14
Hunn, Elizabeth "Lizzie," 235n49,
245n59
Hurston, Zora Neale, 222n37, 233n15

"I Couldn't Hear Nobody Pray" (sacred
song), 153, 212, 244n45
Idea of Africa (Mudimbe), 247n7
intergenerational relationships: children's services, 231n59; church moth-
ers/spiritual mothers, 29, 46, 58, 59,
63, 88–89; culture keepers and, 20;
elders, 38, 52, 53, 56, 87–88, 116, 120–
26, 140, 197–98, 231n60; as exemplars
for other women, 231n64; male roles
and, 231n61; religious leadership and,
59–60; remembering through sacred
song, 169–71; seeking, 121–22; spiritual parents, 121–22; storytelling and,
110–14; sweetgrass basketry, 239n12
Invention of Africa (Mudimbe), 247n7
Islam, 100
"It Is Well" (sacred song), 212

55, 58–59, 230n52; changes within, 62–65; within enslaved communities, 229n34, 229n37; evangelism, 34, 55, 57, 65, 229n18, 231n67; female leadership, 42–55, 57–60, 67–68, 229n52, 231n68; gendered leadership roles, 43–44, 47–50, 57–58, 63–65, 87–90; hypervisibility/invisibility of women in, 59–63; impact of marital status on, 60–61, 62, 118, 232n75, 232n78; informal acknowledgment of women's leadership, 43–47, 55, 57–58, 63–65; intergenerational relationships and, 59–60; liberation theology and, 58; male leadership, 47, 48–49; religious instruction and, 42, 235n50, 235n53, 236n57, 237n76; sanctioned positions, 7; seeking process and, 123–24; Sunday school teachers, 55; through talking to the dead, 104–6, 116; United Methodist Women, 54, 134, 231n62

religious music. *See* sacred music

religious practices: Africanisms and, 5–7, 19, 76–77, 78, 133; changes within, 3–4, 166–68; changing meanings of, 6–7; contributions of women to, 44–47; ethnographic unfolding process, 214–15; faith traditions and, 51–52; folk religions, 76–81; heartfelt expression of, 36; Homemakers Clubs, 48; remembering through sacred song, 169–71; talking to the dead, 2; voodoo (folk religious practice), 19, 76–77, 78, 133

religious syncretism, 220n18

remembering, 2, 112, 169–71, 226n59, 227n60, 247n2. *See also* lived memory

resistance, 101–3

respectability, cult of, 62, 167–69, 246n82

"Rest for the Weary" (sacred song), 151–52

Righteous Discontent (Higginbotham), 66–67

Rituals of Resistance (Young), 7, 8, 15, 101

Rogers, Nikki Lynn, 226n55

"Roll, Jordan, Roll," 136–37, 162

romantic racialism, 13, 59, 221n34, 236n59

root-workers, 7, 23, 67, 68, 70–71, 74, 76; healing/medicinal practices of, 74, 233n20, 234n23; socioreligious power of, 96, 101, 202; use of term, 233n15. *See also* Pinckney, Lucinda

Ross, Rosetta, 5, 50, 219n15, 223n40, 228n12

Rowe, George C., 37

Ruggins, T. Edwin, 246n69

sacred music traditions: African instruments, 248n15; ancestral memories and, 139, 154–55; call and response, 143, 145, 147; choir traditions, 139–40, 148, 156–58, 206, 243nn27–28, 244n39; choral space, 35; creative verbalization, 143–44, 147–48, 156–57; in everyday life, 136–38, 142–43, 153–54; experience of spirits through, 140–41; gospels, xix, 139–41, 143–45, 167, 243n20, 245n50, 246n81; hymns, 148–49, 243n20; language used, 142–43, 144; lowcountry clap, xvii, 5–6, 35, 102, 141–42, 145, 147, 154–55, 164–65, 171, 208, 243n23; overview of, 21–22, 136–38; religious agency through, 64–65, 86–87, 147, 169–71, 237n72; remembering through, 169–71; ring shouts, 208, 245n55, 246n65, 246n67; shouting/seeking, 143, 159–68, 208; soloist feature, 139, 145–48, 156, 158, 206, 243n28, 245n50; spirit possession, 81–83, 165, 245n57, 246n78; spirituals, 143–44, 241n9, 243n20; styles, structures, and tempo, 144–49, 155, 156–58, 243n24; style/structure, 115–56, 245n50; talking to the dead through, 2, 140–41, 155, 158; theological themes and images, 150–53, 156; traditional songs, 116, 138–43; use of diasporic time within, 154–55

Sanders, Ina Belle, 231n65

Santería, 19

St. Stephens, S.C., xv, 2–3
Stuckey, Sterling, 163
Sumter, Evangelist, 57
sweetgrass basketry, 2, 28, 114–15, 180–81, 186, 187, 194, 202, 227n5, 239n12

talking to the dead: African cultural retentions, 132–33, 239n1; Christianity and, 3–4; conjurers and, 133–34; cultural practice, 105; dreams/visions, 108–9, 116, 122, 128, 134; experience of spirits, 105–6, 107, 108, 109, 115, 140–41; haunting vs., xvi, 106; importance of, 3–4, 21–22, 134–35; intergenerational relationships, 110, 112–14, 115–16, 120; as irrelevant, 3–4; listening, 108–16; living/dead coexistence, 207, 208; musical practices and, 140–41; as normative practice, 132–35; prayer, 104–5, 109, 115; overview of, xiv–xv, 21; presumed relationships between the living and the dead/practice at risk, 207–8; as private experience, 116, 134–35; as religio-cultural practice, 3–4, 104–5, 109–14, 133–34; role of elders, 120; seeking and, 21, 117, 120–32; shifts and challenges to, 207–8; shouting, 105; silence and, 105; storytelling, 109–14, 115; sweetgrass basketry, 2, 28, 114–15, 180–81, 186, 187, 194, 202, 227n5, 239n12; through sacred music, 105, 108–9, 140–41; use of term, 2, 104–6; women as culture keepers, 21, 104–6, 109–16
Terry, Faye: author remembrances of, 209; class status, 26–27, 28–31; domestic work, 26–27, 28–29; as elder, 134; faith traditions, 51, 140; folk practices, 80; folk religions, 76; home-going service of, 205–7; influence of church women on, 57; intergenerational relationships, 57; life story of, 26; musical practices, 139, 149, 153, 170–71; on rededication to church, 62; religious beliefs, 51, 102; religious leadership, 53–54,

59–63, 134; religious practice, 53–54, 102–3; sacred music, 140–41; seeking process, 120, 121, 129, 208; shouting, 165–66; talking to the dead, 2, 107, 109, 127; use of blue eyes, 77–78, 80–81
theomusicology, 244n39
Three Eyes for the Journey (Stewart), 223n40, 234n45, 238n92
time: cyclical time, 2, 98, 154–55; diasporic temporality, 98, 154; fluidity of worship time, 97–98; limbo time and, 2; liminal space, 17; linear time, 2, 98, 154–55; sacred music and, 154–55; use of term, 98, 244n48
Towne, Laura: on baptisms, 38; on fluidity of worship time, 97–98; on hagging, 67; life story, 87; on Maum Katie, 87–89; on Mom Charlotte, 89–90; on "Roll, Jordan, Roll," 136–37; on shouts, 41, 160, 161–62
trances/spirit possession, 81–83, 165, 245n57, 246n78
Turner, Lorenzo Dow, 5, 10, 12, 220n20
Turner, Nat, 91
Twining, Mary A., 226n52, 232n78

United Methodist Women, 54, 134, 231n62

Vesey, Denmark, 19, 91, 133
Vodun/Vodoun (African-derived religion), 19, 133
voodoo (folk religious practice), 19, 76–77, 78, 133

Walker, Alice, 10–11, 222n36, 223n38
Walton, Jonathan L., 229n18
Ware, Charles Pickard, 241n9
Warren, Rick, 34
Watch This! (Walton), 229n18
"Way By and By" (sacred song), 212
"We Are Climbing Jacob's Ladder" (sacred song), 152
Weber, Max, 236n65
weddings, 38, 42, 118

Wesley UMC (Wesley United Methodist Church): background info, 26, 31–32, 228n16, 231n62, 242n12; "A Charge to Keep I Have," 212; David Pinckney and, 208; Emancipation Service, 138–39, 174, 181, 201; Faye Terry's homegoing service, 205–6; female religious leadership, 134; "It Is Well," 212; "My Hope Is Built," 212; role of women within, 57, 60; sacred music and, 242n12, 243n32, 245n50; "Sendin' Up My Timbah," 212, 245n50; "Way By and By," 212; website of, 211–12; "When God Calls Me," 212; worship content/style/structure, 34, 51, 53–54, 138–39, 166, 174, 176–77, 201. *See also* Legare, Roberta; Pinckney, Lucinda; Terry, Faye

"We've Come This Far by Faith" (sacred song), 31, 143, 154, 194, 202–3, 242n17

Wheeler, Yenenga: Africanisms of, 179, 247n9, 247n10, 247n12; as business owner, 30–31, 62; class status, 30–31, 62; as elder, 25, 52, 57, 107–8, 121, 129, 149; faith traditions, 51; folk practices, 80, 102–3; on gender norms, 61; impact of church women on, 56; life story, 29, 109–10; lived memories of Africa, 177–80; "Meeting Song

Medley," 212; musical practices, 140, 165, 170–71; "Pure Religion," 243n27; on rededication to church, 62; religious beliefs, 49, 50–51, 102; religious identity, 51; religious practices, 52, 102–3; sacred music, 140–41; seeking process, 117, 120, 121, 125, 126, 127; shouting, 165–66; as storyteller, 27, 52, 109–14, 115, 140, 172, 187, 248n27; talking to the dead, 2, 109–14, 115, 173–74; trees as sacred spaces, 208; "We've Come This Far by Faith," 143, 242n17

"When God Calls Me" (sacred song), 212

Wiesenfeld, Judith, 5, 22, 48–49, 81, 219n15

Wolfe, Michael C., 5, 15, 46, 87, 99, 177, 238n89

womanist theory, 10–11, 15, 58, 222n36, 223nn38–40, 227n6, 228n10

Women in the Church of God in Christ (Butler), 165

Wood, Peter, 226n52

Woodard, Lloyd, 245n50

worship leaders. *See* religious leadership

Yoruba, 133, 220n20

"You Must Have That True Religion" (sacred song), 243n27

Young, Jason, 5, 7, 83, 101, 131, 175